MEMOIRS OF A MUJAHED:

Algeria's Struggle for Freedom, 1945-1962

By

Hamou Amirouche

Translated and Adapted by the author
from his best-selling book
AKFADOU:
Un An Avec le Colonel Amirouche
(Casbah Editions 2009, Algiers)

I

PRAISE FOR
MEMOIRS OF A MUJAHED:
Algeria's Struggle for Freedom, 1945-1962

This elegantly written memoir comes from the pen of a man who joined the Algerian war of national independence as a lad of nineteen. The reader is treated to the engrossing details of a young man's life on the run, proudly serving a humble leader. Because the author grew into a man with wide experience of the modern world, he is able to tell his story wisely: this book is a fine antidote to the nationalistic bombast that rings so false today.

Diana Wylie,
Professor of History, Boston University

... [Hamou Amirouche's] book is a hugely important and compelling work of both sociopolitical analysis and literature— the writing being in turns poignant, lyrical, and humorous, with the unmistakable ring of direct experience and authenticity. ..
... *Memoirs of a Mujahed* is destined to be a classic, completing the film *"The Battle of Algiers"* for whoever wants a deeper understanding of the human condition at an individual level, and sociopolitical forces at a collective level, especially as they pertain to the Middle East and the Maghreb, regions so central to world affairs now and in the foreseeable future.

Milan Kovacovic
Associate Professor of French Studies
University of Minnesota Duluth

The sharpness of the author's recollections as a freedom fighter and memories of dramatic war events going back half a century are impressive. Hamou Amirouche's exceptional literary talent is striking as he evokes a place visited in the dark, a landscape, or a character using the appropriate words, images, and tone.
The powerful and riveting figure of the author's father, as well as that of his oldest brother are compelling. The reader is particularly stirred by the gripping narrative of his childhood and adolescence.

Lucette Valensi, Historian: EHESS
(Ecole des Hautes Etudes en Sciences Sociales)

II

For Hamou Amirouche, a veteran of the Algerian National Liberation Army, everything began with an event he witnessed as a child that changed his life forever: The arrest and savage beating of his nationalist father... He begins by recalling his childhood in a style reminiscent of the unforgettable writings of Mouloud Feraoun... One of Hamou's motivations for writing his memoirs is to convincingly dismiss allegations that Colonel Amirouche, his chief, suspected "intellectuals,"first and foremost of being turncoats in the "Blue Plot..." Hamou Amirouche should be thanked for this lesson in humility, humanism, and also for showing the true face of a national hero, the great Amirouche, even though, as he sternly reminded Hamou, "only God is great."

Lahouari Addi,
Sociology Professor, Institute of Political Science, Lyon;
Visiting Professor Princeton, UCLA and Georgetown
University.

Hamou Amirouche's appeal for the development of a historical consciousness and an honest appraisal of Algeria's history resonates throughout his extraordinary autobiography. Highlighted by his campaigning during the Algerian Revolution as a mujāhid while serving as secretary to the controversial Col. Amirouche (Aït Hamouda; no relation to the author), this book is much more than a war memoir. The author recounts pre-revolutionary social and political conditions while growing up in Berber Kabylia. As an American-educated member of Algeria's technocratic elite, he also offers candid and critical reflections of post-colonial and contemporary Algeria. This is an engaging and an all too rare memoir composed by a thoughtful and perceptive representative of Algeria's revolutionary generation. Its insights will inform and impress students and scholars.

Phillip C. Naylor, Ph.D.
Marquette University
Co-editor, Journal of North African Studies

Copyright

MEMOIRS OF A MUJAHED:

Algeria's Struggle for Freedom, 1945-1962

By
Hamou Amirouche

Translated and Adapted by the author
from his best-selling book
AKFADOU:
Un An Avec le Colonel Amirouche
(Casbah Editions 2009, Algiers)

People speak sometimes about the "bestial" cruelty of man,
but that is terribly unjust and offensive to beasts,
no animal could ever be so cruel as a man,
so artfully,so artistically cruel.

Fyodor Dostoyevsky

DEDICATION

On November 8, 1957, our guerrilla squad was
surrounded by a French Army unit in a small Algerian village.
We managed to break through the enemy circle under a hail of
gunfire and find shelter in the nearby forest before war planes
roared overhead. At nightfall, we cautiously headed back towards
the village, but the French troops had set it on fire. Huge flames
lit up the only living person who hadn't fled or been arrested: an
old woman, pulling a goat on a leash. That woman, who had just
lost everything except her goat, raised her head and whispered,
"May God protect you, my children."

Looking back at my still vivid memories of the Algerian
War, I can't think of anything or anybody that so deeply moved me
as that old woman. This book is dedicated to her.

Acknowledgements

This book would not have seen the day without the relentless encouragements of my wife, Elizabeth, and our children Malina and Djorf, a three-dimensional source of continuous inspiration and support. My brother Lahcene knew how to instill motivation by constantly warning me that unless I wanted my work published posthumously, I had to cut down on hours spent on the tennis court. This is their story too, as well as the story of my sisters; Djamila, and Aziza and my brothers; Sharif, Zouhir, Salah, Nacer and Smaïl

I want to express my heartfelt thanks for the invaluable editorial guidance and suggestions provided by friends and professionals who read parts of, or the entire manuscript: Mustapha Kebiche who patiently designed and redesigned the maps, Alfred Williams a book designer, Ben Brower, Diana Wylie, Lucette Valensi, Julia Clancy-Smith, Phillip C. Naylor, Nabil Boudraa, Milan Kovacovic, Anne Marie Welsh and Larissa Hordynsky, scholars in their own right, who helped improve the form if not the substance of my draft.

Table of Contents

IX

Foreword

. . . Man is a process and, more exactly,
the process of his actions.

Antonio Gramsci

◆

On November 1, 1954, two organizations, heretofore unknown, claimed responsibility for the attacks launching the Algerian War of Independence: the National Liberation Front (FLN) and its armed wing, the National Liberation Army (ALN). I was 17 years old and had just been admitted to a vocational school. The jubilation that met the news reports of the revolt is indelibly etched in my memory. So, too, are the fatalistic comments by those Algerians who derided the plans of the rebels to beat fate. The rebellion, as many called it, was initiated by 22 militants [1] and conducted inside the country by six men: Larbi Ben M'Hidi, Mourad Didouche, Rabah Bitat, Krim Belkacem, Mohammed Boudiaf, and Mostefa Ben Boulaïd. Diplomatic actions outside Algeria were spearheaded by Hocine Aït Ahmed, Ahmed Ben Bella, and Mohammed Khider. In 1954, the average age of the nine leaders was 33 years old.

Their first major diplomatic success was achieved in 1955 at the Afro-Asian Conference. Meeting for the first time in Bandoeng, Indonesia, the 29 independent countries of Asia and Africa granted their full support to the right of self-determination of the peoples of Algeria, Tunisia, and Morocco. More importantly, the Conference was able to place the "Algerian question" on the agenda of the 11th ordinary session of the U.N. General Assembly on October 1, 1956. It was in this international arena that brilliant Algerian diplomats won the war. The French President, General Charles de Gaulle, displayed utter contempt for the U.N. which he called *le machin* (the thing), but even General Maurice Challe, who led the French Army revolt against President de Gaulle in April 1961, recognized that "the Provisional Government of the Algerian Republic now relies on its diplomatic action in the world, action far more vigorous than that of the French Government which is outdated and inefficient." [2]

All 22 revolutionaries who triggered the armed struggle and created the FLN and the ALN came initially from a single organization, the Algerian People's Party (PPA), which had been banned by French President Albert Lebrun on September 26, 1939, and renamed the Movement for the Triumph of Democratic Liberties (MTLD) in 1947. Once the first shots of the Algerian War were fired, the insurgents' sacred commitment to liberate their country never wavered. When the Soummam Convention, organized on August 20, 1956, by Ramdane Abane and Larbi Ben

XI

M'hidi, [3] gave the Algerian Revolution its institutions, the French Army was no longer fighting armed "outlaws" or "terrorists" but a nation at war. Henceforth, this reborn Algeria had an executive and a parliament, the Executive and Coordination Committee (CCE) and the National Council of the Algerian Revolution (CNRA). The Provisional Government of the Algerian Republic, or GPRA, was formed on September 19, 1958.

The Soummam Convention organized Algeria into six military commands called Wilayas and headed by colonels but, mirroring tribal considerations, nominated no supreme commander. This division was to have dramatic consequences and partially explained the near civil war that erupted at the end of the Revolution. On October 23, 1958, French President de Gaulle offered "the peace of the brave" with no conditions other than that of leaving the "knives in the cloakroom."[4]

The GPRA rejected that call for surrender and increased its militant actions in metropolitan France. Ultimate victory, however, was secured only after almost eight years of war, with the signing of the Evian Peace Accords on March 18, 1962. Algeria's independence was proclaimed shortly thereafter, on July 5, 1962. On June 10, 1999, the French National Assembly passed a law officially recognizing the conflict as "a war" and banning the use of "Operations to restore order" in official language and official texts.

PROLOGUE

*We have done nothing for the Revolution,
the best proof is that we're still alive.*

Dr. Lamine Debaghine,
Algerian diplomat during the War of Independence

They [the Algerian nationalists] *concluded that their liberation would not come about through legal channels*

General Charles de Gaulle [5]

◆

XIV

Almost daily, fellow Americans detect my foreign accent, and, prompted by a healthy curiosity, ask me the same questions: "Where are you from? How long have you been here?"

When I answer "I am African American," I am often greeted by a burst of laughter, given my blue eyes and fair complexion.

"South Africa?" is the next question.

"No," I say, "North Africa, Algeria."

Some then think they are speaking to a "Pied Noir," a Frenchman born in Algeria. When I anticipate that question, I hasten to add that I am Berber. Most Americans have heard of something called "Berber carpets," although such rugs are an outright insult to the genuine, beautiful, hand-woven Berber carpets from Morocco, Algeria, and Tunisia. Yet few have heard of the Berber people, the original inhabitants of North Africa, stretching from the Canary Islands south to Mauritania and east to the Siwa Oasis in Egypt. The next question is a subtle way of inquiring, usually with the best of intentions, about *my* religion: "What's the religion of the Algerian people?"

I reply that the overwhelming majority of Algerians are of Muslim faith, adding "But, it hasn't always been that way. Numerous invasions and occupations introduced to Algeria all three Abrahamic religions: Judaism brought most likely by some Jewish Phoenicians, Christianity with the Romans, and finally Islam with the Arabs."

These recurring questions and answers convey, in a nutshell, first the history of North Africa; second, set the stage for my own story; and third, spell out the chain of events that brought me to the United States. This memoir interweaves all three of those elements.

In May of 1945, when I was seven years old, I saw my father tortured and jailed by French occupation forces. A burning hatred of colonialism and the French sparked by that appalling incident consumed me throughout my childhood and ignited my first flickers of political awareness.

When I was still a teenager, the Algerian Revolution gave me the opportunity to seek revenge. I was training to be a mechanic when the war for independence was triggered, rather recklessly, by those 22 nationalists mentioned in the Foreword. Meeting secretly in Algiers in June 1954, those militants believed that provoking revolutionary violence was the most efficient way to restore unity to the ranks of a fractured nationalist party. Sadly, their miscalculation and the hasty declaration of war on "French Algeria" unleashed a war within a war between two rival groups, the National Liberation Front and National Liberation Army (FLN/ALN), on one side, and the Algerian National Movement (MNA), on the other. Thus for four years, Algerians fighting the French Army also slaughtered one another. Because I witnessed the execution of captured soldiers and great patriots of the MNA, I have attempted to explain that tragic episode in the appropriate section of this memoir.

When the world, minus France, woke up to the first shots fired by the "outlaws" of the newly created organizations, no one imagined that November 1, 1954, would be the first day of a savage war that was to last nearly eight years. The insurgent passion of the FLN leaders set the terms of political activism and armed struggle. A generation after independence, when a civil war again tore the country apart, it wasn't because of the failure of revolutionary ideas, but because of the failure of the FLN.

Two days after the war began, on November 3, 1954, my father became my accidental neighbor, for the vocational school I was attending was just a mile from the prison where he was taken. He was betrayed to the French gendarmes (territorial police) by an Algerian municipal constable, a dedicated informer. His arrest led to appalling tortures and incarceration in the same "civil prison" in Bejaia where he had been imprisoned nine years before for about three months. His time served in prisons and concentration camps spanned almost the length of the war for independence (1954-1962). Although my father was subjected to the same treatment and conditions as ordinary criminals, the prison warden denied me visitation rights that were granted to common-law inmates but not to "political" prisoners. Nevertheless, the warden did allow me what he termed an "exceptional privilege": I could bring food to my father. But I was so poor that on weekends the only treat I was able to deliver was a box of plain cookies. It was then that I made the decision to volunteer for the National Liberation Army.

This narrative engages many themes, personal as well as political and historical. My overarching goal is to bring insight to and to shed light upon the ebb and flow of the War of Independence that ended the Fourth French Republic and brought to power General de Gaulle. President de Gaulle then presided over the most lethal "search and destroy" operations of the war in Algeria. We freedom fighters did outwit the elite units of the French Army, well drilled and copiously supplied by NATO, for four years. But by the spring of 1958, we were virtually defenseless. Five-thousand-volt electrified Morice and Challe fences had been erected and millions of antipersonnel mines had been lodged along the Tunisian border, still killing or maiming shepherds to this day. [6]

The fences and the mines asphyxiated us by stemming the flow of arms, but even more vital, of ammunition into the battlefield. We were trapped within the Tunisian and Moroccan borders as if the French had cinched the drawstring of a sack.

Because the war was essentially won in the diplomatic arena, my book also disproves the claim by some historians that President de Gaulle "granted" independence to Algeria. In fact, unchastened by his predecessors'errors and misjudgments, he escalated the conflict and unnecessarily prolonged the agony, all the while proclaiming that he intended to keep Algeria French. Ultimately de Gaulle unleashed a French Army revolt combined with the outbreak of European-sponsored terrorism. These events resulted in the chaotic exodus and resettlement in France of more than a million French settlers and *Harkis*, Muslim Algerians who had served with the French Army.

Other themes will emerge chapter by chapter, but it must be said at the outset that *Memoirs of a Mujahed,* is a pointed indictment of occupation and colonialism not from a perspective of theoretical, abstract insight, but as lived and experienced by a boy who grew up to become a freedom fighter at the age of nineteen. To understand my point of view, I must here offer a word of explanation about my reluctant use of this term. "Mujahed" is derived from the Arabic word *jahada,* to engage in an effort or to struggle. The words mujahed or mujahedeen (plural) were popularized in the U.S. in the 1980s to refer to the Afghans resisting the Soviet occupation of Afghanistan (1979-1989). Unlike the term "jihadist," commonly associated with Islamist [7] terrorism, a mujahed is more usually defined as a freedom fighter.

Our struggle was unquestionably secular, not only because it sought the support of Jewish and Christian Algerians representing one-tenth of the population, but also because the founding leaders had no Islamist inclinations and were resolutely worldly. I knew some of them personally and can affirm that none exhibited the kind of religious fervor, bordering on fanaticism, associated with Islamic fundamentalism. The primary goal of the insurrection was, according to its leaders, the restoration of Algeria's independence, "preserving all fundamental freedoms, without distinction of race or religion." The goal was not to establish an Islamic State, despite the colonialist propaganda that depicted the revolutionaries' actions as motivated by the wish to "return Algeria to the Middle Ages." I cannot stress this fact too strongly, particularly in view of

Islamist claims today that the Revolution was waged "in the name of God." Present-day Algerian Islamists hate to be reminded that of the 22 young men who launched the Revolution, or of the nine historical figures who led it, none came from the "Association of Islamic Scholars."[8]

During the war, the National Liberation Army, to which I belonged, adopted a temporal and secular motto: "It is because we love life [in freedom] that we accept to die [to secure it]." Certainly during World War II, priests offered eve-of-battle prayers, begging for a divine intersession for the recapture of Europe; but during the Algerian war of liberation, there were no *imams* or *sheikhs* accompanying ALN fighting units and no collective prayers before engaging French troops.

The book's narrative is essentially autobiographical, with two figures standing out. The first is the self-educated, humble, but indomitable blacksmith with whom this tale begins: my father. He was the lens through which I saw my first brutal experiences of French colonialism and oppression, and just as important, he was one of the earliest Algerian nationalists. Shortly before he passed away in 1994 at the age of 90, a younger companion during their relentless struggle against colonialism was helping him cross the street when a teenager asked, "Is this old man a relative of yours?"

"This old man," replied the militant, "is the relative of every single Algerian."

The other central figure in my narrative is Colonel Amirouche Aït Hamouda (no relation). He was a true statesman, visionary, and national hero under whose command I had the honor and extraordinary privilege to serve in 1957-1958. Over the years, as I labored to find the right tone to describe Amirouche's greatness as well as his shortcomings, many other books published on the war in both English and French have made my work both easier and far more compelling. For example, Alistair Horne got quite a few things right in his best-seller, *A Savage War of Peace*. But he uncharacteristically erred when he wrote that Colonel Amirouche... "established himself...by a reign of sheer terror."[9]

If that had been the case, the French Government would not have met to "assess the impact on the Revolution" of his death in battle on March 28, 1958.

I came to the United States of America for the first time on February 2, 1962, sent by members of Algeria's provisional government who viewed my potential to earn a university degree as promising for the emerging nation. A ceasefire was proclaimed just a month after my arrival; Algeria's independence announced five months after that.

I then felt great sadness when tragic events unfolded during the race to seize power in Algeria that summer of 1962. After spending the entire war outside the battlefield, the army chief of staff, Colonel Houari Boumediene, led a bloody march from the Tunisian sanctuary, *after the end of the war*, and imposed Ahmed Ben Bella as President, while actual power rested on the army. Recruited mostly from civilians who fled the war, Boumediène's 30,000-strong army which rarely crossed the border to harass French Army camps inside Algeria, fired upon and killed some 2,000 guerrilla fighters who opposed him. Eventually, Boumediene's 13 years in power were blemished by a palace coup overthrowing Ben Bella in 1965, and the assassination of two leaders of the Revolution, Mohammed Khider in 1967 and Belkacem Krim in 1970. The Colonel's peculiar combination of arrogance, hypocrisy, and self-delusion drove him to erase in many Algerians' heart and soul the distinction between just and unjust, right and wrong. His swift journey into oblivion after he died in 1978 of a "mysterious disease" would be worth noting were it not for his disastrous legacy from which Algeria is reeling to this day.

I attended the reception organized in October 1962 by the Algerian Permanent Mission to the United Nations for the admission of Algeria as the 109th member of the United Nations. There I met a lifelong friend, Raouf Boudjakdji. Among other stringent diplomatic duties, he was in charge of helping Algerian students adjust to a new culture and a new way of life. An outstanding diplomat, he went on serve as Algerian ambassador to the Vatican, U. N. institutions in Geneva, and India. Destiny also led this ex-Algerian rebel, like me, to become African-American and Californian. With his characteristic tongue-in-cheek humor, he reminded me recently that top-quality champagne had been ordered for the reception, an historical occasion worth celebrating. But President Ben Bella had ordered its cancellation.

I also witnessed with great dejection the gradual deterioration of Algerian-U.S. relations as soon as Ben Bella landed in New York on October 5, 1962. When the *New York Times* published an October 9, 1962, front-page photo showing Ben Bella embracing Cuban President Oswaldo Dorticos, I sensed immediately that tensions were in the offing. Ben Bella then violated diplomatic protocol by ignoring the State Department's request not to fly directly from New York to Havana to meet with Fidel Castro, the day after "friendly talks" with President John F. Kennedy. As a U.S. Senator, after all, Kennedy was the first prominent American figure to call for Algeria's independence. As a member of the Foreign Relations Committee, speaking on the Senate floor in July

1957, "he antagonized much of the foreign policy establishment by endorsing Algerian independence from the French."[10]

Today, one of the nicest squares in Algiers is still named Plaza Kennedy.

I remember telling myself that Ben Bella was definitely pushing too far his nonalignment diplomatic stand. Instead of using guerrilla tactics in the diplomatic arena, he was waging a frontal onslaught on the strategic-geopolitical interests of a great power; that assault turned out to be very costly. Hearing here and there "Viva Ben Bella," he had forgotten that his legitimacy rested exclusively on a combination of indifference from a people still staggering from almost eight years of a horrific war, and an army which now held that same people at gunpoint after having spent the entire war period in Moroccan and Tunisian sanctuaries.

Living through all these events while I was studying at Georgetown and Wesleyan Universities, I was also gradually introduced to American culture and institutions. The American Constitution fascinated me, especially the Preamble establishing a range of ideals to fulfill and, ultimately, "secure the blessings of liberty." The First Amendment led me to believe that what makes a great nation is not the size of its territory or its natural wealth, but the quality of its leadership.

Today I still wonder whether, if Algeria had been blessed with intelligent leadership, the fringe Islamist movement of the 60s and 70s would have mutated into a mass movement in the 90s, enabling an Islamist political party to use religion as an ideology to win the first-ever democratic elections in a crushing landslide. One can speculate about what might have happened if the disastrous Algerian leaders, who still plague the country, had had the vision of the American Founders who "privatized" religion as early as 1791. Instead, successive Algerian governments proclaimed Islam the religion of the State in all Algerian Constitutions since 1963, thus creating a time bomb that exploded in the 1990s.

Looking back with dismay at the nation's missed opportunities since 1962, I devote a portion of my epilogue to a Revolution hijacked by nonrevolutionaries who led the country into a new Algerian war that prompts the inescapable question: "What went wrong?" Or, as Doctor Ben Brower framed the question in his prize-winning book, "Has a new violence dawned in Algeria or did the previous one never end?"[11]

My narrative spans more than half a century. In a sense, it begins with my memory of American and British soldiers brought to my village by "Operation Torch," the 1942 Anglo-American invasion of North Africa, and ends with this publication. With hindsight and the distance bestowed by age, I am conscious that I may not have perceived events 40 or 50 years ago in the same way that I do today. The past, it is said, is a foreign country: not only do they do things differently there, they also feel and express pain or emotions in a much more subdued way, while the weight of traditional prudery stifles candor.

My book—with its recollections, research, and interpretations—may hardly compare in drama with the life of a militant choosing to die for a cause because he or she loved life, or the harrowing experience of an incarcerated patriot who survived daily humiliation and abuse. The stirring meditation of my father after he was released from prison in 1945, the invasion of our village by warriors wearing what seemed to be pots on their heads, and the sacking of our house by Moroccan mercenaries, for example, have been stitched together from the recollections of an adult who lived these events at the age of seven. Reconstructing historical context for deeper historical understanding, bringing past reality back to life, recounting an incident witnessed or participated in—all these retraced acts are bound to be colored by my present-day knowledge and perceptions.

The author's father in his "disguise" suit before his arrest in Paris in 1960.

Chapter 1
Tazmalt: The Forge of Destiny

We shall patiently bear the trials that fate imposes on us; we shall work for others without rest, both now and when we are old; and when our last hour comes we shall meet it humbly, and there, beyond the grave, we shall say that we have suffered and wept, that our life was bitter, and God will have pity on us.
Masha at the close of Anton Chekhov's *Uncle Vanya*

Anton Chekhov

André Malraux claimed in his novel *Man's Fate* that only death turns a man's life into destiny. I would lay claim to a different assertion. I can state today that it is the unbearable sight of my father being tortured by French troops when I was seven years old that sealed my destiny.

Without that fateful event, which my mother, my brothers, and I could only oppose with our tears, I would not have harbored such a hatred for the French as a child. Perhaps I would not have joined the armed resistance in 1956, would not have met and served with a legendary hero without whose support I never would have attended high school, and, still less, American universities. And these memoirs would have never seen the light of day.

May 8, 1945, which signaled victory over Nazism and Fascism, is engraved in the memory of the Algerian people for a different reason. My father Ahitous, the village blacksmith, could not hear on that day the customary drumbeat preceding an official announcement by the town constable, Monsieur Solbes. And for good reason: he was too busy hammering out the thin blade of a sickle to pay attention to goings-on in the street. I was the one who barged into his shop and informed him that an important announcement was about to be made. As it was the month of May and the harvests were about to begin, my father, sweat dripping from his forehead, had already forged about a dozen sickles since early morning. He gave the final touches to the tool he was making and plunged it into a water basin to harden it. He put down his hammer and his blacksmith's tongs, took off his leather apron, and muttered, "Come with me."

He locked the shop, and side by side we headed towards the public plaza. From every direction villagers, mostly kids, flocked towards Monsieur Solbes and formed a compact circle around him. That guardian of the peace, the drum still hanging from his neck, raised his hand holding a sheet of paper to command silence. Then, in his high-pitched, droning voice, he read, in French, the orders of the authorities: "Order to the population: the residents of Tazmalt and surroundings are ordered to surrender to the gendarmerie all arms in their possession, war rifles, shotguns, pistols, whether they are registered or not, within 48 hours. Beyond this deadline, harsh jail sentences will be inflicted on anyone daring to defy this injunction."

Only a tiny minority, including my father, understood French

24

and was able to translate the order, in a subdued voice, to the other villagers. I watched my father, whose face was expressionless and reflected no particular anxiety. But as I was to learn shortly after, he was far from sure that the hiding place he had selected to bury his rifle—under the grapevine in the vegetable garden—was safe. Sadly for him and for my family, the subsequent events proved he had ample reason to be concerned.

According to a bizarre popular song in the Berber language, the Second World War had just ended with the victory not of the Allies, but of the Russians: *A kaydous, [ak idoussa] Lalman ighelvith ar rous*" ("That's what happened, the Russians defeated the Germans"). However, the news coming from Sétif and Kherrata, some 100 kilometers from Tazmalt, was no cause for celebration. Revolts such as the region had not seen since 1871[12] were confirmed by eyewitnesses. Massacres of civilians were reported to have been savagely perpetrated by the French Army. Then on May 11, 1945, a great tumult seized Tazmalt following the arrival of hundreds of French soldiers and Moroccan Tabors—mercenaries of the French Army. For the first time I saw war planes flying low over the village, generating panic among inhabitants and livestock alike. What might have triggered this sudden invasion was the memory of the 1871 Mokrani revolt against French colonial injustice. Old men told of the bitter punishment they had to endure as our region of Kabylia saw 1,200,000 hectares of its choicest land confiscated by the French. Historians studying that period are clearly justified to observe that "one is reminded of Sparta living under the spell of danger from the Helots and increasing it by the very means employed to dispel it."[13]

Now in 1945, the rebellious area of Kabylia, at the junction of the plains and the mountains, of wretchedness and opulence, had to be firmly dissuaded through a show of force from imitating the insurrection in the eastern part of the country. But the massive deployment of helmeted soldiers did not particularly trouble the fatalistic composure of the villagers. After all, during the past three years the population had become accustomed to seeing hundreds of American and British soldiers come and go and had even witnessed a German literally falling from the sky, apparently parachuting from a downed aircraft. He was captured by a French-Muslim sergeant-major of World War I, who became an instant local hero. I remember catching a glance of the prisoner when he was paraded through the village. I recall the screeching sirens announcing a forthcoming German bombardment and warning the inhabitants to turn off their lights at night. A highly esteemed villager, Azwaw, died of what we can surmise today was a heart attack brought on by one such alert.

The arrival of these Allied warriors who spoke by "twisting their tongue" generated an unusual commerce: eggs were bartered for corned beef or cigarettes, figs for instant coffee or chocolate. There was even a cultural exchange entirely based on swear words—which I didn't realize until I attended Georgetown University—between the soldiers and the young villagers. We learned and repeated such obscenities as "f—ing bastards" and "sonovabitch," as well as milder forms of expression like "Okay Johnny," "gotcha," and "gimme." My older brother Sharif was greatly admired not only for his talent to swear profusely in English, but also for his uncanny ability to relieve the Americans of a great number of cans of instant coffee and corned beef. The whole family relished the meat without worrying, in the acute shortages of the war, whether the canned beast was halal—authorized for consumption by the sacred scriptures. Nearly 20 years later as a student in America, I saw a shelf loaded with cans of corned beef in a supermarket. I began to salivate in anticipation and immediately purchased a can. But no food ever tastes as good in abundance as in destitution.

Soon the attitude that met the new invaders in 1945—indifference, mixed with curiosity—turned brutally violent for our family when a horde of French soldiers and Moroccan Tabors burst into our home. It was three or four in the afternoon and the bright sunshine was eclipsed by dark clouds quite unusual for the season. Flashes of lightning streaked the sky and we could hear intermittent bursts of thunder. Not a single puff of wind stirred in the fruit trees. My brother, a cousin, and I were in the house with an old woman who served as a midwife and had delivered most of the babies in our family. As such, she was like a second mother to us. Pointing to the sky, she explained that the thundering noise was provoked by God's inquisitor, Azrayan, who was rolling his gigantic bludgeon and whom each mortal must confront as soon as he or she is buried. Holding his frightening club in hand, Azrayan asked a single question in Arabic, a language incomprehensible to us Berber speakers: *Ma houa rabbuka?* ("Who is your God?")

The midwife continued. "If you answer 'You,' you are immediately bludgeoned and dispatched to Hell. You must answer, 'My God is your God' to escape this fate."

Frightened beyond imagination, my ten-year-old brother Zouhir asked what would happen to someone who understood only Berber, when my cousin Malha screamed and stood up. I turned around and, in the eerie atmosphere created by the old woman, I half expected to come face to face with Azrayan himself. But no, the new presence was a huge soldier in uniform, with what looked

26

like a cooking pot on his head. He pointed his rifle at us and then proceeded to ransack the room, spearing a sack full of grain with his bayonet.

The soldier asked in Arabic, "Are there any arms?" The old woman replied that there was only semolina for the children. More soldiers barged in, locking us up in another room with my mother and my other brothers. The commanding officer barked an order and two Tabors seized my father and handcuffed him. Then, accompanied by a group of soldiers, the officer headed directly to the grapevine. It took him just a minute or two to dig up a French-made MAS 36 war rifle.

Although I pressed him on countless occasions, my father, to his dying breath, obstinately refused to disclose the name of the person who betrayed him to the French and whom he clearly knew. "Leave him to God's judgment," he would invariably reply. He carried the secret to his grave.

Hoping to spare himself the humiliation of brutalities in front of his family, my father immediately admitted that the rifle belonged to him. But he was not to be spared, not in the atmosphere of hysteria that had seized the French troops following the insurgency that was tearing apart three big cities to the east. The officer angrily brandished the weapon and shouted, "Where are the other arms? To whom have they been distributed?"

"There are no other arms," my father replied quietly.

"You're lying," howled the Frenchman as he struck him with his club. He then invited other soldiers to join him, and blows rained on the blacksmith.

My father confessed to me years later that those repeated kicks and blows, even though they made him lose consciousness, were like caresses compared with the tortures inflicted on him after his second arrest in November 1954 by the notorious General Information Police at the civil prison of Bejaia. There, prisoners were water boarded using toilet water, forced to sit on bottles, and administered electrical shocks. And yet, I never heard him express hatred, nor any desire to find his torturers and exact revenge. He would start to tell his story but never finish it, suggesting rather than describing what intimate parts of the body where subjected to abuse, the prudish character of the Berber holding him back.

"I know that a truckload of arms were distributed in the region. Confess if you hope to save your skin. Where are the other arms hidden?" demanded the officer.

The interrogator then mechanically and relentlessly repeated the same question, striking Ahitous with rage. My father periodically fainted, but a bucket of water quickly restored him to consciousness. He took the blows without a moan or a cry, surely because of my mother and us children, powerlessly watching from the window. At that age I could not understand why the French officer locked us up in a room with a large window facing the garden where my father was being brutalized. Later, I knew he was forcing us to watch the scene, and making sure my father heard our crying to weaken his own resistance. Ten years later, during the war for independence, French troops would cross a new threshold in ignominy. They would force a captured militant under interrogation to witness the rape of his wife, sister or mother. In retaliation, I have to admit that an equally abject practice was used by the mujahedeen: cutting off the genitals of ambushed and killed French soldiers and stuffing them into their mouths.

The Moroccan Tabors, leaning on their rifles, quietly watched the torture, refilling the water bucket and waiting for orders. Occasionally, perhaps troubled by my mother's sobs and screams, they would glance at the window of our prison. I was seven years old but I was not crying. I watched, dumbfounded with shock by what was happening to my revered father.

In the end, realizing that they would extract nothing further, and with no other torture instruments than whips, clubs, and boots, the officer ordered his men to take my father to the military headquarters in Akbou before incarceration in Bejaia prison. Escorted by two soldiers, he staggered past our window. At that point, my mother's cries intensified. Then a new cause for fear hit us when we saw that a group of Tabors was not leaving the house. Some picked our ripe apricots and started eating. Others spread throughout the house and meticulously plundered it. From our war quota of soap and sugar to ancient silver coins and jewelry, every item of value filled the hoods of their *kashabyas* (mantles.) I will never forget the tearful imprecations of my mother against the Moroccan thieves. For a long time afterwards, she held a smoldering grudge against anything Moroccan.

When there was nothing left to steal, the last soldiers left the garden. Silence and a relative peace descended on the house. My mother stopped sobbing. We children naturally turned to our eldest brother, 16-year-old Sharif, to replace my father. Luckily my Uncle Iddir, who lived less than a mile away, appeared and brought us huge comfort. I dearly loved my uncle, my father's second cousin, in spite of his gruff attitude. "Eh, never forget," he said to my mother; "only what is willed by God can happen. Rely on Him. We are leaving Tazmalt. Tomorrow, we will be in Ihitoussen."

Chapter 2

Ihitoussen, the Home of the Blacksmiths

There is no present or future,
only the past happening over and over again

Eugene O'Neill,
referring to Ireland under English occupation.

My father, Ameziane Ahitous Amirouche, took his name from the village Ihitoussen, in the Djurdjura Mountains in northeastern Algeria, where he was born on February 14, 1904. Perched on a rocky and easily defensible peak like all villages in the region of Kabylia, Ihitoussen overlooked tiny plots of land sparsely planted with olive or fig trees. The general indifference with which the men of the village looked upon these barren plots, except when the figs ripened, placed the fields under the full care of the women. Like beasts of burden, they would line up at the fountain at dawn, fill their five-gallon jugs, and carry them on their heads, resting on a cushion, to the fields to water fig trees. The women also cultivated subsistence crops of barley, which required less moisture than wheat, and a few vegetables near the springs. At least once a week they walked five miles to the forest to gather dry wood, the only cooking fuel available.

One could occasionally catch a glimpse of their baggy-trousered shapes harvesting barley, leading a mule or donkey, or trampling sheaves of barley on the threshing ground to separate the grain from the chaff. They picked olives and managed to produce a jug or two of olive oil, doled out with the imperious parsimony dictated by dire poverty to ensure that it lasted until the next harvest. During the harsh snowy winter, the women wove the hooded winter cloaks called burnooses, wool blankets, and the inevitable *akhellal*, the decorative rug that formed part of every bride's dowry. I have a fond memory of my widowed aunt with her extraordinary green eyes, famous for the melons and vegetables she cultivated on the bank of the Sebaou River which she personally sold at the weekly market at Aït Ikhlef.

My father was the fourth son in a family of four boys, Mohand, Arezki, Ravah, and Amezian, and one girl. His sister often fell sick, as if vexed by the lack of affection if not downright hostility that greeted her at birth in spite of her given name, Aziza, "the loved one." Strangely, a few days before she died, she hummed all day the traditional funeral incantation, prompting angry exhortations from her superstitious mother who considered it a sinister omen. Aziza could not overcome the odds she was up against. She passed away at the age of six, victim of a terrible typhus epidemic. She was discreetly buried in a tiny grave dug by my grandfather himself in the village cemetery overlooking the Sebaou Valley, which offered, if one is not starving, one of the most breath-taking vistas in the country. Since Aziza was not entitled to

30

the ritual mortuary invocation or the funeral procession reserved for adults, only the song of the cicada accompanied her to her final resting place. But looking down from heaven, she must have been surprised by the tears on her father's normally expressionless face as he carried her, wrapped in a white shroud, to her tomb.

Natural selection, even if a bit assisted, respected tradition by eliminating a girl, especially a dark-skinned one. Often, for that matter, in a remnant of a pagan practice meant to impact divine sentences, earrings were placed on boys' ears, as if God could be fooled, and, mistaking them for girls, would not recall them to Him.

Of medium height, my father was stocky, with large shoulders reflecting his muscle strength. His deep-set gray-blue eyes, fair complexion, and straight nose, although typical features in his ancestral village, set him apart in the town of Tazmalt, where the average inhabitant looked Latino. A thin mustache, symbol of manhood in Berber culture, adorned his upper lip. When he shaved it, following the end of his military service in the French Army, he provoked an outcry. With a straight face, he explained that the whiskers had been abused by French officers; he needed to regrow a dignified mustache. Unpretentious, he nevertheless projected a martial air, probably derived from the awareness of the challenge he was facing in his efforts to instill a nationalist fiber in fatalistic peasants.

Overcoming the severe deprivations of mountain living, my father and his brothers survived on meager rations of dried acorns, ground and blended with barley, figs, olive oil, and above all, milk, thanks to the goat—often the most important member of the family. But just as happens in any human or animal grouping, when food is barely sufficient to sustain life, some abandon their native land and search for a more promising place to live. My grandfather Boudjemaâ, blacksmith like his ancestors for centuries, decided to try his luck with his four sons in "Arab country," as we used to call any area in Algeria where Arabic, not Berber, was the mother tongue. What urged his departure was the forced military draft instituted by colonial France during World War I, which conscripted his son Arezki, who became the first draft dodger of the region. The family left the rocky confines of their native Kabylia and headed by foot, mule, and train to Saint-Arnaud, now El Eulma, to open a blacksmith's shop. As soon as they arrived in 1916, my grandfather learned, with keen apprehension, that peasant revolts, triggered by the military draft, had broken out everywhere in the Aurès Mountains.

Intensely worried for his draft-dodging son, my grandfather

decided to introduce himself to the Commander of the Saint-Arnaud police brigade. "Here, chief, I am a blacksmith and my shop is located at the eastern section of the town."

"So what?" replied the brigade chief, "First, who are you and where do you come from?"

"I am Kabyle, chief."

"And what do you want?"

"I know," replied my grandfather, "that you own horses. Bring them to my shop any time and I'll forge them brand-new shoes."

From then on, at least once a month, the policemen's horses were brought to the forge to be shod. Since my grandfather never requested payment for his services, and also, perhaps, because his son the draft dodger was blessed with fair skin and blue eyes and looked much younger than his age, my uncle was never called upon to justify his draft status.

Sadly, my grandfather caught an eye disease, most likely trachoma, and lost his sight. He was accompanied back to his native village where he remained secluded except on Fridays, when a family member would guide him to the mosque.

His four sons worked nonstop during the rainy and ploughing season, from October to February, forging ploughshares before returning to their village to spend some two months with their family, helping their spouses prune fig and olive trees. Then, as the harvest season approached, they headed back to Saint-Arnaud to forge sickles, scythes, and pitchforks and shoe donkeys, mules, and horses.

Before engaging in the arduous training to be a blacksmith at the age of 13, my father—unlike his parents and brothers, who remained illiterate to the last day of their life—was given a rare chance to attend the three-room, three-grade school of the region. It served a population of more than 100,000 in an area the size of Rhode Island, which explains the 90 percent illiteracy rate which the "French civilizing mission" left behind in 1962. My father was able to acquire the fundamentals of reading and writing that decisively shaped his life and destiny.

One day he read in the local daily, *La Dépêche de Constantine*, that an acute labor shortage was plaguing France in the aftermath of World War I. A cousin and future brother-in-law from a neighboring village had already bid good bye to his tribe and opened a small restaurant in Marseille. The restaurant owner encouraged my father to emigrate and try his luck. Ahitous promptly decided to talk it over with his father: "You know, Vava [Dad], there is hardly enough of a work load to keep everybody busy in the forge. Arezki and Mohand can manage without Ravah and me. If you authorize us, we could try our chance in France."

"You're too young to travel so far," his father answered.

"No, Dad, trust us," pressed my father. "I speak their language. The two of us will get by."

My grandfather, clinging to tradition, deemed it out of the question for his sons to depart without their father's blessing. Too many sons had been crushed by sudden as well as predictable disaster when a parents' curse was relentlessly released upon them. So he gave in.

Thus my father and my Uncle Ravah, aged 17 and 19 respectively, crossed the Mediterranean in 1921. After a short stay in Marseille, at their cousin's restaurant where they served meals in exchange for room and board, they went to Clermont-Ferrand where they were immediately hired by the Michelin tire-manufacturing plant. Soon, as skilled blacksmiths employed in the metal workshop, they were able to send a substantial portion of their salaries home to Ihitoussen, enabling their older brother Mohand to purchase three plots of fig trees—and the first cow ever seen in the region. When she arrived, the cow was apparently quite bewildered by her unusual escort of a dozen of my father's cousins and relatives. The whole village joined the frenzy, greeting her with buoyant enthusiasm.

"She's the equivalent of ten goats," one cousin observed.

"Maybe," replied another. "But goat's milk is something else!"

Others were looking beyond milk and butter and salivating at the prospect of a gigantic couscous meal. "Okay, you may be right. But cow's meat is peerless in couscous."

In the end, the cow did not live very long in the mountain village. She could not be kept outside exposed to jackal attacks and the freezing winter cold, nor inside the tiny stable hardly large enough to shelter a goat and her kid. Before the cow lost too much weight, she was sacrificed for *thi meshrat,* a traditional feast which gave each family a share of the carcass in exchange for a modest payment.

The two brothers worked three years at the Michelin plant. Years afterwards, my Uncle Ravah was full of praise for Clermont-Ferrand, where pear and apple trees "grew in the forests" and where, on weekends, he would fill a basket with the ripe and fragrant fruit. In 1923 my father was drafted into military service and was forced to sail back home. The Rif War (1921-1926), a rebellion in Morocco, had generated an uncommon, if mitigated, enthusiasm among North African nationalists such as my father.

While doing his service in Dellys, a small port in Kabylia, he wondered whether he would become the second deserter in the family if sent by France to fight Moroccan insurgents. The Moroccan warriors had wiped out a Spanish army 60,000 strong at the battle of Annual; the Spanish commander, General Manuel Fernandez Silvestre, committed suicide. France would not stand by and let Spain lose the war, since it would create a dangerous precedent for their colonies of Algeria and Tunisia. [14]

A French Army under Marshall Philippe Pétain and a Spanish army numbering a total of 250,000 soldiers, using mustard gas against the population, defeated the Morrocans, who surrendered on May 26, 1926.

What spared my father from the Rif War was undoubtedly his level of literacy. Promoted to corporal in charge of supply and logistics for the garrison, he escaped the fearful test of fighting the Moroccan warriors who, according to legend, never pulled the trigger before whispering to the bullet, "You will have to answer to God and His Prophet if you don't hit flesh or bone." Never could he have imagined that one day in May 1945, a horde of Moroccan mercenaries would invade and pillage his home and, without a qualm, assist their French officer in his torture while his powerless family wept and watched.

As soon as my father was demobilized, he returned to France and settled in Paris, where he was again hired as a skilled worker. In Paris, his destiny was reshaped and his life took on a new meaning. His involvement in nationalism began in 1925, when the North African Star (NAS) was formed by a group of nationalists led by the Emir Khaled and Hadj Ali Abdelkader. Created in Paris under the umbrella of the French Communist Party as the Ottoman Empire collapsed and the Rif War was raging, the NAS turned to a factory worker, Messali Hadj, a close friend of Ho Chi Minh, as its charismatic leader. [15]

Messali's Algerian People's Party succeeded the NAS in 1937, recruiting its followers among peasants and workers espousing the idea of nationalism as a class struggle. The dues my father paid for his membership in the NAS were relatively modest, enabling his initiation into the nationalist movement at the age of 22. He was still in France when he heard for the first time of Messali Hadj, the undisputed father of the modern Algerian nationalist movement.[16]

The idea of independence and the withdrawal of French occupying forces from his fatherland, introduced as demands by the NAS, appealed naturally to the fiercely free spirit of my father and his fellow villagers.

The 1871 revolt was still very much alive in the minds of these villagers. The tale of the local hero, M'hand the "Millstone," was told and retold with unmitigated pride. According to the legend, M'hand, hidden behind the millstone of an ancient olive-oil mill which he maneuvered like a turret, repelled dozens of French invaders. An enormous anvil taken from the enemy after a battle, and still used in the village blacksmith shop, was cited as testimony to this victory. The most celebrated heroine, however, was Fadhma N'Sumer. Her fame had crossed the Djurdjura Mountains into the rest of the country, as she led the resistance until she was captured in 1857. In my father's telling of her legend, she carried indelible paint in battle and used it to mark any warrior fleeing the enemy. The tribal honor code did not accept or forgive the shameful stain of retreating and ceding ground to the invaders.

The history of Kabylia reinforced my father's conviction that the "Irumien"or "Romans," as the Kabyles called the French, had to be expelled not only from ancestral lands unsubjugated because they were too poor to arouse any interest, but from the country as a whole. He returned to Algeria in 1927 or 1928 and indirectly saw to it that his father arranged a marriage to an orphan, Fatima Moussaoui.

In many cultures and perhaps in Kabylia more than most, mothers-in-law are viewed with great suspicion. Even John F. Kennedy, paraphrasing Voltaire, made a famous joke about it when, following his election as President in 1960, he declared that, "behind every great man stands a woman and…a surprised mother-in-law." In Algerian society, that bias led to a marked preference for a motherless bride when my grandfather arranged my father's marriage. Tan and short, with brown, sad-looking eyes, my mother always wore, over her long black hair, a yellow headscarf with black stripes matching her full-length, loose-fitting dress of brighter yellow. Strong-willed and hardworking, she never complained about the hardships of life in the village.

Although the tradition of a wife's submissiveness to the husband was rarely questioned, my mother had constant heated arguments with my father, always over her children and particularly the oldest, Sharif, whose rebellious and unruly nature was a cause for concern. I remember one day when, after a particularly harsh dispute, my father turned to me and asked me to state who was right. Taken aback but thinking fast, I replied that it was forbidden by religion to judge parents. A stalwart and unconditional supporter and ally of her children, whenever my father set out to punish one of us for mischief, my mother would interpose and say, "Don't

35

you ever raise a hand against *my* children." Occasionally, if we misbehaved, she would threaten to tell my father, but she never did.

With meat rarely affordable, she cooked delicious vegetarian dishes. Homemade pasta with zucchini flowers is one of my favorites to this day. She was also a peacemaker whenever tempers flared in our neighborhood over windows broken by kids and their slingshots.

In Ihitoussen there were, strictly speaking, no social classes as there was no real division of labor. Nonetheless, one could detect differences in standing and social rank linked to the number of olive trees or fig trees a family owned and, in the case of my mother, to the prestige bestowed on her father by the fact that he was the first, or one of the first villagers, to go on pilgrimage to Mecca. I can't vouch for the claim that it took my grandfather, in the early 20th century, close to one year to accomplish the only optional duty in the Islamic scriptures: pilgrimage. My mother acquired even more authority later in life when God gratified her with seven sons out of nine children.

Soon after his marriage, my father and two of his brothers opened a forge in the Aurès Mountains, among the Shawiya Berbers. They stayed in the region nearly ten years, adapting their Kabyle dialect to the local tongue, saving centime after centime thanks to my Uncle Ravah, a scrooge such as the world has never seen, who held the purse strings tightly closed. He kept the same notorious reputation until his death: he never spent a franc without regretting it.

Depriving himself and his brothers of virtually everything that could have improved their diet and daily life, Uncle Ravah cut back on staples, on fruit and vegetables, constantly looking for ways to live on less. He never allowed himself or his brothers the least amount of leisure. If anyone dared criticize him for excessive austerity, he always made the same reply, "There are those who have experienced hunger only with their stomach, and those who do so with their memory."

One day, my father told me, they entrusted Uncle Ravah to buy some meat for their daily couscous. He returned after a few minutes and declared with a somber expression that the butchers had not slaughtered any lamb that day.

"What are you talking about?" retorted his older brother. "I saw plenty of meat at the butcher's this morning."

"Okay," replied Uncle Ravah. "You saw, I saw. Now it's Ameziane's turn to go have his share of meat…looking." They all laughed and rallied behind Uncle Ravah's harsh economic policies.

They were not going to regret it. Soon they had saved enough money to purchase a property closer to Ihitoussen, for each time they returned home, the journey took a toll on their health and expenses. The trip took a full day by bus and train to Ighzer Amokrane, where they spent a night at a cousin's home, a blacksmith like them. At dawn the next day, they crossed the mountains in five hours by foot or on rented mules.

Ahitous and Fatima had their first son, Sharif, in 1929. Next came two daughters who died in infancy before two other sons, Zouhir and myself, completed the pre-World War II family. Three years before I was born, my father made a decision which flew in the face of Kabyle tradition: he decided to move his entire family to the Soummam Valley, settling in Tazmalt at the foot of the Djurdjura Mountains.

He knew that some of the most beautiful farms of the French settlers were located in that valley. The tractor had not yet been introduced, so wooden ploughs remained the only means to till the land. The prosperous farms of the French aroused burning desires among the local peasants, but for the time being, as they settled in Tazmalt, my father and my uncle did not see beyond the opportunity to work full time and earn a living so much closer to their home.

The village of their ancestors, Ihitoussen, supplied virtually every blacksmith practicing the trade in Algeria. According to legend, they inherited the trade from Sidna (Lord) David. And what a trade! They were actually metallurgists, not just masters of their craft. My grandfather made sure he transmitted his noble but arduous craft to his children. They made their own anvils and tongs, the latter in a wide range of shapes according to the tools they had to forge, repair, or sharpen. They welded metal pieces, using handfuls of sand to prevent the metal from melting away. They also engraved on mule bridles the extraordinarily intricate geometric designs made famous by the Berber rugs women have been weaving for centuries.

These skilled artisans departed their village on the eve of the rainy season in early October, leaving their family in the custody of elderly tribal members. When my father and my uncle settled in Tazmalt, they were far from imagining that it would be forever. The rainy season lasted longer than in the Aurès, and the Sahel/ Soummam River enabled the French settlers and two indigenous Francophile farmers to cultivate some of the best vegetables, oranges, tangerines, and olives in Algeria.

The peasants never readied their tools in advance because they lacked the funds, and subsistence agriculture never benefited from any type of credit. As a consequence, as soon as they assessed that it had rained enough for them to begin ploughing, dozens of farmers rushed to the forge. My father and my uncle worked from dawn to late at night to enable the peasants to plough their land while it was still moist. My grandfather often exhorted them to ease up for their health and to take some rest. "It's not work you are going to bring to an end, but yourselves," he would say, but to no avail.

The blacksmiths were often reimbursed in kind: grapes and fresh figs in the summer, a basketful of dried figs in the fall. From humble renters of a room which served as both shop and bedroom, they became owners of a splendid five-room house with a separate forge. The huge garden included a grapevine, half-a-dozen orange and tangerine trees, two lemon trees, an apricot and a peach tree, and of course the obligatory fig tree, without which no Kabyle would consider himself the owner of a property of any sort.

Henceforth, my father was ready to challenge the tenacious Kabyle tradition that perpetuated the unfortunate separation of the work place from tribal residency, weighing painfully on families several months during the year. True, choosing Tazmalt as a permanent residence and moving his family there would signal the end of the tribe. So what? My father had lived many years in France, had been an activist in the North African Star, and thought now of building a nation, transcending tribal loyalties. He was aware of other ways of life and other ways to bring up children. He felt more pity than condescendension towards his fellow Berbers, who survived in wretchedness, and yet continued to render gratitude to God for their fate of a hardscrabble life.

Besides, my father had had enough of a life locked in the universe of the clan, distrustful and frozen in time, stifled by its traditions, belittled by its religious references, wrapped in its superstitions and its occasional *eheshkulen* or black magic. I was barely ten years old when I heard for the first time in Ihitoussen a story which made me shudder. This was the tale of a woman who was in the habit of digging up a cadaver, rolling couscous with its hand, and then serving the meal to the man whose willpower she had elected to control.

My father's release from the clan began one Friday after prayer, when most of the village affairs were conducted in the village assembly. There, he solemnly asked to be heard. "God be praised," he said. "As you know, our hard work led us to the light: we acquired a property on the other side of the mountain. We installed a forge separate from the house. I decided, with your authorization and blessing, to move with my wife and children and make Tazmalt our permanent residence."

When my father told me of his announcement, he said it was as if a bomb had exploded in the midst of the assembly. Leaving tribal land with wife and children was unprecedented. The act represented a threat to the traditions, the language, and the culture obstinately kept alive for thousands of years. Such a gesture could signal the disintegration, the end of the tribe.

"You want to take our hood off [bring shame to the village], oh Boudjemaâ's son; is that what you want?" shouted the village chief.

"Real dishonor is rolling couscous like a woman and abandoning wife and children several months of the year. My wife will no longer line up at dawn at the fountain and walk into the forest to fetch dry wood. Use your imagination: permanent running water in the house and firewood delivered to the home. And electricity!"

When the village chief had no immediate response, my father told me that he was barely able to abstain from adding, "I was one of the first, and still one of the very few, who introduced latrines into the village—yet you and your wives continue to shit in the bushes. I reject this primitive way of life."

The majority of the villagers had never heard of running water and still less of electrical power. Those who had traveled to the city attempted to explain to those who had never ventured out of the mountains all the advantages of plumbing and electricity. But doing so was akin to describing colors to someone born blind. My father nevertheless made a final attempt. "Think of your own fountain in your house. There is a key, which opens or shuts the fountain off as needed. As night falls, you push a button and the house is filled with light as if it were daylight, without the stench of burnt petrol or oil."

Questions and appreciative comments in subdued voices met this introduction to the great benefits of civilization epitomized by running water and electricity. My father took advantage of another silent pause and pressed his case, "Believe me, it is with a heavy heart that I am taking my wife to Tazmalt where she will live practically sequestered." My father knew and respected tribal traditions, and he had no intention of questioning or undermining them. Women went out in their own village and traveled miles to the forest to fetch dry wood. They tilled plots of land often located several miles away. Some of them even attended the weekly market to sell their produce. The veil was unknown. But as soon as a woman left tribe and family, she had to don the traditional white Berber veil whenever she went out of the house.

39

"I only plead for your blessing," continued my father. "Wherever we live, we will never allow our culture, our language, our traditions to be threatened. Besides, who can contest that Tazmalt is settled by Kabyles and is located in Algeria?" When he realized that the majority of the assembly, fearing a dangerous precedent, was denying him permission to take his family with him, he rose and, undeterred, declared: "I am sorry, but my decision is made and it is irreversible. *Ejighken thilahna* (goodbye)." And he left the meeting.

From Jijel, where he had been established for years, my Uncle Iddir, at my father's urging, also moved with his family to Tazmalt, where he set up a forge at the south entrance of the village. With my father positioned at the north entrance, competition was decisively discouraged. Ahitous was far from imagining that he turned out to be a trailblazer among tribal members. Very quickly, all blacksmiths originating from Ihitoussen, one after the other, rented homes and shops all over Algeria, installed rudimentary forges under the encouraging or indifferent stare of French settlers, and ended up buying properties and moving their families to towns where they earned a living. Naturally, they kept their modest home in the village of their ancestors where they returned during summer, celebrated weddings and circumcisions, and buried their dead.

Still today, one can find such blacksmiths in virtually every town or city in Algeria. All these ingenious craftsmen spoke Arabic with a strong Kabyle accent and fiercely clung to their language and culture like their fellow Berbers from other regions.[17]

Given my family's recent history and our traditions, once my father was arrested, Uncle Iddir immediately took charge and organized our speedy return from Tazmalt to our native Ihitoussen where we still owned a house, and a few small plots of land planted with fig and olive trees.

From Tazmalt to Ihitoussen, as the crow flies, the distance does not exceed 50 miles. But the two villages are separated by the Djurdjura Mountains. There was only one mountain pass, often clogged with heavy snow. In winter it was virtually impossible to reach Ihitoussen. Villagers remembered the fate of reckless travelers who, unable to find their way in a snowstorm, vanished forever. Legend told of peasants encountering lions in the pass before the Roman and Byzantine occupations from 200 BCE to 700 CE. In their tales the peasants always insisted that no one was ever killed by a lion if he or she did not show signs of panic.

Even in summer, however, it was not easy to discover the path meandering through the rocks and ravines of the Chrea Pass. In general, an hour-long train ride to Ighzer Amokran, followed by a five-hour mountain crossing by rented mule, was the fastest route. However, given the dramatic circumstances which forced my family's flight to Ihitoussen, Uncle Iddir opted to rent an old pickup truck. We were piled into the jalopy, my family and Uncle Iddir's—ten people and one goat.

But a minute after the driver gunned the engine, the terrified goat leaped over the side rails of the truck and crashed onto the roadway. My uncle did not waste time. Realizing that the animal was in agony, he seized a knife and slaughtered the goat as prescribed by scripture, to make it halal. I will always remember the blood gushing from the slashed throat. Tears welled in my eyes as I watched the poor animal frantically thrashing its legs before death stiffened its body. My uncle waited a moment for the goat to shed all its blood and then loaded the carcass into the truck. During the three-hour trip, I was under the impression that the goat's wide-open eyes remained accusingly focused on Uncle Iddir.

The old pickup, overloaded and sputtering, strained across the mountain pass and begin the descent towards Acif Oussardhoun, where the road ended. From there to Ihitoussen, the distance did not exceed ten miles. We would continue the journey by mule. We unloaded clothing, blankets, a bag of maize meal from the U.S., a can of olive oil, some hastily packed cooking utensils, and the goat carcass. Uncle Iddir paid for the trip, heartily thanked the driver, and watched as he turned the truck around and head back to Tazmalt.

Then, turning to my eldest brother Sharif, he said, "You are going to walk to Ihitoussen. Find Uncle Mohand Ouameur and if his mules are free, tell him we will be waiting at Acif Oussardhoun. Don't come back unless you can't find someone. And remember! Not a word about your father!"

The wait for Sharif was long. Fortunately a jug of fresh water was always available at the edge of the path—a centuries-old tradition for the relief of thirsty travelers. The sun was already declining when we saw, with a sigh of thankfulness, a thick cloud of dust on the horizon. It was the expected mules.

Sharif had not obeyed my uncle's orders and very quickly, the whole region had learned of Ahitous' arrest. Details of his detention and the brutalities he suffered at the hands of the savage Iroumien ("God curse them") began to spread among the villagers, who offered a hearty welcome to our family. Their greetings were all the warmer because news brought by the blacksmiths fleeing the massacres of Kherrata, Sétif, and Guelma had caused great concern. The tales of summary executions of entire families, the bombing of villages by heavy artillery and military aircraft,

41

bewildered the villagers and aroused a mixture of revulsion and revolt.

But France, instead of generating fear or provoking awe and terror, was projecting instead a pitiful image of itself. Its crushing during World War II, followed by four years of German occupation, dealt a fatal blow to French prestige even among Francophile Algerians who advocated Algeria's full integration with France.

Patriots of the Algerian People's Party knew that French sovereignty was nearly compromised for years. The ruthless repression ordered in May 1945, to reaffirm "the will of victorious France not to allow French sovereignty in Algeria to be jeopardized," as General de Gaulle put it in a message to Governor General Yves Chataigneau, [18] inspired more hatred than fear.

"There can't be any hope invested in a heartless race," became one of the nationalists' slogans, echoed by the peasants' fatalistic "God has the power to bring them to reason." Reason was not the lofty quality for which colonial rule was known. A powerful revolutionary current was pervading every corner of Algerian soil, but France failed to see it. The villagers who greeted our return to Ihitoussen may not have been fully conscious of that revolutionary current, but their reactions to my father's arrest show that they were inevitably swept along on the same tide of revulsion and revolt.

Once the welcoming celebration ended, Uncle Iddir and his family went directly to their home located some 50 yards from ours. Our one-story house, built of stone with a red tile roof, consisted of two rooms on the ground floor and two rooms on the second, accessed by an outside staircase leading to the balcony. I retain a dreadful memory of this balcony from which I fell when I was only four years old. The house had been under construction when, venturing onto the balcony, I stepped on a board that was not nailed firm and yielded under my feet. I fainted when I crashed into the yard and terrified my poor mother, who, overwhelmed by her two other toddlers, had momentarily lost sight of me.

The cemented ground floor was covered with woven *alfa* grass mats, occasionally topped with a woolen carpet for visiting guests. The rooms faced inward like all houses in Ihitoussen, a wall concealing residents from the eyes of strangers. Anyone was considered foreign if he or she was alien to the village or to the 150 families bound by real or imagined ties of kinship or consanguinity. With firewood as the only cooking fuel, the kitchen was outdoors in the courtyard, next to the wall built around the house, and topped by a sort of veranda sheltering it from bad weather.

As soon as we settled in, a procession of villagers lined up to comfort my mother. The first to appear was my Uncle Ravah. He wore his eternal baggy pants of indefinite color, a shirt, and a cap of doubtful cleanliness. Casting his eagle-like gaze on his brother's kids—we were five boys in 1945—he whispered, "Only God is eternal."

Then, raising his voice, he said, "I always told my brother that he couldn't have children and simultaneously engage in militant politics. Not with these miscreants. He never listened. We must pray God now that he stays alive."

This customary outburst from Uncle Ravah did not fool anyone. Married for 15 years but childless, everyone knew, and he more than any other, that if his brother died, it would be his responsibility to support our family. In fact it was rumored that he planned to marry a second wife who could give him an heir. The cultural system always blamed the wife for a couple's infertility, encouraging the childless husband to divorce and remarry. More frequently, the husband simply opted for an additional wife. In such a case, it was not uncommon for the first wife to arrange her husband's marriage to a second, naturally never pretty, woman. This is what exactly happened a few years later in Uncle Ravah's family.

For the moment, because of my Aunt Zahwa's extraordinary blue eyes and voluptuous form, Uncle Ravah at 43 years of age may have been childless but still remained fiercely loyal to his wife. For him an unappealing prospect loomed. He would have to care for all of his brother's sons should my father not return alive or be sentenced to a long prison term. Turning to the visitors and seeking their approval, he said, "The French race is ruthless because it does not fear God. What can the Algerian People's Party do to stop the carnage? With what?"

Murmurs of approval greeted his words. "I am telling you, it's a race that denies God, and God Himself doesn't seem to give a damn."

As his words rang out, strong calls to order came from all sides. "Curse Satan, oh Ravah! Don't let the devil take hold of your tongue." My uncle, who had a reputation for picking a fight for no reason, raised his arms, pointed them to heaven, and left the house filled with people who had come to show their solidarity with the bereaved family.

It was not until dusk that the crowd of visitors, mostly women, gradually left the house. The days were long, certainly, but two hours of each day were taken up with the task of rolling the couscous.

43

Invitations to dinner were not a part of village custom even in rare times of plenty, let alone the scarcities and famines of World War II. However, if one unexpectedly stumbled upon someone having a meal, the rules of hospitality required offering to share even the meagerest of repasts. The ritual formula of exchange in this case was, curiously, the opposite of that in the West. If a French person comes across a compatriot having a meal, the conventional salutation is *bon appétit* ("litterally I hope you are hungry enough to enjoy your meal"). An Algerian in the same circumstances wishes a fellow Algerian the exact opposite: "*May God fill you,*" implying "*with the little you have.*" Furthermore, returning from the weekly market, the privileged few who could afford a few morsels of meat absolutely had to hide them from view when crossing the village. If by chance an impoverished person were to see the meat, tradition required the more privileged person to bring the poorer neighbor a share of the meat at dinner time.

It was, however, fairly common for visiting relatives to bring food. Indeed, less than half an hour after sunset, just as my mother, after breast-feeding the baby, was about to prepare the traditional flat bread, there was a knock at the door. My grandmother, panting with old age, appeared with a wooden dish full of couscous already mixed with sauce. As far as I remember, it was a real treat. The couscous was generously seasoned with olive oil and cooked with lentils, for green vegetables were only available on market day. My grandmother had added a piece of dried fat to the sauce, giving it a smoky flavor we had not tasted since we moved to Tazmalt. We made a circle around the common dish as Grandmother, sitting in a corner, watched with a mixture of sadness and emotion.

My brother Sharif quickly ate his spoonfuls of couscous and then approached her. "Grandma, tell us a story."

He knew she had an inexhaustible repertoire of tales pitting the wily, legendary Bel âjjout against Tseriel the ogress. At these words, a smile lit her somber features, adding a few wrinkles to her face. "Not tonight, my children, not tonight. You are tired. Tomorrow, maybe."

Because rumors and wild speculation, fueled by eyewitnesses to the massacres at Kherrata and Sétif, aroused the greatest concern for the fate of her son, Grandmother's heart sank as she surveyed her five grandchildren. The oldest was only 16 years old; the youngest, a baby still at the breast. Would they be orphaned? To disguise her anxiety, she rose and lit the oil lamp, which began to smoke profusely. The halo of flame lit up her wrinkled face and created an unfamiliar atmosphere, with our monstrous shadows projected on the walls by the pale light. Outside, hungry jackals began to howl, causing an energetic concert of barking dogs. We inched closer to Grandmother and yawned without restraint. She ran her hand over our heads, shaved as was the custom, and held back her tears.

I have a fond memory of her angelic sweetness and unalterable dedication to her family. Articulating her phrases with some difficulty, she turned to my mother and said, "You have become a city girl. You have lost the habit of lining up at the fountain or collecting bundles of wood. But you have to resume mountain living. For tomorrow's meals, I will give you enough firewood."

"Thanks, Yemma," whispered my mother.

"But for water," continued my grandmother, "you will have to line up at the fountain at dawn. Otherwise the line will be too long, and you can't leave your children alone that long. You remember, not so long ago you could wash clothes in the Oued Zemaâ River. Not anymore. It's dried up. Your neighbor Djedjiga will show you the way to the forest, where you can pick up dead wood and bring back a bundle. It will not be easy with your five children, but just think of them and nobody else. Courage!"

According to the legend, M'hand "Vougharaf," hidden behind the millstone of an ancient olive-oil mill which he maneuvered like a turret, repelled dozens of French invaders.

Chapter 3
Liberation and Commitment to the Cause

"No one can make you feel inferior without your consent"
Eleanor Roosevelt

For nearly three months, my mother slaved to support her young family. She arose each day at dawn. She had to fetch water every other day and gather dead wood at least two or three times a week. While preparing the daily couscous, she would occasionally kick the cradle hanging from a beam to calm her crying one-year-old, while keeping a watchful eye on her active three-year-old. The hardest part was carrying her youngest on her back while balancing a jug of water on her head. Her eldest son was not always there to look after his younger brothers. More than once, my mother regretted that two of her daughters had died in infancy. My two surviving sisters, Jamila and Aziza, were not born until 1949 and 1952.

All this time, her mother-in-law displayed exceptional solicitude. Not only did she often take us to her home, but she also put aside for us the lump of fresh butter she made once a week. In addition, she seemed to have an endless supply of dried figs for us. Everyone knew that she took great care of her goat and fig trees. Early each spring, she put on trousers and using a pick, aired the soil around each fruit tree. As for her goat, it followed her around like a trained dog. Every day she led it near the fountain where grass was abundant. At night the leaves of ash trees completed the lucky animal's diet.

But in May 1945, the grass was scarce and villagers were forced to hire a shepherd to take their flocks to pasture earlier than usual. Those who owned a goat brought their animals, at daybreak, to the village square. The shepherd led the flock to a mountain pasture. After a few days, the goats knew the routine. Once released from their tiny stables, they headed on their own to the meeting place. In the evening, the shepherd brought them back to the village square. Sometimes a family waited in vain for their beloved animal. Outwitting the vigilance of the shepherd, a jackal would attack and kill a goat straying into the woods. The loss was met with a grief that put the entire village in turmoil. The villagers organized a hunting party but would find no more than the cleaned skeleton and skin of the goat.

To alleviate his boredom, my older brother Sharif and other boys his age accompanied the shepherd to the mountains. If I was lucky, Sharif might condescend to take me with him. At lunchtime, the shepherd would milk a goat or two and concoct a delicious drink with a few drops of fig tree sap poured into the warm milk. We each got a share, elegantly served in a fig leaf.

Nearly three months had elapsed since my father had been taken into custody but still, no one knew exactly where he was incarcerated. Towards the end of July, my mother, busy washing diapers, heard shrill cries outside. A few seconds later her neighbor's daughter burst breathlessly into the house and said, "He has arrived! Uncle Ameziane has arrived!"

My mother could not believe her ears at first, but two children in the neighborhood confirmed the news. She quickly washed her hands and retrieved from a crate a rug, which she spread in the master bedroom. She cut a piece of bread and placed it in a wooden dish, next to a small bowl of olive oil and a water pitcher. A few minutes later, my father appeared on the doorstep surrounded by a swarm of noisy children. He was barely recognizable: pale and skinny, his usually rosy cheeks were as ashen as parchment and bristling with black hairs. His gray eyes and thin lips forced a smile before he collapsed on the carpet. He found the strength to pull us towards him, my brothers and I, one after another.

"Greetings, oh son of Boudjemaâ," my mother murmured.

"Greetings to you too," he replied.

These were the only accepted salutations permitted in public between husband and wife.

Soon the news of my father's release spread at the speed of the small legs of children. The grueling five-hour walk through the mountains had utterly exhausted him. He, whom nobody ever heard complain, leaned against the bare wall of the room and confessed in a whisper, "I am spent."

Retiring to rest was contrary to local custom, so he forced himself to get up and begin the interminable, traditional hand-kissing with men and women. When he was finally able to sit, a blacksmith from Kherrata was the first to speak. It was only years later that I was able to reconstruct the dialogue and grasp its real meaning.

"God has visibly protected you," the blacksmith said. "What these monsters have done, there are no words that can tell it."

"I know," replied my father. "Bejaia's civil prison was packed with Algerians who, like me, had the chance to stay alive and tell what they witnessed or experienced."

"You see something in this? How can we explain this extraordinary outburst of ferocity?"

My father paused and then, in a barely audible voice, tried to explain: "The French have completely lost their minds. They panicked at the sight of a few thousand Algerians waving flags. Flags, not guns! Not yet, but that's coming soon. But flags are perhaps more frightening than guns."

Breathing hard, he added, "The police inspector who interrogated me howled in my face, 'No use revolting, nothing will change. It will always be the same. We will smash you as we have done each time you rebelled.' But he is mistaken. We will now defy history and intrude in it. To make it and not repeat it."

"What do you think will happen now?" asked a villager.

"I don't know," replied my father. "But one thing is certain: the massacres signal the end of politics, the end of the assimilationists, the integrationists, and the fusionists of Algeria with France. We will no longer wave flags and get slaughtered. It's going to be another form of struggle, a merciless struggle."

"But," observed a visitor, "with what?" He did not need to clarify his thinking. Everyone had in mind the overwhelming number of French soldiers and their enormous military potential. For these blacksmiths, any attempt to challenge colonial oppression with force was an expression of despair akin to suicide. Even a suggestion of rebellion prompted visions of tanks and fighter planes ruthlessly dropping their bombs on wretched villages. The whispers that accompanied the question all asked the same thing: "With what?"

"With all the people," said my father. "Never again with fragmented ranks as with Mokrani in 1871, or the Ouled Sidi Sheikh tribes in 1881. Last May's uprisings showed that Algerians are ready. No corner of Algeria has been spared the turmoil, and the blood of patriots flowed everywhere. The days of colonialism are numbered."

His words, as we know, proved prophetic. Two years after the massacres, the first armed group, the Secret Organization (OS) was set up nationwide. And seven years later, on All Saints' Day in 1954, the bell began to toll for French colonialism in Algeria.

For now, the villagers paraded one after the other before my father, pronouncing the usual formula "Thank God you're safe." It was nearly six o'clock before the last visitor left the house and calm returned. Moving slowly, my father made an effort to get up and go outside the house. He sat down on a large rock and indulged in thought. The months he had spent in civil prison were a nightmare ordeal of interrogation and torture, using sophisticated techniques like water boarding. And he recalled his testimony to the judge at his trial.

"Where did you get that rifle?" the judge asked.

"A peasant from the mountains sold it to me, sir."

"What is his name?"

"Belkacem is the only name he gave me."

"You lie," roared the judge. "Did you know that it is a

prohibited weapon?"

"Yes, sir."

"Then why did you buy it?"

"To protect and defend the honor of my family, sir."

"What do you mean?"

"I am a stranger in Tazmalt. I am from Grand Kabylia. Thugs can threaten the honor of my family."

"And the authorities and the law, what do you make of that?"

"There is only a one-eyed village constable that nobody fears, sir."

"Why didn't you purchase a shotgun?"

"It's too expensive, sir. I am only a blacksmith and have five children to feed."

Curiously, at no time did the judge or the police question my father about his activities within the nationalist party, which were totally secret at the time. Neither did they ask about the mysterious truck loaded with arms, the subject of relentless questioning in our garden at Tazmalt. He was returned to the cell he shared with common criminals and never questioned again.

The news of the massacres at Kherrata and Sétif had been confirmed throughout Algeria and deemed beyond comprehension. But it was to be years before the world learned what had happened because elsewhere May 8, 1945, was a day to celebrate the Allied victory. In Algeria, however, thousands took to the streets in major cities, brandishing flags and demanding independence. The leaders of the nationalist party who organized the marches had been encouraged by the 1941 Atlantic Charter establishing a vision for a post-World War II era, a document that proclaimed that all peoples have a right to self-determination. But for the Algerian people, the celebrations turned into tragedy.

Under the benevolent or indifferent eye of the colonial authorities, and foreshadowing the Secret Army Organization (OAS) 17 years later, French settlers organized into militias and conducted punitive expeditions to avenge the killings of some 88 colonists in local uprisings. Many colonists boasted of having made great hits at the opening of hunting season. One settler claimed that he alone killed "83 ravens," a racist term for dark-skinned Algerians.[19]

According to André Prenant, geographer and specialist in the demography of Algeria, who visited the region three years after the Sétif massacres, "the region was struck by grief. There were deaths in every family... The repression of May 1945 was, in the unanimous opinion of all historians, something terrible. I think there were between 20,000 and 25,000 victims. The families kept quiet and did not even dare report their dead."[20]

Algeria had experienced for more than two weeks an outbreak of murderous and hysterical madness. Many leaders and activists were arrested. Military courts handed down 2,000 convictions, 151 of which were death sentences. "Pacification," a euphemism that would later be resurrected during the revolutionary war for independence, only ended with the "official" declaration of loyalty towards the French of the tribes "organized as a great show" on a beach between Jijel and Kherrata on May 22, 1945. [21]

Gradually, in a gesture of appeasement, most of the prisoners including my father were released. What most likely spared my father a long prison sentence was his humble condition of blacksmith. He was assumed to be illiterate. He knew well how to conceal his level of culture and education and, although he spoke perfect French, he called for an interpreter, which allowed him time for reflection before answering questions. Many who were considered "too educated" among the insurgents were sentenced to long prison terms, and 20 of them were mercilessly executed. [22]

Watching the sun set as he relived his ordeal, my father was already planning a new phase of the struggle ahead. The song of cicadas subsided as the crickets took over with their own concert. A light wind began to stir the tops of the ash trees. He looked out on the countless tiny fields of fig and olive trees bounded by stone walls which, as tenaciously as the sturdy villagers themselves, survived due to the meticulous care of women.

He thought of us all, he told me years later, and what would have happened to us if he had been executed or sentenced to a long prison term. He weighed the pertinent and sometimes sharp criticisms of my mother, who urged him to abandon politics and stop jeopardizing the future of his children. "What future?" he replied. "Making out of them blacksmiths? Maybe. But office clerks bossed around in the colonial administration? Never!

"The people have just proved that they are cured of the disease of fear. Thousands of irrepressible breaths, I am convinced," he told me, "will soon unleash a tornado that will sweep the colonial order. The storm will spare no part of this sacred land. It will carry and disseminate all kinds of seeds, fertile or sterile. They will all germinate and the most useful and most tenacious will ultimately prevail, by the will of men and women and God's gracious help. We will make a huge bonfire of old, dead oak trees, of superstitions and fatalistic traditions. But the green wood, the tender and fragile shrubs that want to live, will not always be spared.

"We don't remember who we are, what century we live in, for how many centuries we have been in this state. But that's irrelevant! Now history begins. We are going to redeem it. We will be reborn through and by a new battle. The last one! And we shall overcome, because we are not alone as we were in 1830 or 1871. We will win by the force of circumstances and history which lie on our side rather than by the strength of our arms or the number of our combatants."

In those moments, my father briefly saw himself from the outside, detached from time and place. He recognized his own conflict between the sacred call to liberate his fatherland and his love and concern for his wife and children, overwhelmed by the hardships of village life. He knew he belonged to an indomitable race torn from ancestral land by the sheer necessity to survive. He saw the unspeakable madness of France's ruthless rule, just because men like him were peacefully demanding some dignity.

Humiliated in the Second World War, France had taken revenge on a defenseless people. The onslaught of a powerful, massively equipped and precisely disciplined German Army had overwhelmed the nation in just a few weeks. Whole contingents surrendered, shamefully, by telephone. Without the intervention of the United States, England and the Soviet Union, World War II would have been the end of France's sovereignty for decades.

Algerian militants had begun to sense that France was vulnerable and could be forced out. Learning from the mistakes of Emir Abdelkader,[23] any new guerrilla leader would establish his headquarters not in the Sahara Desert but instead at Ihitoussen, in the forests of Akfadou, or on the crests of the impregnable Djurdjura or Aurès Mountains. My father surveyed the wild and barren countryside, inhospitable and inaccessible. Poor and miserable though it was, this village of his ancestors gave him an uplifting sense of irrepressible freedom, security, and invulnerability. The need to act weighed as heavily on his mind as on the day he dared to defy the tribal leaders, leave his native Ihitoussen, and settle in Tazmalt.

Night had fallen by the time he made his decision. Reentering the house, he called my brother Sharif. "You know where my cousin the mule herdsman lives. Go see him and ask him if his two mules are available for tomorrow morning early. We're going back to Tazmalt. Hurry up, it will soon be too dark."

The prospect of again enjoying electric lights, running water, and above all, the itinerant cinema which came to Tazmalt every Thursday, sped Sharif on his way. After half an hour he was back. "Vava, he tells you that he will be here with his mules tomorrow right after the dawn prayer."

"Very well, kids, it's bedtime for you," my father said. Then he turned to my mother. "Fatima, you must bake two loaves of bread for us and Mohand and fill a bottle of olive oil for the road. I'll go say goodbye to my mother and my father. It won't take too long."

The author's parents.

Chapter 4

Return to Tazmalt

Man forgets sooner the death of his father
than the loss of his property
Niccolo Machiavelli, *The Prince*

*Any authority, resting on force instead of law,
is in the end overthrown by it.*
Louis-Philippe de Ségur

The small town of Tazmalt, built at the foot of the Djurdjura Mountains in the valley of the Soummam, was a model of French colonial architecture. The main street crossed the principal thoroughfare connecting Algiers and Bejaia. Known as "The Four Ways," it extended to the railway station, a quarter of a mile further south. Nearly all the French settlers in Tazmalt lived on this street.

First and foremost among their houses was the most opulent one owned by the Barbauds. Their one-story residence with shutters and a wrought-iron balcony looked the most impressive, if not the most beautiful. Facing inward, with a large courtyard, the house left the impression of being uninhabited, as no sign of life filtered from its closed windows. This absence of vitality reflected the mentality of its haughty and conservative owners, who sequestered their females in the same way as bourgeois Muslims.

Except for the rare moments when they sneaked into their black Citroen to go to their country mansion, no inhabitant of Tazmalt ever caught sight of the Barbauds' wives and daughters. The women's education was entrusted to carefully selected Catholic nuns. The men, proud and contemptuous even with their less wealthy fellow Catholics, spoke to no one and greeted no one.

Across from the Barbauds, the Cartaillers' house symbolized their openness and lack of visible distrust towards the Algerian community. The house entrance revealed, through a wrought-iron gate, a staircase leading to the second floor and a large, well-maintained garden planted with rose bushes, jasmine, and bougainvillea. The Cartailler men and women went about their business peacefully or lounged on comfortable chairs, reading *l'Echo d'Alger*, the newspaper of the French settlers.

Further south, towards the railroad station and across from the town hall, the Lilles' house was a perfect replica of the Barbauds'. The widowed Madame Lille, an occasional substitute teacher, owned the only irrigated farm on the outskirts of Tazmalt. In the blazing heat of the summer, with refrigerators still unheard of in Tazmalt, the clear, icy water from Madam Lille's well delighted the villagers, who rushed to it with their gerrycans as soon as they heard the deafening roar of the diesel engine pump.

About 300 meters farther south resided the poorest French families. The Haubins, my Uncle Iddir's neighbors, were humble wheelwrights before changing their trade to mechanics.

Occasionally, they resumed their former work and repaired the horse-drawn carts still used by farmers in the region. The Haubins were not averse to associating with Algerians and spoke our regional language, Kabyle, with almost no accent.

Near the Haubins lived the Widow Parrot, keeper of a bar that was always packed. Her two daughters, Genevieve and Christianne, both very pretty, were the primary draw for customers, mostly French males. Their cloistered females, like Muslims, did not frequent the only bistro in Tazmalt.

Recessed in a side street lived Monsieur Merlot, owner of a vineyard two kilometers from Tazmalt on the banks of the river. Naturally, given his name, he was the owner of the only winery in the region.

Adjoining the Merlots lived Berthola, the handyman for the municipality: plumber, trench-digger supervisor, hydraulics expert. He was constantly on the go, repairing leaks and maintaining water pipes. Big and fat, always breathing hard, he was often forced to sit down to supervise the work of excavation. In doing so, he exposed his ruddy testicles through his shorts and triggered the laughter of scoundrels like me.

Finally, on the same street as our family's forge, between the European and Algerian districts, there stood a mission of the Anglican Church. Attracted by the sweets offered to potential converts, many children attended the sermon delivered in the Kabyle language by the very popular Mr. Griffith. I still remember, half a century later, a rhyme street kids my age learned and repeated while laughing: "Sidna Aïssa, dhamaksa (Christ is a shepherd)." In retrospect, I am surprised that our parents, who often debated religious issues with Mr. Griffith, never prohibited us from celebrating Sidna Aïssa, the Lord Jesus. Perhaps because they were reminded by the Imam that Jesus was a prophet like Mohamed and Christians were People of the Book, a remarkable tolerance prevailed between the Anglicans and the Muslim villagers.

The roads were not paved, so mud in winter and dust in summer made for heavy going. Traveling salesmen never ventured into such inhospitable, squalid places. On the main street, a few grocers, two cafés, two butchers, and a tailor were the only businesses owned or run by Algerians, struggling to cope with the cruel shortages of World War II. The first bakery appeared only in 1948, along with two or three beaneries. At the south and north ends of town, Algerians were crowded into houses built for the most part of unfired mud brick. Their complaints protesting their utter wretchedness fell on the deaf ears of the French settlers.

The worlds of the settlers and of the Algerians mostly

obeyed the absurd yet understandable logic of mutual exclusion. The two communities had their own grocery stores. With the exception of a few Algerian families who were landowners and subserviently Francophile, and a few artisans, the vast majority of the people were seasonal workers or laborers.

Before the advent of the reaper-binder, hundreds of workers were employed to harvest wheat, barley, and hay with sickles and scythes forged by blacksmiths such as my father. The grape harvest used almost exclusively child labor. Picking fruit such as oranges or tangerines, harvesting vegetables and olives, created seasonal jobs which, though insecure, at least allowed poor people clumped around the farms of the settlers to make a precarious living.

The famous olive groves of the region supplied half-a-dozen small olive-oil processing plants. Part of the production was delivered to Monsieur Tamzali, who refined and exported the oil. After pressing, the seeds were crushed again to allow for the recovery of secondary oil. Somewhat unfit for human consumption, it was nevertheless used for frying. It also formed the base of the soap manufactured in Bejaia and commonly referred to as "Marseille soap."

Most of the settlers' farms were large and irrigated, and the settlers became quite prosperous thanks to abundant and cheap labor. But every fall and winter, floods from the Sahel-Soummmam River swept away huge chunks of arable land. Hence, some settlers' farms lost tens of acres each year. Reinforcing the riverbank was not of much use, as the capricious course of the stream, combined with a fairly steep slope, made control of the flow after a rainstorm virtually impossible.

My father was astute to settle in the area and convince his brother Ravah to join with him to acquire a property. Located at the invisible borderline separating the settlers' quarters from the indigenous section and facing the mission of the Church of England, their forge was ideally placed. Mountain farmers had to pass by it on their way to weekly market. They often left their farm tools to be repaired and their pack animals to be shod. Some of them, sick or injured, stopped at the English mission for free medical care provided with extraordinary dedication by the sisters and brothers of the Anglican Church, speaking their strongly accented but fluent Kabyle.

Such was the town to which our family returned just one day after we were reunited with my father. We left Ihitoussen at the first streaks of dawn, traveling towards Ighzer Amokrane. This took us more than five hours, marked by frequent halts to change and breastfeed my baby brother. As we approached Ouzellaguene,

58

my father decided to make a slight detour for lunch at a famous mountain spring, whose abundant year-round flow was a mandatory and most pleasant stop for all travelers. Its crystal-clear glacier-fed water was so famous that the government started bottling it immediately after independence.

With our thirst quenched and our corn cakes devoured, the youngest were mounted on mules, with my father or my mother taking turns holding on to us. We began our slow descent towards Ighzer Amokrane, arriving shortly after nine in the morning. We still had an hour or two before the Bejaia-Algiers train, so we rested in the waiting room of the station while my father settled up with his muleskinner cousin. He paid the few francs due and watched his cousin take out the hay from bags hanging on each side of the saddle and carefully spread it out in front of his animals. He took off their bridles and watched as they eagerly devoured the dried grass.

"You know," Cousin Ouameur said, "I should feed them barley. But even for us, it is too expensive and not easily available."

"I confess that I miss the good barley cakes of yesterday," said my father. "We're fed up with corn flour. But we must be thankful to the Americans that we are able to survive on it."

"You can say that. In Ihitoussen, there are no ration vouchers for even maize flour. We have to stay alive on barley bran and acorn flour. It really is a severe dearth."

"Now that the war has ended," my father observed, "maybe the situation will improve. By the way, why don't you wait for the arrival of the train? There may be customers for you to at least as far as Ouzellaguene."

The mule herdsman lifted his cap with one hand, and scratching his head with the other, asked, "What time is the train is scheduled to arrive?"

"Oh, in an hour or two, it depends; the station master himself does not know."

"In that case, I'll wait." Cousin Ouameur sniffed the air, looked at the sky and the leaves of the ash tree, and concluded, "It is not going to be too hot today. The mules will be exposed to about an hour of heat."

He unsaddled his animals and led them to a stubble field, where they began to graze. Using a saddle for a pillow, he lay down under an olive tree and fell asleep.

Impatiently, I waited for my first train ride. Zouhir, Sharif, and I went out and scrutinized the horizon eagerly, watching for the coal-fired engine and its plume of black smoke. But Salah, two years older, sickly and hungry, would not stop moaning. Baby

59

Nacer would not stop crying. The piece of corn-flour cake and dried figs my mother had consumed had not produced much milk. She nonetheless gave the baby her breast, and he soon fell asleep.

The screeching brakes of the train entering the station alerted everyone. We boarded while Ouameur approached a few travelers and proposed his mules for hire. When Ahitous saw that a family seemed interested, he gave a sigh of relief. As the train started, he leaned against the window to wave goodbye to his cousin. The broad smile that lit up Ouameur's face was a clear indication that his mules—and his pockets—were not making the return trip empty.

After three stops in less than an hour, the train entered the Tazmalt station. It was almost noon and the blistering heat in the valley was overwhelming. My father carefully avoided the main street and the bar swarming with settlers and their informants. He sent my brother Sharif by the shortest route to inform Uncle Iddir that we were back in Tazmalt. "You just tell him I was released and ask him to come see me this afternoon."

It took a quarter of an hour for the whole family to reach our home, abandoned for nearly three months. With an unsteady hand my father unlocked the outside door. Without a word, he handed the baby and the room keys to my mother. She opened all the doors and windows and began to thoroughly wash the dust-covered floors. Her exhausted baby found his crib and immediately fell asleep.

The garden was in terrible shape. The corner, where peppers and tomatoes used to grow, was trampled; other areas completely ransacked. Here and there were the imprints of studded shoes, cigarette butts, and brown spots from chewing tobacco. My father crossed the garden and his eyes hardened when he lingered at the spot where he had been beaten with such incredible ferocity.

His heart sank at the thought that he would never again see his beloved MAS 36. I did not yet know how to read but my older brothers, Zouhir and Sharif, had been able to decipher on the cylinder head, *Manufacture d'Armes de Saint-Etienne*. My father remembered the times when he lovingly stroked his rifle, disassembled it, greased it, and put it back together in a flash. Once, during the holiday commemorating the birth of the Prophet Mohammed, he could not resist. Under cover of large firecrackers, he amused himself by introducing shells into the barrel and ejecting them while explaining, "You open the breech like this, you push the cartridge into the barrel like this, you aim like this, and you pull the trigger like this." He fired a shot into the ground which left a cavity that enormously impressed us boys.

Now he felt naked and vulnerable. But never mind, he was a blacksmith after all, and would not remain helpless for very long. He could easily forge a sharp sword, a saber, or even a spear as he had in the early days in Tazmalt. He would keep it in a corner of the forge, ready to use.

He looked at the apricot tree which the Moroccan Tabors had attacked like a swarm of locusts. Some branches had been broken, and he felt the pain that a Kabyle always experiences towards a wounded fruit tree. But the wound was not fatal. Apart from the sacking of the house and the huge fright caused to his family, the damage was bearable. More than anything, the honor of women had been preserved. It was time to forget the past and look unflinchingly into the future.

He heard a knock at the door and knew immediately that it was Uncle Iddir. They embraced affectionately and sat on a bench in the shade of the fig tree.

"You know, with what happened in Kherrata and Sétif, we thought we'd never see you again," Iddir said.

"My hour has not yet come, that's all. Have there been any arrests of militants here?"

"Not recently to my knowledge. They apparently went after Larbi Oulebsir, but he was nowhere to be found. He must be hiding in the mountains. But your neighbors Boho Oulebsir and his brother Ali were arrested and beaten. Ali even got a broken nose."

"Ali? That's a real surprise. They know he fought bravely for France against Nazi Germany. Being released from the French Army with the rank of warrant officer when you can barely read and write is not something everyone could do."

Ali Oulebsir was demobilized in 1944. His bravery in battle had earned him great prestige in the French community in Tazmalt.

"Besides," added my father, "he and his brother flirt openly with the Ulama (Association of Islamic Scholars), not with the Algerian People's Party. The Ulama never take any extreme positions and therefore are ranked second everywhere."

I remember well my father's assertion that day about the Ulama, but it was not until years later that I found out that Article Three of the bylaws of the Association unambiguously stated, "Any political discussion and, moreover, any intervention in a political issue, is strictly prohibited within the Association."[24] Later I discovered an even more significant letter written by the Islamic reformer Sheikh Mohammed Abdu, who explicitly cautioned in 1903 "against criticism of [French] government policy... Such a subject is very dangerous..."[25]

However, during this period of insurgency in May 1945, the French made no such fine distinctions among their Algerian subjects. As they were to do again on a massive scale a decade later, especially during the Battle of Algiers in 1957, the French randomly arrested any Algerian and subjected him or her to abuse or torture. No specific charges had to be brought: the Algerians were assumed to know the cause of their arrest—and many proved it by denouncing anyone to bring their ordeal to an end.

The brief silence that crept between the two cousins was broken by Uncle Iddir, who said to my father, "If I may give you some advice, drop your political activism. You have five kids and you cannot afford to defy the French with impunity. The French are miscreants who do not acknowledge God."

My father felt his temper rising and was tempted to say that he had enough of being reminded all the time that having children meant he must submit to French occupation forever. But he checked himself and calmly replied, "You're surely right, Iddir. I'm seriously considering it. I'd better drop all this. If something happened to me, who would take care of my family?"

He did not mean a single word of what he said, of course, but he decided to wrap all his militant activities in total secrecy. Since the officer who had led the search operation against him had moved, without hesitation, directly to the grapevine to dig up his beloved army rifle, he suspected an informant. Besides, the less the members of the family knew about his activities, the more they were protected from any collective punishment.

The call to prayer ended the cousins' discussion. My uncle got up and invited my father to accompany him to the mosque. But Father politely declined. "I will pray at home. Besides, I am two prayers behind schedule. Go ahead. It's needless to tell anyone that I'm back. The informants will learn that soon enough. For my part, I will appear in the village only when I really have to."

Since his release from jail, my father had become a different man. He would constantly mutter to himself: "It's finished, it's the end of politics. We will never again take to the streets, wave flags, and get slaughtered."

At this point I would like briefly to digress into American history to show how revolutions tend to be triggered by the same pattern of events. The May 8, 1945, massacres were to play the same role in the Algerian insurrection as the Boston Massacre did in 1770. The tragic death of American patriots had intensified the tensions generated by the Townshend Acts and set in motion a series of events that ultimately produced the Declaration of Independence in 1776.

Two years after the massacres at Kherrata, Sétif and Guelma, the first armed group, the Special Organization, was formed. Nine years later, on November 1, 1954, the death knell began to toll for French Algeria. Absolute patriots were convinced, after the May 8 massacres, that the scandalous injustice of colonial oppression would only disappear the way it had been imposed, by armed force. To cite a delightful understatement by General de Gaulle, "They concluded that their liberation would not come about through legal channels."[26]

By the same token, tyranny could only be attacked by the militant portion of patriots closest to the occupation, not by submissive Francophile families. The two years that followed the dramatic events of 1945 were marked by heated arguments within my family. My mother, citing the number of children to look after, continued to press my father to quit his militant activities. My older brother Sharif, unable to find a worthwhile occupation with the departure of American and British troops from Tazmalt, took to smoking *kif*, the local variety of marijuana. When my father found out about it, he ordered my brother to don a leather apron and begin training as a blacksmith. He then asked my mother to arrange for Sharif's marriage, which was celebrated in 1947 but quickly fell apart. After a second arranged marriage failed, Sharif sent a messenger to my father indicating whom *he* wanted to marry. This time the union lasted until death.

My brother Zouhir and I continued to attend primary school under my father's watchful eye. I do not know if the dramatic events of 1945 had something to do with it or if I was solitary by nature, but I very rarely mingled with other kids or participated in their games after school. Outside school, my favorite pastime was hunting birds. I cannot resist recounting an incident that still makes me laugh more than 50 years later. Before returning to afternoon class one day, I made a detour through the olive groves and captured a goldfinch. Not having enough time to take it home, I put it in my pocket and rushed to school. In the middle of the history lesson, the bird jumped out of my pocket and limped between the desks to the cheers of my comrades, unleashing the wrath of the master. Monsieur Avril punished me with "bad points," although these took into account the fact that I was his best student at the time.

Zouhir, the first of the tribe to be admitted to the Bejaia High School, convinced my father that racist Pied Noir professors would never grant him a degree in Algeria. He was sent to France to the Reims Ecole Supérieure de Commerce.

Politically, the years that followed the bloody repression

63

of nationalist activists in 1945 at first served to radicalize the 19-year-old nationalist movement marked by arrests, harassment, and suicidal shortsighted policies of the French settlers. Then one day, Si Larbi Oulebsir met with a companion in their secret office and revealed a project that was drastically to change the lives of the nationalists.

Installed on two wooden chairs behind a small table, Si Larbi announced to my father, "Ahitous, you are the oldest member of the militant nationalist cause in Tazmalt and you're the first to hear the news. The Directorate of the Algerian People's Party [PPA] has created a paramilitary outfit called the OS [literally "the bone"], the Special Organization. The OS will be an elite entity and the armed wing of the party. First and foremost, it will train the freedom fighters. The PPA's top leadership has drawn conclusions from the killings of two years ago. The era of peaceful demonstrations met by aircraft bombings and hails of machine gun fire is over. We won't take to the streets any longer and get slaughtered. We must take up arms. You know our motto: 'Independence is not granted, it has to be snatched.' "

Si Larbi considered war an unalleviated misfortune, but he also knew that it was an unavoidable continuation of failed and hopeless politicking.

"Yes, I know the slogan," said my father. "And if I were ever to forget it, the torture and humiliation I suffered while my wife and my children were watching, will remind me of it every moment of my life. I will be an implacable adversary."

"Good. Now, we have to prepare a list of party members who could be proposed for the OS. We need young militants, absolutely reliable, who have never been arrested and therefore are not known to the police, if possible—young men who can be trained to use weapons."

"You already have Ravah Mahia," said my father.

Nicknamed the "Bald One," Mahia had acquired a reputation for bravery from a simple fist fight with the eldest son of Mayor Robert Barbaud. Well fed and powerful, weighing twice as much as his adversary, the young Barbaud had grabbed Mahia by the collar and was about to punish him. But Mahia, with a mighty head butt, knocked out the settler. It cost Mahia dearly since he spent 24 hours in jail, during which time he was beaten by the police under the mayor's command. Since then, the Bald One had become the idol of youngsters and commanded respect from adults.

This incident served as a model to explain the principle of guerrilla warfare. Mahia used a ruse and surprise to defeat a much stronger opponent. We would do the same with guerrilla tactics against a powerful and well-equipped enemy. Ravah was therefore added to the list as a leading candidate, along with Si Larbi himself, to be proposed for the OS. In all, my father and Si Larbi decided upon a dozen people who were trustworthy and able to form the nucleus of armed resistance in the region.

"I think the Directorate will be satisfied," Si Larbi said. "We can start training with shotguns at the cemetery as soon as the hunting season starts. Ideally, we should find and recruit a veteran of World War II, the ongoing war in Indochina, or even World War I."

"I know one," said Ahitous. He is a true patriot. But there is a hitch. He lost a leg in the war."

Si Larbi burst into laughter.

"For the 'snap to attention,' 'stand at ease,' and clicking of heels, a wooden leg is not very practical."

So, for the time being, they were content with the list they had just established.

During the years after the massacres of 1945, it was not easy to enlist the support of many farmers in our region and inspire them to join Si Larbi Oulebsir and my father in the nationalist party. Many conformed to the image projected of them in the French textbooks as hopelessly fatalistic. They were easy to defeat because they had forsaken the true path of God and disobeyed His sacred injunctions. Colonialism was nothing but atonement for original sin.

"Si Larbi and I," my father told me years later, "were like doctors without patients or merchants with no customers. The vast majority of the population lived in utter poverty, but they were resigned to their fate." He reminded me that such fatalists endlessly repeated, like mantras, such statements as "God has willed that," "The French are too powerful," or "Resist them with what?"

By contrast, my father expressed a very different sentiment. "Certainly, if the forefathers were defeated, it was not for lack of courage or bravery. No, foreigners subdued us with their heavy artillery and their war machinery. But if their superior organizational skills, their armament, and their numbers made the difference, it was because our ranks were disorganized, disunited. Then, again, it was in the forests of Akfadou or on the crests of these imposing, inaccessible Djurdjura or Aurès Mountains that you should have planted your camp, oh Emir Abdel Kader, and not in the Sahara Desert."

Family life and hard work at the forge, interspersed with meetings with Si Larbi Oulebsir and other militants, continued unabated for Ahitous. Unfortunately, he was confronted almost immediately by constant hostility and harassment from the

65

mayor of Tazmalt, Robert Barbaud. First, the mayor decided it was against the law, meaning his law, to use the shop front of the forge to shoe, or even to tie, animals. Never, at the time, could my father have imagined that soon he was to establish a forge on the very lands Barbaud owned. But for now, the blacksmith was forced to shoe the animals inside his cramped workshop. Whenever he did so, a dull anger lifted him and increased his determination to continue the struggle whatever the cost.

During the years Barbaud was mayor, the hatred and suspicion he exhibited towards my father was accompanied by close surveillance. Thus, a post office employee "rented" a room in a building owned by the mayor, a hundred meters from the forge, and this spy spent most of his time observing the comings and goings of peasants who stopped at our forge. Although the age difference was considerable, the man tried to befriend me and extract information on my father's travels, particularly to Algiers. He also wanted to know about the outsiders who came to see the blacksmith. The postman ideally complemented the servile collaboration of the spy-in-chief of the village, the constable M. M.

I was about 12 and still in primary school when this pitiful character barged into the classroom and whispered something into the schoolmaster's ear. Then he barked to me, "Come with me." I followed him, filled with apprehension and assuming, incorrectly as it turned out, that my exploits with my slingshot had prompted his notice. As we walked out of the school, I looked sideways at him and told myself that M. M was definitely the person I hated most in the world.

On a previous day, I had been hunting birds when this peacekeeper of the village emerged like a devil from a box and grabbed me by the arm. He confiscated my slingshot, then undertook a body search and triumphantly waved a spare slingshot that he also confiscated. To be sure, the slingshots of young rascals, including myself, often targeted the glass windows of the settlers.

My diabolical marksmanship with a slingshot enabled me to kill several birds each time I went hunting. I would string them through their bills and make myself a belt of multicolored chickadees, finches, sparrows, and warblers, returning triumphantly to the village under the admiring gaze of young and old alike. Certainly none of the latter would blame any teenager for seeking an alternative source of protein. We kids even devised a barbaric way to cut, according to religious rites, the throats of those poor, beautiful birds with one of their own feathers. By the time I read years later that "God accompanies with an angry stare the fall of a bird that gets killed," my exploits with a slingshot, combined with the use of DDT, meant that there remained very few birds in Kabylia.

When M. M. took away my hunting weapons the first time, tears of helpless rage welled in my eyes, though I did not cry. It took me a while to find an olive branch in the shape of a V, to flame it to stiffen it, and then find an old inner tube near the car garage of the European quarter, carefully cut it into strips, and make a slingshot worthy of the name.

There was precisely such a slingshot in my pocket as I walked silently next to M. M. and wondered why he had not yet searched me and emptied my pockets. My anxiety increased significantly when I realized we had started climbing the hill that led to El Bordj, the Fort, which housed police headquarters. The large blue metal gate was opened after M. M rang the bell. Soon I found myself facing the police chief in a bare room where a few wooden chairs were scattered.

"Here you are. What's your name?" began the police chief.

"Hamou Amirouche, sir."

"Chief, you call me Chief."

"Yes, Chief."

"How old are you?"

"Twelve years, Chief."

"What class are you in?"

"The diploma class, Chief."

"You study hard at school?"

"I am first in my class, Chief."

At these words the police chief sat upright in his chair and turned to Constable M.M., who confirmed my status with a nod. This obviously put the chief in a bad mood, because there were five French pupils in the class.

"What time do you get out of school?"

"At four o'clock, Chief."

"What do you do after school?"

"I do my homework, Chief."

"And after your homework?"

"I go for a walk in the village, Chief."

"I know. You've were seen last night." My face must have expressed surprise, but I said nothing.

"We saw you talking to the driver of a black Citroen. What's his name again? I forgot it."

"I haven't spoken to anyone, chief."

"Do not lie, otherwise you'll go to jail. What did the driver of the car ask you?"

"Chief, I have not spoken to anyone."

"Then the constable is a liar?"

"I don't know, Chief, but I haven't talked to anyone."

I was telling the truth. At that age, I would have cracked under pressure and threat of jail if I had actually contacted anybody from outside the village. The police chief kept silent for a moment, then got up and, pointing his forefinger at me, said. "Go home. And if we ever found out that you lied, you'll go to jail. Understand?"

"Yes, Chief."

I went straight home and told my father. He listened silently and was surprised that his son has not had a fit of tears during the questioning, I, who was usually so sensitive. Then he gently placed his hand on my head and murmured: "That scoundrel, M.M., has absolutely no sense of decency. He is going overboard in treachery and cowardice."

Many years later I understood the meaning of my father's words: the Constable was the chief informer of the village. My father resolved then not to include me in his militant activities and allowed me quietly to prepare for my Certificate of Primary Education which symbolized, at the time, the summit of knowledge.

The teacher, Monsieur Fernand Avril, driven by an uncommon dedication, had taken on the task of bestowing on Tazmalt its first graduates in history. For this purpose, he selected the six best students in his class and made us study really hard. Even weekends, with the exam date approaching, were spent on reviewing arithmetic, geography, history, poetry recitation, and writing short essays.

To be sure, Monsieur Avril had temporarily dropped in my esteem two years earlier, following an unprecedented revolt by three students about to graduate, including my brother Zouhir. For the commemoration of the Armistice on November 11 ending the First World War, graduating students were taken every year to the War Memorial opposite the town hall to sing the French national anthem. The colonial press never failed to write that "the parade on November 11 allowed the French Muslims to show their unwavering attachment to France," in other words, to their masters.

In 1948 or 1949, three students rebelled and refused to attend the ceremony. My 14-year-old brother received a suspension of a week. The other students, both aged 16, were permanently excluded from school. Referring to this defiance, in a speech full of self-importance and bitterness at such ingratitude, Monsieur Avril even denounced, without naming him, "the father of a student in this classroom"—and I knew immediately that it was my father—

68

"who engaged in anti-French activities."

But I would forgive the master when the fateful day of the exam arrived. Monsieur Avril arranged with the school principal to transport us all in their personal cars to the examination center in Akbou. In the late afternoon, when the results were announced and all candidates from Tazmalt received their certificates, our joy was incredible.

Diploma in hand and beaming with pride, I crossed the main street of the village, and almost all the grocers and merchants invited me to stop, offering me cookies, fruit, and candy. They showered me with praise and murmured, "You have the chance to read and write. We, we are like animals."

But soon, the hopes aroused by my success in primary school were dashed. I was an intelligent child, almost constantly at the top of my class throughout grade school, spurred on by my father who constantly reminded me that unless I studied hard, I would end up shoeing mules and horses in his forge. The prominent French settler and mayor of Tazmalt, Robert Barbaud, saw to it that I did exactly that: He vetoed my application for a scholarship to attend the only high school in our region, in Bejaia, 60 miles from my hometown. His veto was punishment for my father's militant activism. While this cruel decision might have pleased the mayor, it illustrates one great dilemma of colonialism: to socially promote the indigenous population could have been a way to moderate nationalist aspirations and prevent a popular movement from acquiring a revolutionary dimension. But to increase the number of graduates through mass education also implied inevitable demands for power sharing and equal rights through universal suffrage. And this, of course, would eventually result in the political marginalization of the French minority. The settlers' lobby in Algeria was never able to disentangle from its contradictions; their foolish shortsightedness ultimately bred, with great ease, the people who became their gravediggers—the men and women who destroyed the myth of "French Algeria."

As my father could not afford to send me to a high school which required money for room and board, I found myself forced to consider something else. I wrote to the Merchant Marine, to Caterpillar, and a few other large companies, requesting of their "high benevolence" a position as an apprentice. It was then that I discovered the unbridgeable gulf separating the native's from the colonist's worlds. They were not only totally different, but antagonistic: on the one hand, the world of peasants, artisans, and small businessmen upon whom a primary-school certificate bestowed great prestige; and on the other hand, the closed world of

69

colonists which a modest primary-school degree could not open. Understanding that my opportunities were entirely foreclosed, I had no other option but to join the family forge. After a year of hard training, I began to shoe donkeys and mules—but not yet horses—and to repair small agricultural tools such as axes and hoes, while developing a genuine love for this noble profession.

The nationalist party, the PPA, had been banned in 1939 but reappeared in 1947 as the Movement for the Triumph of Democratic Liberties (MTLD). The creation in the same year of the OS thrust Ahitous to a new kind of activity: because he was one of the very few literate activists, he spent most of his time at night painting slogans on the walls of the region: "Release Messali Hadj," "Long live Free Algeria," "Free the Political Prisoners."

In 1950 a major event shook the region. A betrayal within the OS resulted in its dismantling by the notorious General Information Police and the arrest of more than 300 activists. Of course, Tazmalt activists did not escape repression. A dozen of them were arrested and had the rare privilege of enjoying the company of Ramdane Abane in the civil prison of Bejaia. Abane was sentenced to a five-year term. Being one of the very few militants holding a baccalaureate degree, he read extensively in prison. Unfortunately, his superior knowledge bred in him an attitude of contempt towards his peers. He had no respect for the militants who, although barely educated, triggered the Revolution while he was in jail. These same peers assassinated him in 1957, a year after he masterminded the Soummam Convention which gave the Revolution its institutions.[27]

As for my father, he was repeatedly arrested and taken to Akbou for interrogation, each time causing us great concern; but he was always released, probably saved once again by his profession, his many children, and the fact that, unlike Si Larbi Oulebsir, he was a recruiter for, but not a member of, the OS. His trade was also ideal as a cover for his political activities, since it could explain the perpetual line of peasants in his forge, including militants. His alibi was also always the same: "Inspector, I am a blacksmith. I have six kids and my elderly father to feed. I don't engage in politics."

One of his most implacable enemies was the French sycophant A. T., a villager who socialized only with the settlers. To celebrate his election to the City Council, A.T. ordered all the village cafés not to charge their customers and bill him instead. I remember vividly the gloomy expression on my father's face as he muttered "renegade," cursing A.T.'s election by traitors. That day, no nationalist ventured into the village cafés, even though the

70

logic of the struggle might have implied encouraging activists to eat and drink there, thereby contributing to the financial ruin of a Francophile bootlicker.

The months following the mass arrests of activists after the OS was dismantled gave my father more work. To help the needy families of incarcerated militants, he often left his forge in the care of my eldest brother and traveled tens of miles to ask for donations, always in kind: semolina flour, wheat, barley, olive oil, carefully avoiding the wealthy Francophile farmers. Whatever he collected, he distributed to the families of political prisoners.

On Fridays, he engaged Abdelmalek Foudala, the director of the Arabic school and imam of the mosque, to use his legendary oratorical skills and convince the peasants to express in-kind solidarity towards the families of prisoners. The mosque, a magnificent building erected as if to mock the Catholic Church across the street, was packed every time Abdelmalek Foudala officiated. It was built entirely with funds donated by citizens on land donated by the Chebbi family. The French vice-prefect in Bejaia had apparently offered financial assistance, immediately rejected by the association of citizens responsible for the project.

"They fight in God's name," the Muslim cleric pleaded as he asked for donations. Ahitous privately acknowledged that he would have preferred the use of the phrase "on behalf of the fatherland," but never contradicted Abdelmalek, who, in his Friday sermons, would often focus on the devastating effects of colonialism and the crucial importance of unity of the Algerian *nation* rather than the *Islamic* community. Thanks to these sermons, delivered in a subtle blend of Arabic and Kabyle, even the poorest families showed solidarity towards activists' families and helped feed them. The bourgeois landowners or the affluent merchants were never approached since they had set up a coalition to defeat the nationalist candidates in the local elections of 1947.

I rarely missed these Friday orations although their boldness worried me, especially as Constable M.M., the very man who had taken me to the police station for questioning, never missed the sermons either. Sadly, my concerns were well grounded. In 1957, our revered imam was assassinated by French paratroopers during a trip to Algiers. Before he left Tazmalt, the imam received a peremptory message from an Algerian gendarme, delivered by his young daughter: "Do not travel to Algiers." But we cannot escape our fate. I cannot help but think of a story I read a long time ago every time I remember Abdelmalek's tragic end.

One day the sultan of Damascus was resting in his palace when his favorite servant burst into the living room and cried out,

"Your Majesty, lend me your fastest horse; I beg you. I must leave at once for Baghdad." The sultan asked why the youth was in such a hurry. "As I passed through the palace garden just now," replied the servant, "I saw a horrible figure standing there. It was Death. When he saw me, he stretched out his arms as if to take me. I must lose no time in escaping from him; I am too young to die."

The sultan allowed his servant to take his fastest horse and leave. When the young man was gone, the sultan went into the garden and found Death still standing there.

"How dare you frighten my servant?" the sultan demanded.

"Your Majesty," Death said, "I simply threw up my hands in surprise at finding him here in your garden. You see, I have an appointment with him tonight in Baghdad."

The discovery of the paramilitary OS in Tazmalt proper had an unexpectedly dramatic effect on the settlers of the region. Most of them began to sell their farms and initiate a steady exodus to Algiers. The first to put their farm up for sale were, of course, the most unpopular: the Barbauds. But as one might expect, no individual Algerian, except perhaps a fistful of Francophile landlords, had sufficient resources to purchase their farm , assessed at 20 million francs, some $200,000 in 1952 U.S. dollars.

One day a peasant friend came to see my father. "You know," the visitor said, "the Barbauds put their farm up for sale. I worked for them as a laborer for years. I planted myself many of their beautiful orange and clementine trees. The country is ours, but the land is theirs. I told myself many times, how can we plant so many fruit trees in a land that no longer belongs to us?"

First, my father only smiled. "The Barbauds' farm for sale! Big deal! The 'big tent' Francophile families will acquire it and the same laborers will continue to plant trees in the same land that still belongs to others."

Nevertheless, my father asked, "And who do you think will purchase the Barbauds' farm?"

"Us," the farmer replied without hesitation. "Many of us. They are selling it for 20 million. With 1 million each, 20 of us can acquire it."

My father took only a moment to think: here was a way to get even with the mayor. He broke the brief silence and said to his friend, "Deal me in." In the next few days, he made an inventory of his assets and came to the conclusion that he had only his home in Ihitoussen and his small olive-oil mill with a single hydraulic press operating next to the forge. Selling the house in Ihitoussen presented a major problem: you might be able to shake an age-old tradition and leave the tribe with your family, but you could not sell your family abode in the ancestral village.

He went to see his cousins on his father's side in Bordj Bou Arreridj, offering them the Ihitoussen house for a ridiculously low price, on condition that he could buy it back if any recurrence of violent events such as those of 1945 made such a repurchase necessary. (In fact, the new owner took up arms at the beginning of the Revolution and, as soon as the French Army was informed, our beautiful home was razed.)

With money from the sale, my father soon transformed into a farmer-blacksmith in Allaghan, four miles from Tazmalt, along with the weakling son that I still was at the age of 14. Of the colonial family's mansion, he inherited a bedroom and a storage room that we used as a kitchen. The first thing my father pointed out to me was a loophole that the settler had cut directly into the window hardwood.

"You see that hole cut in the panel? This helps to get a gun out and fire if necessary. The Barbauds never felt safe in the area. They hated us all and vice versa. No surprise that they were the first to clear out." This was two years before the Revolution!

Ahitous entrusted his workshop in Tazmalt to my brother Sharif and, using mud brick as a building material, erected a blacksmith shop on a piece of his newly acquired land bordering the Bejaia-Algiers highway. I served as his aide, apprentice, and occasional confidante.

While learning the blacksmith's trade, I often cursed the mayor whose unconscionable dismissal of my scholarship application became an additional reason to revolt. The fact that I could not continue my studies like some of my school friends filled me with a profound sadness. But I could also understand that with my older brother Zouhir at the Ecole Supérieure de Commerce in Reims, which cost my father a fortune, I could only resign myself to mastering my ancestors' trade and helping my father attend to the needs of his large family.

I worked hard to learn how to shoe the beasts of burden, and, with a sledge hammer, shape, under my father's direction, a plowshare, hatchet, or pickax. At first, farmers were reluctant to entrust their donkey or mule, let alone their valuable horse, to an inexperienced apprentice. Indeed, if you were not careful, the nail hammered into the hoof could pierce the flesh and seriously hobble the animal, to the great displeasure of its owner.

Therefore, my father often asked farmers to tether their animals to the rings in the wall in front of the forge and go do their shopping. Now he could laugh at the memory of the mayor, who had forced him to shoe the animals inside his crammed forge in Tazmalt, rather than on the space outside deemed the exclusive property of French settlers. "Well done, Mayor. You forbade us to shoe our animals outside the forge. Well, we'll shoe them on *your* land."

Ihitoussen: The author's ancestral village.

Chapter 5
From Farmyard to Schoolyard

Luck is the residue of design.
Branch Rickey, baseball innovator

Along with acquisition of the mayor's property came a new profession with unexpected hardships for my father—farming. First, he had to monitor closely the distribution of irrigation water. When his turn for his share came, sometimes very late at night, watering had to take place immediately for his orange and clementine trees and the few rows of tomatoes and peppers at which he successfully tried his hand. But the hardest part of farming was the olive harvest on the 12 acres of land he now owned. He used a tall ladder to climb to the tops of the trees and dislodge the olives, which fell onto a tarp on the ground for my sister and me to collect.

One day the ladder tipped and he managed to grab a branch, narrowly avoiding crashing to the ground. This incident triggered a long meditation on the organization of his professional life. Finally, one evening after dinner, he declared, "I have a very nice trade and I am currently hanging onto trees and balancing like a monkey." Shortly thereafter, he sold his share of the farm and used the proceeds to expand the family home in Tazmalt. I was the first to rejoice because now I could have a room to myself. I was 15 years old; it was about time.

Furthermore, life on the farm in Allaghan was not particularly thrilling. In fact, I was so despondent at times that I began seriously to consider getting married. According to tradition, I had been engaged since the age of eight or nine to a distant cousin in Ihitoussen. Fortunately for me, my older brother Zouhir angrily dissuaded me from marriage, adding a few choice insults that verged on blasphemy.

Not that life in Tazmalt was very exciting either, but at least I could see an occasional movie featuring Tarzan or Zorro or enjoy an old Western. But very often the films shown in Tazmalt were Egyptian soap operas, most popular among peasants of the area. So I devoted myself to reading the novels that my brother Sharif brought home by the dozen: *The Saint* by Leslie Charteris, Agatha Christie mystery stories, the Biggles books by W. E. John, and, most fascinating of all, *The Arabian Nights*. As I read and reread the tales, I was often shocked in my religious beliefs. For example, a shipwrecked prince rescued by a mysterious old sailor had been instructed in a dream never to invoke the name of God. When the prince finally spotted land, he forgot about the warning and cried out "God be praised!"

Immediately his boat sank and he escaped drowning by a hair.

I was in great need of those moments of relaxation after an exhausting day that started after dawn prayers and did not end until dusk or even later. The work at the forge, essentially handling a heavy sledge hammer, took a toll on my abdominal muscles. I suffered two consecutive hernias, requiring two surgeries. At Dr. Brechet's clinic in Bejaia where I was operated on, I told myself that my work in the forge was all but over and I had to find some other way to earn a living.

In the early 1950s, with the Tunisian and Moroccan nationalist insurrections in full swing, our colonial administration perceived the warning signs that an Algerian revolution might be imminent. Although always too late in enacting reforms to improve the lot of the Algerian people, the authorities nonetheless inaugurated a Vocational Center in nearby Bejaia. My brother Zouhir suggested, or rather ordered me, to start preparing for the competitive exam to gain admission to the Center. But as it turned out, I had no cause for concern. I ranked second among the hundreds who sat for the exam, and, with the cursed Mayor Barbaud now self-exiled in Algiers, my application for an internship was duly approved.

My destiny took on a new course and my life would be drastically altered. If a fortune teller had dared to predict that a blacksmith would find himself, exactly 10 years later, a graduate of major American universities, or that he would be accepted as a Visiting Scholar at Harvard University's Center for Middle East Studies after 20 years in the Algerian Government Service, I would have reported the charlatan to the police for the fraudulent practice of fortune telling.

I spent the summer of 1954 shopping for my boarding school wardrobe. Although it was quite a financial burden for a blacksmith, my father made sure that the two suits and other items of clothing required for admission as an intern to the Vocational Center were of top quality.

When we arrived in Bejaia in early October, there was great excitement on the "Plain," the nickname for the great expanse of flat land across from the stadium on which the Center stood. Columns of students formed from the train and bus stations and started walking the two miles to the school. Many of them, mostly highlanders who were leaving their villages for the first time in their lives, were fascinated by the sea, halting to gaze at it before resuming their march with their heavy cardboard suitcases balanced on their shoulders.

Flanked by three of my comrades from Tazmalt, memories

of my first trip to Bejaia made me smile. My father had brought me with him when he went shopping for my school wardrobe. I remembered my first coffee with cream and the croissant that I savored at a luxurious café normally reserved for Europeans. With our blue-gray eyes and fair complexions disguising our ethnicity, we were addressed as "Messieurs" and served with a smile. I remembered the breathtaking view from Gueydon Plaza to the bay surrounded by mountains. As if he read my thoughts, my friend Omar Hocine remarked: "You, Hamou, have already been here. You can guide us, I hope."

"Not really," I answered. "I came only once with my father. But in Bejaia, all roads lead to the old town. The Plain where our Center is located is less interesting except for its stadium and green areas. The more recent buildings are built there as the city could not expand elsewhere because of the mountains."

Halfway to the Center, a sinister-looking building made me stop short. "What's wrong?" asked my friend.

"You see before you the civil prison. That's where my father was imprisoned in 1945. Beaten and tortured in Tazmalt first, then locked up there behind those walls. He could very well have been shot."

"Forget it. Forget all that," advised Hocine. "We are here to study and learn a trade. Forget about the French. Only God is more powerful than they are."

Only God? God was invoked at every turn to hold Him responsible for everything. Until when? And the Indochinese peasants? What was their religion, that allowed them to overthrow their masters? But I remained silent as the memories of that fateful day in May 1945 flowed back into my mind. Little did I suspect that, a few weeks later, that same penitentiary would again close its heavy doors behind hundreds of patriots, including my own father.

We passed the entrance to the prison, where men and women carrying baskets and packages were sadly lining up. Soon the Vocational Center, painted in beige, appeared before us, adjoining the Municipal Stadium. The stout little supervisor, Monsieur Ranouil, with his small plump hands and metal-rimmed glasses, greeted us and, after a close inspection of the clothing we had brought, showed us to our dormitories. It was barely 11 o'clock in the morning.

Roll call was at noon, just before we headed to the dining hall. When the name Zemmouri was called, two students responded angrily. "Which one?" Paul, a Jew, and Abdelhafid, a Muslim, had the same last name and hated to be mistaken for one another. As might be expected in a colonized country and ethnically segmented society, contacts between the French and the indigenous population were exceedingly rare or reduced to a strict minimum. It wasn't always that way, I found out years later.

Berber Jews and non-Jewish Berbers, some converted to Christianity, some remaining partly pagan, formed basically one— tribal—people until the Ummayad Muslim invasion in the seventh century. Led by Jewish Berber Queen Al Kahina, who rallied under her leadership all the Berbers of the Aurès region, the invasion was successfully contained for five years. Unfortunately the French conquest, by granting French citizenship to all Algerian Jews but not Muslims, had driven a wedge between Muslims and Jews. This divide-and-conquer tactic was enshrined in the ill-famed 1870 Crémieux Decree. By accepting French status, the Jews distanced themselves from the rest of the Algerian population, and by 1962 most had left Algeria.

But in fact, at the beginning of my school year, we all preferred to socialize exclusively with our peers from the same village, then the same region. It took a few months to forge friendships between students from the Sétif or Khenchela areas on the one hand, and the Kabyles of the Soummam Valley or Great Kabylia on the other.

For my part, I soon found myself making friends with Abdelhamid Naili from Akbou, some 12 miles from Tazmalt, and we quickly became inseparable. At the time, I never imagined that our friendship would compel him to follow me into the bush two years later when I joined the guerrilla fighters. Another student from Akbou, Jean-Pierre Nicolai, a Pied Noir or French-born Algerian whose parents had left Russia after the 1917 October Revolution, was also becoming a close friend when the Algerian insurrection stopped short the process.

Our first months were filled with studious competition marked by a continuous but courteous rivalry between Nikolai and me. The two after-dinner hours devoted to reviewing our lessons and doing our homework often proved inadequate. Nikolai and I watched each other as we went to bed. If one of us stayed too long in the bathroom, the other knew he was using the bathroom lights to study after curfew and did the same in an adjoining bathroom. Despite this rivalry, healthy after all, Nikolai and I began as good friends, essentially because we came from the same social stratum in neighboring villages. But the revolutionary earthquake, November 1, 1954, dealt a mortal blow to our budding camaraderie.

Abdelhamid Naili, my buddy at the vocational Center;
killed three months after he joined in 1957.

Chapter 6
Arrest and Betrayal

Today we say we are here. We are the forgotten souls of the fatherland.
A member of the Zapatista Army of National Liberation
in Chiapas, Mexico, 1994

―――――――――――◆―――――――――――

The Algerian dormitory superintendent brought the news to us the next morning. "There are serious troubles in the country," he whispered, his air of gravity contradicted by the glee in his eyes. "There is armed fighting. There are attacks across the country against the French. We don't yet know what that means. But there are fears of a new May 1945. Be careful. Don't raise the topic with your fellow French trainees."

Yet it was Nicolai who broached the subject with me the same day. "You know, Hamou," he said, "I really fear for my dad. He is a truck driver who is constantly on the road and exposed to all risks."

I tried to reassure him, but without much luck.

I must point out that at the beginning of the uprising, it was difficult to get a clear picture of the strategy adopted by the militants or the objectives of their struggle. Furthermore, and this is often understated, in 1954 the population at large was hardly brimming with revolutionary fervor—although French repression on a massive scale would soon turn the people into active supporters of the insurgency. I did know from my father that the revolt of 1945 was initiated by the activists of the Algerian People's Party, and I assumed that the nationalists were once again at work.

Soon after, my worst fears were confirmed. A fellow student who had spent the weekend in Tazmalt brought the news that my father had been arrested on the evening of November 3 at the entrance of the mosque and was detained in the civil prison of Bejaia. My older brother Sharif had not informed me, aware that it would upset me and seriously affect my studies. We also heard that armed groups calling themselves "mujahedeen," intent on liberating the country from colonialism, were gathering in the mountain villages at night.

Deeply disturbed and depressed, my first impulse was to abandon my studies and return to Tazmalt to help my brother at the forge and monitor closely the evolution of the insurgency. Then I remembered the two hernias. Pulling myself together, I thought about the opportunity I would deny Nicolai: if I stayed, he would not be able to establish supremacy among the first-year student-apprentices.

I waited for the weekend to quietly slip away from the Vocational Center and walk to the civil prison, less than two miles away. It was a typically gray day, for the season and for the region. Intimidated by the imposing frame of the prison and the guards who communicated with visitors through small portholes, I hesitated a long moment, imagining my father's physical and moral state, taken from his family and locked behind these walls like a common criminal. I tried to imagine myself deprived of liberty for months, unable to walk along the shores of the Mediterranean, lingering in front of the fishermen who were "bromiching"—throwing bits of stale bread to the sea to attract fish—or removing red mullets, snappers, porgies, and groupers from their nets. I would no longer hear the sound of waves crashing on the rocks, go to the movies, take the train on weekends to see my family and friends in Tazmalt. Nor would I walk to the river to play ducks and drakes; rolling up my pants to catch small mullets while moorhens scampered along the river.

Then I banished these thoughts from my mind, reminding myself that my father, since I had known him, had never been to the movies, had never listened to the sound of the surf, had never stopped in front of fishermen pulling from their nets what God had so sparingly placed in them. I slowly walked to one of the portholes and in a small and hesitant voice addressed the warden. "Sir, my father is here, I don't know if I can see him..."

"What did your father do?"

"I don't know, Sir. He was arrested in early November."

"Ah! He is involved in politics! No, no visitors are allowed. But you can bring him food if you want. Next!"

I walked away slowly, gloomy and powerless, and immediately began counting the few coins I had. I stopped at a grocery store, but all I could afford was a carton of biscuits. I returned to the prison and said to the guard, "These are for my father, Ameziane Ahitous Amirouche."

"Write his name on the box."

I wrote my father's name and handed the box to the warden. For a moment I remained standing in front of the prison to observe the comings and goings of families with their bundles. Then I slowly walked back to the Center, vaguely aware that something was changing and that I had to determine the extent and nature of the change taking place. What impact would the attacks of those men called *fellaghas* or bandits by many, have on the country? I knew that in Tunisia and Morocco the *fellaghas* had been giving French law enforcement a hard time for the past two or three years. I knew that since my father had been arrested, it was clear evidence that the nationalist party, as in 1945, was behind the insurgency. But something also told me that this time was different.

There were no mass demonstrations displaying banners and chanting "Release Messali" or "Long live free Algeria."

I remembered my father's jubilation only a few months earlier, in May, when the news of the collapse of the French Army at Dien Bien Phu in Indochina made the headlines of *Alger Républicain*, the only daily newspaper he read. Then I heard him say, "What a people! What Indochinese peasants accomplished, the Algerian *fellahin* [peasants] can achieve too. It took them eight years, 1946 to 1954. What are eight years in the life and history of a nation?"

Did this mean that we would adopt the same tactics as the Indochinese? In any case, it was apparently out of the question to storm, armed with no more than flags, the machine guns of the French Army as in May 1945. No doubt this Sunday would not be like any other ordinary Sunday for me. I was not going to walk along the sea. I was not going to see the Jeunesse Sportive Musulmane de Bougie in a fierce battle with the Football Club de Bougie, the Pied Noir soccer club we derisively called "Football Club of the Limping" or "lame duck football."

Back at the Center, my friend Abdelhamid Naïli was playing soccer with some other students. I declined the invitation to join them, and Naïli knew immediately that something was amiss with me. He led me away, asking "What's wrong?"

Naïli was an orphan raised by his maternal grandfather, a veteran who lost a leg in World War I. Naïli had an exceptional awareness of his identity as an Algerian, and an astonishing knowledge of the history of the country. He never forgot that, despite his great sacrifices, his grandfather lived out his life in abject poverty. Before answering his question, I wanted to test my friend.

"Do you see this coin? *Travail, Famille, Patrie* ["Work, Family, Fatherland," the Motto of the Vichy Regime during the German occupation of France: 1940-1944]. Do we, Algerians, have a Fatherland?"

Naïli did not answer.

"You can see all over the walls of Bejaia this ad," I continued: "*Chaque pays a son drapeau, l'Algérie les pâtes Audureau* [Each country has its own flag, Algeria has Audureau pasta]. Is it macaroni that symbolizes and carries the emblem of our country? We don't know who we are, what century we live in. We have forgotten how long it's been that way." I was repeating words I had memorized from my father.

"What are you talking about? Are you raving or what?" said Naïli.

84

"Listen to me. You know that the Tunisians and Moroccans started their struggle against French colonialism. Well that's exactly what the Algerian 'rebels' are doing." I continued my diatribe in the voice of my father. "Now begins history. We will be reborn for one last fight. And we will win because we are no longer alone. We will win by the sheer force of circumstances and the heroic sacrifices of men and women. In the mountain villages they are called the mujahedeen. They are all from the nationalist party."

Naïli, frightened by my passion, kept looking around to make sure no Frenchman was within earshot. We spoke in Kabyle, but a Kabyle peppered with French and Arabic words.

He did not answer at first. Then he lowered his voice and asked in a whisper, "Do you really think we have the power to expel the French from our homeland? Remember all the uprisings crushed in blood since 1830. Think of the last one. How many thousands of men, women, and children were massacred just seven years ago? You say we are no longer alone. Who came to our rescue in 1945? They could have wiped us all out like the American Indians, while the whole universe was watching or looking the other way. They'll do worse this time around than in 1945."

I argued back. "No, Naïli! This time we will use the same tactics as the Indochinese. No more demonstrations or mass uprisings. We will use guerrilla fighting as practiced by Emir Abdelkader against the French invaders or Jugurtha against the Roman occupiers."

"What are you talking about? I don't understand."

"Well, it's simple. What happens if you are threatened by a boy bigger and stronger than you? How do you fight back? You use guile and surprise. You pretend to whine and you undermine his vigilance. Then you suddenly knock him down with a head butt to the jaw. You don't throw a punch, you use your head. We must do the same with the French. They are much stronger and more numerous than we are. They already were in 1830 when they invaded our country."

I went on. "My father told me we were perhaps 4 or 5 million at the time of the invasion when they were 26 million, practically seven to one, can you imagine? Despite that, it took them 17 years to defeat the Algerians. In fact, it took them 27 years to occupy Kabylia. Subjugate it is another question. In addition, the gap in the sophistication and quantity of weapons has considerably widened since then. We cannot open a front with them."

Naïli looked at me dubiously, "You sound quite knowledgeable on the matter, you!"

"Oh, if I do, it's thanks to my father."

"But I remain skeptical," said Naïli. "Look at our Valley, at Bejaia, look at their beautiful farms, their mansions and palaces, you think they will give all that up? They would rather massacre us to the last one."

"Perhaps," I said, "but our brothers will not relent now. Those who decided to initiate these violent actions had nothing to lose. Most of them were wanted by the police, some even put on trial and sentenced to death in absentia.

"You know," I continued, "my father always told me that the massacres of 1945 sounded the death knell of politicking, that the Algerian patriots would trigger a hurricane that would carry men and women like seeds, some good, some bad. According to him, they will all germinate. No one can help it. But my father is sure it will be the good seeds that will prevail."

At that moment, the bell announcing lunch began to ring and we made our way to the canteen. As usual on Sunday it was two-thirds empty, and because each table had to be filled, forcing an Algerian-French mix, meal times had become increasingly tense since the announcement of the armed insurgency. Given the tension in the air, the noisy chatter that usually accompanied each meal gave way to a silence broken only by the intermittent sounds of forks and knives on plates.

I surveyed the dining room, looking for my buddies from Tazmalt and Akbou. I harbored a special affection for my childhood friend Athman Bahloul. Like me, he was 17 years old. We had attended primary school together and shared in the mischief that inevitably followed misbehaving boys. When I saw him two tables away, I waved to him to join me in the yard after lunch. In the courtyard, we isolated ourselves from the French, as usual, to discuss the issues of the day.

"Tell me, Athman, you live in the mountains, how are things there with the rebels? Have you ever seen them?"

"No, I haven't seen anyone," my friend replied sharply. "By the way, did you find the solution to the assigned algebra problem?"

I understood at once that it was an excuse to be alone together and I answered, "Yes."

"In that case come with me one minute to the study room. Then we will perhaps improvise a soccer game." We excused ourselves and headed indoors.

"What's wrong with you to ask me reckless questions like that?" Athman reproached me as soon as we were alone. "I don't know your friends."

He was suspicious. Athman spoke only when he was forced

86

to and possessed the quality that later made him a brilliant officer of Algerian Military Security, that essential quality called "a passion for anonymity" by Winston Churchill.

"First of all," he continued to scold, "where were you this morning?"

"At the prison," I replied in a muffled voice.

"What?"

"Keep it to yourself, Athman. My father is now our neighbor, incarcerated in the civil prison. I walked there this morning but was told that I could not see him. I brought him a box of cookies, I hope they will deliver them to him."

Athman kept silent for a moment, then asked, "Who is taking care of the forge and the family?"

"My older brother. Today, I was really tempted to drop everything and go lend a hand to my brother at the forge, or to join the rebels. Next time, you can talk in front of Naïli Abdelhamid. We can trust him, I am sure. In any case, every one of us must identify with either side and quickly. No one can afford to sit on the fence."

As usual, he paused a moment and then murmured. "You're probably right. But for now we must exercise caution."

"Well," I said, "your reaction earlier shows that you know something."

"Yes, I spent last Sunday in my village. They came at night and they assembled the men at the mosque. There were about 30. They were led by Abderrahmane Mira. It was he who spoke. He asked us to help them because they took up arms to liberate our country from colonialism. He threatened those who might be reluctant or would choose the French side, pointing at his pistol. Here's basically what he said: 'The French claim that we are bandits who must be denounced. You all must be very careful, do not believe them.' [28]

Those who remain loyal to France will be mercilessly punished. It's your duty to support the mujahedeen in proportion to your means. The colonial administration ordered all holders of hunting rifles to hand them over to the police. You must defy that order and hand them to us. For those whose shotgun has been registered, there is a ready excuse: The 'bandits' stormed the village and seized the rifles by force."

"What kind of weapons did they carry?" I asked.

"Shotguns for the most part. Abderrahman had a semiautomatic rifle. There were also a few submachine guns. They handed out a document entitled Proclamation of the First November 1954 and asked those who could read French to translate it to the

87

others. I hid a copy in the trunk of an olive tree in my village. We'll read it together during spring break."

We did not need to. A few days later, the leftist daily *Alger Républicain* provided wide coverage of the Declaration of the First November and revealed the emergence of a new organization, the National Liberation Front (FLN). Its declared aim was nothing less than the independence of Algeria. The slogan repeatedly affirmed by my father and Si Larbi Oulebsir was being carried out: "Freedom is not granted, it has to be snatched."

The few weeks leading to the 1955 spring holidays were marked by passionate discussions after meals in the large soccer field, away from the French who could only throw sidelong glances, frustrated at not understanding the Berber language. However, midterm exams were in the offing and failure was not to be contemplated. Our parents—farmers, artisans, and small shopkeepers—were bled dry to pay for the mandatory school wardrobe in addition to pocket money for the weekly movie, the stadium tickets, and the spicy lamb sausages after the soccer games. Those who could not afford the sausages treated themselves to a bowl of chickpeas seasoned with cumin.

Immediately after the exam, Athman and I took the train to Tazmalt. We were filled with anxiety and apprehension. One of our buddies from primary school, who had not had a chance to attend a vocational school like us, had been shot dead by a patrol of French soldiers. The French spread the rumor that he was mentally deranged and had a habit of leaving his home and wandering aimlessly through the night, breaching the curfew hours. But we learned as soon as we arrived that our friend had been killed before the curfew went into effect, without a warning shot being fired. He was 18 years old and is remembered as the first martyr of the village.

A swarm of soldiers was now occupying the town. It was exactly as it had been in May 1945: the same green locusts were wearing the same green helmets. Again the soldiers were full of arrogance and disdain during the day, tense apprehension at night.

But this time, instead of the Moroccan Tabors, the French Army had brought contingents of intriguing soldiers of color whom the villagers referred to as "Senegalese" even if they were from the Ivory Coast, Chad, or Gabon. With few exceptions, these troops showed remarkable affability, presumably acknowledging the deference that Algerians, or merchants in any case, paid them and to which they were clearly not accustomed. But they could also exhibit fierce savagery, as happened in Aït Hamdoun in early 1956. That day the Senegalese gave vent to their bloodlust and slaughtered many civilians in retaliation when one of their own was cornered and killed with an ax in the village.

As soon as I arrived in Tazmalt, I learned that my father, accused of "undermining the internal security of the State" had been tried in February 1955 and sentenced to 16 months in prison, followed by 5 years of house arrest. He decided to appeal the sentence. The retrial, expected to take place in Algiers, required the transfer of the prisoner to the capital. It was the Easter holiday and, as the counsel had not notified my family until the day of the transfer, my brother Sharif and I headed to the station, hoping to catch a glance of our father.

Soon the train appeared, blasting its horn. And there, at a window, appeared my father flanked by two policemen. He raised his chained arms to greet us. He was terribly thin, but a sad smile lit up his face and the sight of his children gave a special brightness to his gray eyes.

"To Beni Mansur," he shouted before being roughly pulled back and forced to sit down in the compartment. Without missing a beat, we proceeded to the old taxi parked behind the station and took off in a cloud of black smoke and dust to Beni Mansur, five miles away by train and more than double that by road. Arriving at Beni Mansur station, we walked to the platform and, not knowing where our father and his guards were waiting for the Algiers train, stood in front of the waiting room.

Soon my father, held on a leash by the two gendarmes, came out of a room adjoining the bar and all three headed to the bathroom. When he saw us standing 20 meters away, the same sad grin appeared on his pale face. Fists clenched, he raised his chained arms and saluted. Seeing my father wearing handcuffs like a common criminal who had to be escorted even to the toilet seized me with an uncontrollable rage. I remember that image of him at the train station as if it were yesterday. No doubt I would have attacked the police and attempted to release my father if I had had a gun, whatever the consequences for my family. Burning with a helpless hatred, I watched as they returned to the room reserved for them.

"He looks terribly thin, our old man," whispered Sharif.

"I don't even know if the warden handed over to him the boxes of cookies that I brought to him almost every Sunday," I said.

We waited nearly an hour before the train finally entered the station. Under escort, Ahitous boarded. Other prisoners, also being transferred to Algiers, appeared at the windows of the compartments and began to ask questions to the peasants in local code.

"How is the country?"

"Dust is rising from mud," answered a voice. "The fire is blazing. It will grill the locusts," said another. Others shouted "This blaze will devour Fafa [France]."

Laughter rang out from every side and my chest swelled with pride. "These peasants are not intimidated by the show of force," I told myself. "Or at least they are no longer afraid."

Soon the monotonous voice of the station master announced over the loudspeaker, "Passengers to Algiers on board, please. The train is about to depart."

And two minutes later the train departed. The blacksmith once more raised his chained arms from behind the window and saluted. This time his face remained expressionless but his fists were clenched. My brother and I watched as the train disappeared over the horizon, then headed to the parking lot and boarded the taxi. We exchanged not a word during the entire trip to Tazmalt.

But as soon as we were alone, still fuming with rage, I gave vent to my feelings. I turned to my brother, and said in a trembling voice: "You know, Sharif, I want to volunteer and join the... You think they will accept me?"

"What are you talking about? Stop talking nonsense. You're too young and besides you are studying. Do you at least know what it means, studying? God willing, one day our country will be independent." Then, putting his arm around my shoulders, he started laughing. "You will perhaps be appointed the constable of the village and it will be your turn to confiscate slingshots."

After the buildup of so much nervous tension, I couldn't help but release it by laughing myself. Then, still reeling from bitterness, I headed to my room, leaving to my brother the sensitive task of telling my mother about our father's condition. I sat on my bed and began to think about the topic of the essay the French teacher, Monsieur Lasserre, had assigned for the holidays: "Comment on and discuss Victor Hugo's claim that 'Those who live are those who struggle. They are those in whom a firm design fills the soul and spirit.' " I was tempted to draft a firm rebuttal, saying that Victor Hugo has never experienced the humiliation and brutality of occupation. Those who struggle do not live. They end up in prison experiencing appalling degradation and unspeakable torments. Or they are slaughtered without mercy, disappearing from the earth without a smile ever lighting up their face. But although Monsieur Lasserre was born in France and was probably more liberal than a Pied Noir born in Algeria, I did not want to take any risks by being provocative. I reduced my ambition to pursuing a distinguished career as an auto mechanic.

The following days were uneventful, if one excludes the arrival of additional French troops who seized a warehouse from a neighboring family not 50 meters from our home and turned it into barracks. The shock for my family came when the French soldiers established an observation post on our neighbor's terrace, adjoining the roof of our house.

A drama occurred when the youngest of my brothers, Smaïl, a six-year-old who had never seen a black man, began to make fun of a Senegalese who was on duty on the terrace. The soldier first threatened Smaïl by stomping and shouting to scare him away. But when Smaïl began pulling his lower lip down with both hands and sticking out his tongue, the guard became enraged, loaded his MAS 49, and screamed insults in his native language. The commotion brought my mother out into the yard. She immediately realized the danger, and making sure the soldier witnessed it, slapped her son on both cheeks.

I spent my spring break leafing through the *Alger Républicain*, a newspaper that was as much a part of everyday life as the loaves of bread that the baker delivered each morning on his squeaky two-wheeled cart. I rarely ventured into the street, especially since I had started to wear a red fez to dispel any doubt about my ethnic identity. I loathed being stopped and forced to exhibit my identity card of "French Muslim," and I did not want to fall afoul of one of the raids the French troops staged from time to time in the hope of capturing a wanted militant, liaison officer, or armed "terrorist" who had infiltrated the village to carry out an attack.

In the last raid I had been taken at gunpoint along with all the faithful as we came out of the mosque. We were forcibly directed to the weekly cattle market and ordered to sit on the dung-covered ground. Then began body searches and identity verification, which lasted over two hours.

Sometimes I detoured through the village to visit my cousin Hamzaoui at my Uncle Iddir's forge. I was there one day as he was shaping agricultural tools under his father's guidance, when a captain in the Special Administrative Sections (SAS), which specialized in the French lies and propaganda dubbed "psychological warfare," burst into the shop. He was alone, and I remember that for a few minutes, oblivious of the consequences, I imagined attacking him, snatching his weapon, and joining the resistance. Those Algerians who joined the armed struggle with their own weapons, particularly a highly prized U.S. Garand or French MAS 49 taken from the body of a French officer, were considered heroes. But I did not have the courage. Furthermore, the captain carried only a pistol fastened to his gun belt, which was of little interest. If he were armed with a MAS 49, I told myself, it would probably have been worthwhile to sacrifice my uncle and my cousin in the inevitable reprisal.

Meanwhile, the officer had completed the exchange of civility with my Uncle Iddir, who, pointing to me, said, "This is a nephew who is lucky. He was spared the hard work of the forge."

The captain turned to me. "What's your name, young man?"

"My name is Hamou Amirouche and I am a student in Bejaia."

"In high school?"

"No, sir, in a vocational school."

"Call me *mon capitaine* (literally my captain)." Then, turning to my uncle, he continued, "You see, Iddir, France's achievements. It builds schools, colleges, technical schools. Your nephew will surely succeed and help his family."

"Yes, he is lucky to be able to read and write. Not like me. My son could also have continued his studies, but he could not get a scholarship and in Bejaia, room and board are not so cheap."

The captain ignored my uncle's remark and continued, "France has accomplished great things in Algeria. And the *fellaghas* want to expel France from Algeria. A bunch of bandits armed with shotguns!"

A stony silence greeted these remarks. My uncle chose that moment to take out of the furnace a white-hot sheet of steel and, helped by my cousin, began to shape it into a plowshare. The sparks of melted steel that filled the air, and the deafening noise of the hammer on the anvil, were probably too much for the SAS officer. He left the forge and rushed into the store across the street to resume his standard stump speech on the "rebels" and the "French accomplishments in Algeria" which, inadvertently, had bred them.

The introduction of the SAS in every village with its relentless propaganda was part of a new French strategy: winning the hearts and minds of the population. Their counterinsurgency and counterterror experts had warned that arbitrary arrests and daily abuse created more enemies than they destroyed. But once the French realized that the enemy lived among the people like fish in water, they launched "regrouping camps," removing on a massive scale the people from their habitat in order to kill the fish.

The year 1955 was marked by further arrivals in Tazmalt of an impressive number of soldiers, the Alpine Corps and the Foreign Legion, to the great delight of at least one group of villagers: the merchants, seeing new recruits to swindle.

These newly arrived "locusts," as they were called, prevented most mountain peasants from entering the village with their mules or donkeys to market their agricultural products at the weekly market, for fear they might be smuggling weapons. One day a friend of my father's left his mule at the entrance of the village not far from the checkpoint and came to ask us to go get it and replace its worn-out shoes. Believing that the sentry who knew me would let me pass, I led the mule by the bridle, but was halted nonetheless. The sentry ordered me to turn back, punctuating his order with a kick that made me shake with a fury that I still feel today, more than 50 years later. The idea of joining the guerrillas, which had been haunting me for the last few months, really began to take shape in my mind. So I devoted the last days of spring vacation to spying on the guardhouse.

I knew that to be accepted into the ranks of the National Liberation Army, I might have to undergo the terrible initiation of killing one of the enemy. The test was just too horrible for an 18-year-old to contemplate. But shedding blood in almost ritualistic manner might be the only way to irretrievably cut all ties with civilian life—or indeed, with life itself. I quickly discovered that three soldiers manned the checkpoint from morning until dusk. Half an hour before closing the gate that gave access to the village, only one soldier was left on duty. A surprise attack, to snatch his rifle or submachine gun a few minutes before dark, was possible. But attack him with what? I had to find a contact with the mujahedeen, volunteer, and offer to stage an attack under their guidance. Would they accept me? Would they trust a teenager, and a puny one at that, with a gun? What would happen to my brothers and sisters in retaliation?

In terms of contacts, I knew that the best source was my brother Sharif, a fundraiser for the National Liberation Front, as I discovered when he had been arrested, tortured, and imprisoned in a notorious camp north of Akbou. But I'd rather keep my efforts secret. This is why I decided to get in touch with a former activist, member of the paramilitary OS, and my father's former companion in the nationalist party. I walked to the south section of town where he resided but, as might be expected, did not find him at home. He was surely a wanted man, like all activists of the nationalist party still at large. His son appeared suspicious, but when I informed him that I was the son of Ahitous, he relaxed and told me that I would find his father on the farm, a small orchard located on the riverbank two miles from Tazmalt.

I found him busy pruning an orange tree. He recognized me

93

right away and asked about my father. "He's fine," I replied. "He was transferred to Algiers, where he will be retried. He may have a chance to see his sentence commuted. He has a good lawyer."

"And you, Hamou? Are you still studying in Bejaia?"

"Yes," I replied.

"Study hard. Sooner or later, Algeria will be free and will need you." He paused and asked if I needed anything.

"Amrane, I have a friend who wants to join the mujahedeen but has no contact with the mountain."

"And who is this friend?"

"He is a student like me."

"And where is he from?"

"Uh, Akbou."

"And why didn't he seek his own contacts in Akbou?"

"He doesn't know nor trust anyone."

The militant stared at me for a few seconds before asking point blank, "This friend wouldn't be you, by any chance?"

"Okay, it's me. Please don't tell anyone in my family. Can you help me?"

He considered for a while and then said, "When you volunteer to die for your country, you don't do it lightly. First, have you talked to your brother? Do you know that you will be forced to stage an individual attack? And that in reprisal, some members of your family, your big brother, in the first place, will probably be executed? And what about your studies and your training?"

I did not answer right away. I confess that the prospect of exposing my brother to being shot shattered for a moment my determination. My mother would be fatally traumatized. As for my "studies," drawing spare parts on a drawing board, training on machine tools, and solving basic geometry problems had sapped my motivation and willpower. Only my intense rivalry with Nicolai kept me at the top of my class.

"Anyway," he said, "give me a week or two, and I will get back to you."

He never did. I returned wearily to my school and took wicked pleasure in beating Nikolai's grade-point average throughout the rest of 1955 and the first quarter of 1956. However, the idea of going underground continued to haunt my evenings, fueled by the news of primary school classmates from Tazmalt being accepted into the ranks of the National Liberation Army.

Many heroic legends had begun to appear among the peasantry to inspire me. One resistance fighter, for example, surrounded by French soldiers, took out of his pocket what looked like a matchbox and patted it. A few minutes later, it was the guerrillas who encircled the French soldiers. Another mujahed shot an officer and, to cover his flight, sprinkled cayenne pepper on his tracks to fool the dogs launched in his pursuit.

But more than these stories, the thought of my father again tortured by his captors, nine years after 1945, and the image of his arms chained like a common criminal's, kept alive my intense desire for revenge. Looking back at my motivations at that age, I can say that retribution and hatred, rather than the lofty ideal of freeing my country, were my primary reason for taking up arms.

My father's appeal confirmed his sentence. He was released in the summer of 1956 after serving 16 months in prison and being subjected to all kinds of tortures. And this time, except for uncles and cousins, no visitor dared to show solidarity by paying him a visit. The war was changing quite a few customs and behaviors. As soon as he was released, my father received a threatening message from the "brothers," as the insurgents were called, requiring him to pay 350,000 francs (the equivalent of more than a year's earnings) or be exposed to terrible punishment. When my father told me about it, he could not repress a feeling of righteous anger."They know I just got out of prison. They know I'm a blacksmith. They know that what they demand is beyond my financial means."

I said nothing, but the incident further strengthened my resolve to join the National Liberation Army as soon as possible, to protect my family from the arbitrariness of these "brothers." Such contributions demanded by the mujahedeen were one more injustice against which we were powerless, unless we joined the French Army as part of a vigilante group, the Harkis or Goumiers, who had to abandon their villages and live practically in French Army barracks. My father's fortune amounted to a few thousand francs, for in the summer blacksmiths didn't have much work. He contacted the revolutionary political commissar of the region, who established a schedule of payments. Years later, I learned that a number of peasants had joined the Harkis or Goumiers to shield themselves from the extreme demands and abuses of some of the guerillas.

My father remembered a meeting held shortly after the schism that fractured the nationalist party in 1954, with tragic consequences. The split led to a senseless fratricidal war which pitted the National Liberation Front against the Movement National Algérien (MNA), the rival organization, for six years. An activist leader traveled from Bejaia to Tazmalt to probe local militants on their allegiance towards Messali Hajj, the leader of the MNA.

At the time, the vast majority of grassroots activists vowed loyalty to the charismatic Messali, promising unswerving dedication. This was especially true of former emigrants like my father who had witnessed the birth of the first nationalist movement in France in 1926. But when he was asked to take sides in the conflict (spelled out by footnote # 47, chapter 10)) between Messali and the Central Committee of the Movement for the Triumph of Democratic Liberties, my father wisely replied that he wanted unity and preferred not to commit himself to either side. When he received the message directing him to pay that exorbitant sum of money, he wondered whether the revolutionary leadership was not testing his loyalty to the National Liberation Front. Fully aware of his personal friendship with Si Larbi Oulebsir of the MNA, the local National Liberation Front leader may have suspected him of being a Messalist.

Whatever the reason, my father's banishment from Tazmalt by the French Police, which was a part of his sentence, left him no time to linger in the region and reconnect with former militants who knew him and had joined the armed resistance. He left Tazmalt and settled in his native Ihitoussen. But he soon realized he was far from welcome. The village chief served him with a virtual expulsion order after a meeting of the village assembly. "You will soon attract the gendarmes to the village," the chief said.

"How is that?"

"Well, you're the only one in the village to engage in politics. You just served a prison term. They are sure to come around here. And they will begin to suspect everyone and to conduct house searches all over the place. Is that what you want?"

"And what do you advise me to do?" my father asked.

"Leave the village," said the chief replied.

My father stared at his questioner with a look of the utmost contempt and, in a voice barely containing his rage, said, "Hundreds of soldiers are already camping at your doorstep, in Bouzeguène and Horra, and you tell me I'm going to attract the police! Soon they will search your shacks and ransack them, perhaps rape your wives and your daughters, and your main concern is Ameziane Ahitous Amirouche! You and your fellow assembly members are like mules who deny their father, claiming to be the offspring of a horse, not a donkey. You are sound asleep and you turn your back to the storm instead of facing it. 'Girl with braided hair, stay asleep, stars are still shining in the sky.' " He concluded with the insulting refrain of a village song.

When my father told me about this incident, I felt my chest swell with pride. But at the same time, I knew something had radically changed in Ihitoussen. The Revolution that was taking place was shaking up many traditions. Calling the village chief a girl with braids

96

would have constituted a mortal offense before the Revolution.

My father left the assembly seething with rage. He felt doubly betrayed. The first betrayal involved tribal solidarities, which compelled members to provide unconditional help and support to one another under any circumstances. Village tradition required that, if one of your kinsmen intended to commit a crime, you did everything in your power to dissuade him. If you failed, you helped him commit the perfect crime. The second betrayal was national, for the chief had failed to comprehend the nature of the struggle that patriots like my father were waging.

Although most of the villagers were far from sharing the views of their chief, my father did not feel safe any longer. At 53, he was too old to go underground. Besides, who would take care of his family? He decided to flee to France. But before leaving the country, he had a conversation explaining his situation with an old nationalist comrade. Encouraging my father to leave Algeria, his friend gave him the names and addresses of National Liberation Front activists in Paris.

Colonel Amirouche behind a group of officers holding machine guns "Bren", which had just been routed from Tunisia (October 1957.)

Chapter 7
Waiting for the Call to Arms

◆

With an additional diploma, we will not make better corpses.
Strike call of the General Union of Algerian Muslim Students,
May 1956

French Soldiers in Algeria, 1956

The year 1956 would prove to be a decisive turning point in my life. As soon as I returned to the Vocational Center after spring break in April, I learned that a fellow student had been murdered, burned alive by French soldiers in a small mountain village near Bejaia. The first effect of the news was to nurture ever deeper suspicion between the Algerian students and their French counterparts.

The assassination triggered a student general strike. When we received the strike notification from the National Liberation Front, many trainees advanced the pusillanimous argument that the call to strike did not concern us: we were apprentices, not students. But from the outset, along with several classmates, I declared my solidarity with students across the country. Another trainee, now a retired senior executive of Air Algérie, recently reminded me that I had planned the strike at the Center. I was both touched and flattered: I was 18 years old in May 1956.

For us students, our challenge was how to organize a strike without attracting the attention of supervisors, in particular the general superintendent, who was constantly snooping and listening to conversations—and before switching off the lights each night, checking that our underpants were hanging from the bunk bed. He made little effort to conceal his bias in favor of the French.

It was not easy for us, who had virtually no way of communicating with the Bejaia high school, to coordinate our actions. We informed all those willing to participate that the strike would begin on May 19 at six in the morning. "Do not take your bags, do not walk in groups, take the first train or the first bus leaving for your village. Otherwise, get lost in an isolated cove outside Bejaia until late afternoon before traveling. The police will be alerted an hour after our departure. They will surely search for us and forcefully bring us back in police vans."

Early on the morning of May 19, dozens of students surreptitiously left the Center, hands in pockets. Some were caught at the railroad or bus stations, thrown in police vans, subjected to interrogation, and forcibly returned to the Center. But most of us, like my brother Lahcène and I, were able to return safely to our village. I decided it was safer for us to go to Ihitoussen and avoid, for now, the small town of Tazmalt.

The easy part was taking the train to Ighzer Amokrane. But from there, we had to walk to Ihitoussen, which was not so simple.

We had never completed the journey without our father. At first, aided by locals, we were able to orient ourselves by following a path that zigzagged between rocks and boulders. But just beyond, the wilderness that characterized this deserted part of the Djurdjura Mountains was more problematic. For nearly three hours, we tried to find and follow the trail through ravines and ditches leading to the mountain pass. Once we crested the pass, we would be able to descend towards the village of Horra, some two miles away from Ihitoussen. When we finally saw a flock of goats, we let out a huge sigh of relief before even catching sight of Horra. We reacted like the traveler who lays eyes on a boat and exclaims, before seeing the water, "the sea!"

But Ihitoussen was not the haven of peace and security that I had expected to find. The French military's Alpine Corps had already infested the region and begun to crisscross the country. The unit was trained for mountain fighting, and wore white uniforms in winter when they also indulged in cross-country skiing. The Alpine Corps installed a fortified camp in Bouzeguène, a strategic location that could control mountain traffic and the activity of a dozen villages. The base overlooked the large village of Taourirth, known to be a place of resistance to the occupation, which had twice been set on fire by the French invaders, in the 1850s and again in 1956. The French camp was facing the north side of the Djurjura Range, where a second military base was established. The third base camp, Horra to the east, controlled the mountain pass.

I had hardly settled in the village before I was subjected to my first humiliation. One morning around 11 o'clock, French soldiers burst into our house and, shouting, brutally pushed every one out at gun point to search for arms. All adult males caught sleeping at that late hour, automatically suspected of having engaged in nocturnal sabotage and harassment of military posts, were taken in for interrogation. On the way back to their bases, the French soldiers wrote in white paint on every rock. *"Kabylie, Terre Française"* (Kabylia Is French Land). I had to repeatedly translate for the locals that arrogant and provocative phrase. The reaction was almost always the same: a puzzled nod or resounding laughter, negating a negation.

This was still the time when "From right to left, all the heads of our governments and our passing governments and transitional Republics successively claimed that there was no other than French Algeria, which was basically a way of saying there was no Algeria at all or, if there was one, it does not belong to Algerians."[29]

Was it any wonder that during the Nazi occupation of France, a popular slogan was "Algiers, capital of Free France"?

I shared a room on the second floor of my uncle's house with my brother Lahcène. Very quickly, I discovered that the village of Aït Salah a few miles away had provided many of the guerrillas in the region. If I wanted to join the resistance, I had to find a contact with someone from Aït Salah.

My opportunity came in the summer of 1956. One night a group of guerrillas entered Ihitoussen in search of supplies. Their leader, a native of Aït Salah, gathered the villagers and addressed them in these terms:

"Dear brothers, I will be brief. We took up arms to liberate our country. We need support from everyone. We need money, we need to be fed, and we need to be protected. You must be ready to help us, according to your means and abilities. Do not believe the French propaganda calling us bandits or outlaws. We are mujahedeen. Spread the word everywhere. You must stand unconditionally by our side no matter what happens because if we do not unite, we are lost. It is everyone's sacred duty. Those who turn a deaf ear to our cause or have sworn allegiance to the colonial administration..." He began to fondle the pistol hanging from his belt, sending an unequivocal message.

The guerrillas left the village as they had come, like ghosts. The next day the village assembly convened to discuss the issue. The village chief, the same one who had driven out my father, did not beat around the bush. "Giving money to a gang of highwaymen is out of the question. Liberate the country!" he sneered."With shotguns. Who does he think we are?"

The majority of the village assembly first rallied to their chief, but their loyalty did not last long. A few days later, he was found in a ravine with his throat slit. The shock was considerable in this quiet village, but the dreadful message was clear. Now two villagers, among the most educated, were appointed and made responsible for raising funds and supplying food to the area's armed groups. It was naturally to one of these leaders, Madani Chikh, that I turned.

"You know," I said, "that students have obeyed the order for a general strike. The instruction urges us to join the armed struggle. I need a contact. Can you help me?"

He stared at me for a long time as if to gauge my determination and replied, "You are the first volunteer from the village. You're young and I assume you know the test you will be subjected to prior to—"

"I'm not so young, I interrupted him. I'm soon going to turn 19. And I know about the test." I knew I was frail and looked younger than my age, but I hated to be reminded of it at every turn.

"In that case," he said, "get ready to accompany a group that will take supplies to the mujahedeen in a few days. You can talk to the leader."

A week later, just as night was falling, Madani came to fetch me. I was extremely surprised but thrilled when he handed me an automatic pistol, explained how it worked, and showed me the safety catch. "There are lookouts around the village. In general, the French soldiers never go out at night. Use this gun only if necessary to raise the alarm. Other group members are also equipped with three pistols and two shotguns. This is mainly to familiarize you with a gun."

I thought it unnecessary to point out that my father had always possessed, in addition to the MAS 36 that we had been forbidden to touch, a revolver which we had been authorized to handle unloaded. I had fun as a child squeezing the firing pin with my two index fingers and watching the round container revolve after each "shot." Nor did I say that I had some compulsory military training at the Vocational Center with a .22 rifle, during which I had shown that I was an excellent marksman. I felt the cold metal in my palm, and resisted the temptation to place a shell in the chamber and shoot a cactus.

On the village square, I found a half-dozen young men prancing with impatience. "Attention," Madani said in a muffled voice, "each and every one, in rotation, carries a basket. We form a column. Maintain a distance of at least ten meters from each other. Remember the passwords 'aqarmoudh' [tile] and 'abakal' [of clay]. 'Aqarmoudh' is the call, 'abakal' the response." The passwords were chosen with the guttural consonants that French soldiers could not pronounce without betraying their accent. Unfortunately, the Harkis and other local auxiliaries soon solved this problem for the French army.

Our small group began to move under the moonlight to the east, heading to the forest bordering Aït Salah. We walked for over two hours in silence when a voice pierced the night: "Halt! Who goes there?"

Madani gave the password and from behind the bushes sprang a dozen uniformed men, immediately followed by a large group armed with shotguns, two or three machine guns, and rifles. After the usual greetings, the guerrillas began to eat the food we were carrying, and Madani took the leader aside and spoke to him for a few minutes. The guerrilla chief motioned for me to come forward.

"So you want to join our ranks?"

"It is my dream, if you will accept me. I am a student. We

103

were ordered by the National Liberation Front to go on strike and join the National Liberation Army. Here I am, on strike and volunteering."

"I hear you are from a family of great patriots. But this is not always a guarantee for us. The warranty is the test that all volunteers are subjected to. Those who are drafted for military service in the French army or who are wanted by the police for their militant actions are exempted from the trial. The police are not looking for you, are they?"

For a second, to spare myself the forthcoming ordeal, I was tempted to claim that I was the organizer of the strike at the Center, that I had been drafted by the French army. But what evidence could I provide? While I felt totally incapable of killing anyone, I wanted to prove to myself that I had the courage to accomplish what thousands of other Algerians had done before me, sometimes at the cost of their lives.

"No," I replied in a trembling voice, "I'm not wanted by the police."

"In that case, you know the test."

"Yes, I know the test."

"Here is how it's going to be," said the leader. "We will point out a person to you who is sentenced to death, whom you will have to execute. It could be a French officer, a policeman, a traitor, a member of your family, even your own father if the organization sentences him to death." He stopped when he saw me freeze and then added, "You're young and you can decline."[30]

Utterly shaken in my resolve, I remember that I literally choked when I answered, "I am not young and I accept."

"Fine. From now on, you're not allowed to leave your village. You will be picked up at your house. The person sentenced by the National Liberation Front will be pointed out to you. This can be anywhere: Bouzeguène, Horra, or Azzazga. You will have the opportunity to observe his movements, his habits. When you're ready to stage the attack, we will tell you where to retrieve the weapon, usually an automatic handgun. A bullet will already be in the chamber and the safety catch lifted. You will have only to pull the trigger. One or two bullets to the head or chest."

He paused and I knew it was to study my reaction, having realized that my voice was a bit unsteady. Then he continued, "We will tell you where to drop the weapon immediately after the action, in a grocery store or butcher shop nearby. Do you have any questions?"

"Is it possible to practice a little shooting before the attack? I have already fired a .22 caliber rifle but it's not a handgun."

"No, it is not possible. Ammunition is very scarce. Besides, that's noisy and needlessly attracts attention. Again, you're young, you could get shot. You can still change your mind."

"No, I won't."

"In that case, stay put. Someone will contact you shortly."

He turned on his heel and joined his group, eating couscous out of a large wooden bowl. I threw a sideways glance at those guerrillas who, most of them, were hardly older than I was and told myself that, if I accomplished my mission without getting killed or captured, I would soon be sharing their hopes and hardships.

I started thinking about the tragic death of a youth I was told about in Tazmalt who, like me, had been subjected to this inhuman test marking the almost ritual jump from civilian life under the colonial order to the life and perhaps death of a freedom fighter. The mission of the young volunteer was to shoot a police officer known as a vicious torturer in Algiers. The young man had carefully observed the officer's habits and decided to shoot him on Lyre Street, not far from the Casbah.

But there were soldier patrols everywhere; the streets were looped with barbed wire to render virtually impossible any escape after an attack. Striving to find a solution, the young recruit noticed that he could possibly climb a utility pole, jump over the barbed wire, and put this barrier between himself and his eventual pursuers.

The day of the attack, he waited at a distance for the officer to appear. Discreetly removing a chair from a café, he placed it against the utility pole. When the police officer approached, the boy faced him and pumped two bullets into his chest. He then began to run towards the pole—but the chair was gone. The patrol, alerted by the gunfire, found him helplessly standing in front of the fence. In a futile and desperate move, he pointed his pistol towards the soldiers but did not have time to pull the trigger. A burst of submachine gun fire pinned him to the barbed wire.

I imagined this martyr so frail, the revolver so pitiful against the weapons of the patrol. I identified with this young militant, an actor in a one-act tragedy, too young to die. I saw him contemplate, for one last time before expiring, one of the inscriptions that covered the walls of the city: "Algeria Will Live Free."

The soldiers who had surrounded him, probably young conscripts themselves, were, according to witnesses, utterly shaken by the extreme youth of the teenager whom they had just shot dead. The platoon leader barked orders and they all turned and, heads down, quietly left the scene of the drama. I observed for a moment the guerrillas standing with me and wondered how many of them had been executioners before becoming combatants.

Madani walked towards me and tried to read the expression on my face, but it was too dark. He said instead, "Well, let's gather our baskets and go home."

We shook hands with each of the guerrillas and silently headed back to the village. It was past midnight when we reached it. I handed the gun back to Madani and walked home. Lahcène was sound asleep and I lay down fully clothed beside him on the mat of woven alfa grass that we shared on the bare floor.

I will never forget that dreadful night. I realized suddenly what an infernal cycle I had thrust myself into. Would I have the courage to shoot a man in cold blood whom I was most likely seeing for the first time? If only it was one of those who had savagely beaten my father under the sight of my sobbing mother and brothers in 1945, or his torturers in the civil prison of Bejaia, or one of the policemen who dragged him like a dog on a leash to the bathroom in Beni Mansur, or the infamous constable who confiscated my slingshots and delivered me to the police for questioning even though I was only a child, or the sentry who kicked me just a few months earlier.

What if the gun jammed and they captured me? What would happen to my family? The French followed the notorious practice, after an attack on one of their own, of shooting several civilians at random in retaliation and as a deterrent. Such events had occurred in Aït Hamdoun early in that year. "Chop off ten heads of natives for each beheaded Frenchman"[31] was the known practice.

I tossed and turned on my mat all night. It was hotter than usual, or maybe I was feverish. Moonlight slanted in through the only window of our room, casting a faint lozenge of light on the cement floor. I looked out and contemplated the eerie landscape, formed of shadows and strange figures dominated by the majestic Djurdjura a few miles away. I could not discern, in the pale light, the markings on the rocks but I knew they were there: "Kabylia Is French Land."

I wondered what the reaction would be if I wrote in Marseille, "Marseille is a Kabyle city," or better yet, "Marseille, the land of Islam." Through the tiny window, I could see to the east the dimmed lights of the fortified camp of Horra. I thought bitterly that it took only a few hundred soldiers armed to the teeth, strangers to this land, to dispose of, as they pleased, thousands of indigenous people. They smashed the doors of our modest homes, ordered out the old and the young at any time of day or night, and took away suspects who were often never to be seen again. Finally, for good measure, they decreed the wretched, desolate, but proud

106

Kabylia as French land. They could vandalize, kill, burn, and rape without qualm, all this not because they were braver in battle or endowed with superior intelligence, but because they were so well armed. Many peasants were resigned to the occupation of their country as a manifestation of divine wrath.

Since the arrival of these helmeted invaders, we no longer heard the lullabies of mothers, no one danced at weddings or circumcisions. The flutes of the shepherds were silenced, no longer playing the melody so little remembered today, "My love with the beautiful braids, sleep a little more, the sky is still filled with stars."

What could the Kherrata peasants do against the savage bombing of their villages by the French Air Force in 1945? Who could defend them from those soldiers who pierced with a bayonet the bellies of their pregnant wives? "God alone can counter them," they muttered after each execution of hostages in reprisal for a guerrilla ambush. God was more powerful than they, certainly, but He needed a helping hand, and it was this hand that those who called themselves mujahedeen had dared to offer to God.

I stood at the window for a long time. Gradually, I felt less feverish, and perhaps because of lack of sleep and mental exhaustion, less terrified at the prospect of killing someone. My anguish dwindled as I whispered to myself the fatalistic formula, "what's written is written." The day was breaking, and at any moment the imam would call the faithful to the dawn prayer. At the Vocational Center I had stopped the practice, but I suddenly felt the need to kneel and communicate with the Almighty. I performed my ritual ablutions with as little noise as possible so as not to wake my brother and recited my favorite verse of the Koran. As soon as the soft voice of the imam rose above the village without the detestable loudspeakers of today, I headed for the small room near the village plaza which served as a mosque.

I began to count the days and weeks that followed, marked by restless anguish, fearful anticipation of the test I had to pass, and the honor of becoming part of a group of heroic fighters. I was surprised not to receive any news and mentioned it to Madani.

"You know, they may think you are too young or they may fear reprisals against the population. In the latest attack against a French soldier, a civilian group was taken hostage and shot dead."

"What do you advise?"

"Patience; in the meantime you can help the Moussebline."[32] This was the name given to volunteer civilians in charge mostly of sabotage missions. Kabylia, however, was not only too proud to intimidate and too autonomous to buy off, it was also too poor to attract French settlers.

Although they tried to persuade the Kabyles that the French administration harbored no ill feelings towards them, the propagandists of the Special Administrative Services realized that theirs was a hopeless task after an act of sabotage. There were no electricity nor telegraph poles, no orange trees nor grapevines to cut down; no farms belonging to the settlers for the "terrorists" to set on fire. There was nothing to sabotage that could harm the settlers since there were no settlers. But there was the dirt road that connected the two military camps of Horra and Bouzeguène and extended as far as Azzazga.

"You can be part of a team that digs trenches on the road," Madani told me. The idea was far from thrilling, but I could not decline. So I participated in my first mission of sabotage. I was assigned sentry duty due to my small physique, while those with picks and shovels worked on the hard and compact soil of the dirt road. But the next day at about 10 a.m., a platoon of Alpine Corps soldiers stormed the village and ordered us, at gunpoint, to fill in the trenches we had so laboriously dug the night before.

For two or three nights, we set about the Sisyphean task of digging trenches at night, under the orders of the guerrillas, and refilling them the next day under the command of French soldiers. But one night our watchmen were fooled by a simple tactic that we learned to elude only after a terrible tragedy. A small convoy of French trucks with their headlights on moved from one camp to another at twilight. When they reached the ditches filled in during the day, a few soldiers jumped out without the trucks stopping to avoid alerting the sentries. It took only a few minutes for these soldiers to plant mines in the soft earth of the refilled trenches.

My time had not yet come, because I was not a member of the team of saboteurs assembled that fateful night. The first pickaxe stroke triggered a landmine and blew to pieces the closest saboteur, whose hand was found a few dozen meters away. I heard the blast from my room, but it was not until the next day that I learned the terrible news. It put an end to our sabotage of the dirt road.

I stayed in the village most of the summer of 1956, waiting in vain to hear from the guerrilla leader. During all this time, I resisted the nearly irresistible temptation to get married. I had just turned 19 years old. None of my fellow villagers my age was single, and each one told me about a very pretty girl who was still unmarried, a rare occurrence for a girl at the age of 16. But my older brother Zouhir angrily dissuaded me once again. "If you were busy studying for an exam," he wrote to me from Reims, "you would not be in the process of messing around with this stupid idea."

Therefore, I decided to leave the village and return to Tazmalt. I made a stop at the Vocational Center to say goodbye and collect my meager belongings. The French trainees and some Algerians were back at school, but the place appeared to me strangely empty, unusually silent and sad. Although some French students looked at me sideways, no one spoke to me. I headed straight to the dorm and slowly packed my suitcase, overwhelmed with melancholy. I was leaving the Center where I had been happy overall. The "mountain" remaining ominously silent, I wondered what I was going to do with my life.

The few Algerian students who had ignored the strike order kept a low profile and pretended not to see me. When I passed one of them myself, I put in my expression as much contempt as I could muster as he lowered his head and looked away. But the future was probably on their side. None of them would die, weapon in hand, or experience the indignity of the infamous colonial jails. A non-striker has even reached the eminent position of Prime Minister in post-independence Algeria; he presided over the organization of the first "clean and honest elections" in sad memory. [33]

One French instructor, Monsieur Aubert, master of machine tools, saw me and asked, "What's wrong with you? Why did you leave?"

I shrugged but did not answer.

"I don't understand your behavior," he continued. You have a unique chance to get a diploma in one year, at the gracious expense of the administration. You are sheltered and fed and taught free of charge. And you're leaving? You're giving up all this?"

"Yes, Monsieur Aubert. I'm leaving."

He stared at me silently for a moment, his bright blue eyes boring into my soul. Then, lowering his voice, he made a strange remark that left me speechless, "You know, if I were you, I'd join the guerrillas."

I stood open-mouthed, unable to utter a word. Monsieur Aubert was one of the most solitary and least talkative of all the Center's teachers and it was virtually impossible to decipher the expression on his face. It was only years later, when I read the Pied Noir writer Jules Roy's words, "If I were a Muslim I'd be in the bush," that I understood the true meaning of my teacher's words.

"Goodbye, Monsieur Aubert. Thanks for everything and God bless you," I said.

The Emir Abdelkader led the resistance to the invasion and occupation of Algeria by France, 1832-1847

Chapter 8
Guerrilla at Last

Each of us has one day more or less sad, more or less distant,
when he must finally accept to be a man.
Jean Anouilh

Joining the guerrillas, as we have seen, was unfortunately not as easy as one might think. Dejected, I returned to work at the forge, helping my older brother Sharif. But I could not put my heart into it. I learned that other classmates had been recruited without going through the initiation rite of killing a man—but not me.

I understood later that they had been drafted by the French army, and it was enough to take the mobilization order to the regional political commissar of the revolutionary forces to be immediately integrated into a guerrilla group. To be sure, when I was summoned to the French review board and examined by the military doctor, I hoped that I, too, would be declared fit for service, opening the door to the National Liberation Army. But such was not the case. The two scars from my hernia operations did not escape the notice of the doctor. My 127 pounds also worked against me. To my great disappointment, I was exempted from military service.

That was when, at the height of frustration, I decided to force the hand of destiny. I met a young peasant from Aït Hamdoun one day while I was shoeing his mule. I told him about my fruitless efforts to join the freedom fighters. He looked at me thoughtfully, as if to assess my determination, and then offered to introduce me to a group leader in charge of sabotage.

"There are a dozen of them," he said. "They really are the handymen of the Revolution—lookouts, saboteurs, food providers, intelligence agents."

Two or three days later, I told my mother that I was leaving to look for work in Algiers. I bought myself a pair of army boots and climbed to the village of Aït Hamdoun to join the saboteurs. It was 1956, and I wasn't to see my family again for seven years. I'll never forget the hospitality, warmth, and outright assistance of the Aït Hamdoun villagers, who immediately understood my plight and adopted me.

In Aït Hamdoun, my first act was to indulge in a symbolic ritual, burning my French-Muslim identity card. I mentally said a fervent prayer to be spared that other ritual act of killing a man in cold blood. Then began long months of dashed hopes and bitter frustrations.

In Aït Hamdoun, often stormed and ransacked by French soldiers, we organized our own guard. Since the village was a transit area between the eastern and western sectors of the Wilaya III revolutionary military command, I met a large number of officers, political commissars, and National Liberation Army guerrillas passing through the village. I recall looking with envy at their modern arms, which I quickly learned to identify: U.S. carbine, Garand rifle, Thomson submachine gun, German Mauser, British Sten, Bell rifle, French MAS 36 and 49 rifle, MAT submachine gun. To all of the guerrillas I met almost nightly, I conveyed my frustration. "We are asked to go on strike and join the ranks of the National Liberation Army, and we have been completely ignored as if we did not exist." From all, I asked for help enrolling in their ranks. To all, I declared myself ready to submit to the ordeal that I can never mention, even 50 years later, without a chill in my spine—to kill a member of the enemy. I even enlisted a help of a cousin, Lieutenant Mohand Saïd Metouchi (unfortunately killed in 1957), but to no avail. Month after month went by. And then I met, in the early summer of 1957, a sophisticated expatriate on vacation who impressed me immediately.

Weary and fairly demoralized, I followed his advice to take advantage of the literary skills that had earned me first prize in French composition: I wrote numerous letters to officers and political commissars. Displaying my youthful impatience, if not outright anger, I reminded those I wrote to that it was not fair to order us to go on strike and join the ranks of the freedom fighters and then abandon us, defenseless, to French soldiers. Being exposed to indifference or rejection by the guerrilla leaders, I had decided to address the very top of the hierarchy.

At the outbreak of the Revolution Aït Hamdoun was living in relative peace, but the regional guerrilla leader soon brought the village into the turmoil besetting the rest of the Kabylia region. Mounting an ambush within the village itself, he resorted to a tactic as old as humanity: attracting repression and thus swinging the last recalcitrant villagers to the camp of the National Liberation Army. This proved to be the end of the tacitly established agreement with colonial forces in a village that naively believed it could remain neutral. The ruthless repression that befell Aït Hamdoun turned every villager into an implacable enemy of the French. The French troops had cleverly been put to work as the main recruiters of insurgents.

One night on patrol, we had barely left the village when a harsh voice suddenly broke the silence of the night. "Stop! Who goes there?"

I could barely discern the barrel of a weapon shining in the moonlight. We quickly recovered from our surprise and gave the local password before disclosing our identity. Immediately, four uniformed men emerged from the shadow of an olive tree, two on each side, and walked toward us, weapons in hand.

A fifth one, taller, wearing a camouflage shirt and trousers with his rifle slung over his shoulder, led the way. On his orders, we turned back towards the village, answering his questions about the movements of French troops. After all, we were the watch guards and intelligence agents. Each day, the peasants going down to the town reported troop reinforcements that indicated an imminent sweep in the region, and we immediately alerted the guerrillas or the National Liberation Front militants in the village.

I was startled when the leader asked, "Is there a young student here called Amirouche?"

I replied that I was that student.

"You wrote me a letter," he said.

I was speechless. Not knowing whom I was addressing, I stammered, "I wrote several letters, including one to the great Amirouche."

"Only God is great." Abruptly, he cut me off, before continuing with an amused smile, "I am Amirouche." One of my letters had finally done the trick! I did not learn till much later that my letter angrily signed "Amirouche" petitioning the head of the Wilaya III Military Command intrigued and motivated him to meet his namesake.

I could conceal neither my surprise nor a tremor of emotion. Was I dreaming? Colonel Amirouche had often been described to me by guerrillas passing through the village, and I had read many articles in the colonial press about the "bloodthirsty Amirouche." The image I had constructed of him was far from reflecting the reality standing before me. Here he was, not armed to the teeth but carrying on his shoulder a light U.S. M1 carbine; not dressed in a fancy uniform but wearing the simplest, most inconspicuous shirt and trousers; not ferocious looking but smiling fraternally.

He was tall and lean, of upright posture, with a black mustache. His wide-set black eyes, shining with extraordinary brilliance, were piercing and fierce. With his finely drawn eyebrows, high forehead, and straight nose, he was ruggedly handsome. A front tooth broken by French police during a Paris demonstration in 1953 gave him a ferocious look until he smiled. What seemed to dominate in him was energy and willpower. His walk was supple, fast, and silent like a cat's. I felt my chest swell with pride and joy as, mentally, I threw out a challenge to the French soldiers.

In this modest narrative, I do not pretend to draw a definitive historical portrait of a revolutionary figure who has left his mark on the Algerian Revolution, at whose side I had the rare privilege of living and serving for nearly a year. Although he has excited strong emotions, Colonel Amirouche has still not received much scholarly attention. His reputation has been somewhat negative, essentially because it was created and sustained by French writers. Algerians such as Boumediene, who never fired a shot during the war but later highjacked the Revolution for their own ends, did everything they could to erase Amirouche's name from the history of the war of liberation. When the army chief of staff Boumediene ordered that Colonel Amirouche's remains be secretly buried under the archives of the National Gendarmerie headquarters, he showed a sad lack of character that only jealousy can explain. [34]

Amirouche made history and Boumediene didn't.

A range of epithets, nearly all of them hostile, has been used over the years to describe Colonel Amirouche. The historian Alistair Horne did concede, however, that Amirouche was "of remarkably quick and decisive intelligence." [35]

My spirited defense of Colonel Amirouche on TV shows and in various articles in the Algerian press [36] is, I believe, a timely corrective to a generally false and negative picture. In this account I will describe him as I knew and observed him in the heat of the moment. A straightforward reporting of the events I was privileged to witness will explain my admiration for this giant of the Algerian Revolution, an admiration which does not, I hope, affect the objectivity essential to true testimony.

But to return to my tale, we guided the group to the village Koranic school, deserted by night but vibrant by day with the singing of boys and girls led by a young teacher with a pistol in his belt, whose pedagogy consisted of teaching patriotic songs. The school was a shelter for guerrillas passing through at night or for auxiliaries like us during the day. On this night an oil lamp hung on the wall, oriented so no light filtered outside. The acrid smell of burnt oil filled the air. A woven alfa mat was spread on the cement floor. The Colonel and his companions settled somehow. He gave instructions to post sentries around the village, not just in front of military camps from which a threat might come. Then he unbuckled his ammunition belt, placed it under his knapsack which he used as a pillow, and fell asleep. His four bodyguards did the same, and I noted that they did not take off their boots. Nor were they assigned to guard the entrance of the school. Such was the Colonel's power that among his people, his reputation was obviously the only protection he needed.

I remained awake a long time, sitting against the wall and watching him and his bodyguards sleep in the profound silence of the village night. I stared with an irrepressible envy at the automatic weapons that I could now identify but had never handled. I wondered what Amirouche's inquiry about me really meant.

Outside, the animation generated by the arrival of Amirouche had gradually subsided. The stillness of the night created the illusion that there was no war, that Aït Hamdoun was not likely to be ransacked the next day, its people humiliated, hostages massacred, the village set on fire, as always happened when a bloody encounter occurred within a village sheltering insurgents.

How could I get any rest in a room where the most famous Algerian revolutionary himself rested quietly? It was only in the wee hours of dawn that I finally lay down in a corner. But the excitement caused by the faint hope of joining Amirouche prevented me from sleeping comfortably.

Amirouche and his companions awoke at dawn, buckled their belts, and stood ready for any contingency. It was usually at the first light of day that the French Army mounted their seek-and-destroy operations against the rebels. Local sentries would alert the guerrillas, who immediately dispersed in small groups into the rugged terrain, vanishing before the arrival of aircraft or transport helicopters.

Coffee was brought with flat bread and olive oil. At about 10 o'clock, as no suspicious movement or aircraft had been observed, Amirouche relaxed again, unbuckled his ammunition belt, and summoned the regional leaders, including the political commissars and village storekeepers, from Aït Hamdoun and the surrounding villages. With each, he discussed the morale of the population and the budget, assessed food supply problems, and checked their accounts. At one point, he noticed that coffee consumption by a platoon was overstated and did not match the number of cups that normally brewed from a 250-gram packet. Asking for a coffee pot and a packet of coffee, Amirouche used half of it to brew the coffee himself. He then asked everyone to taste it, including the storekeeper. All agreed, of course, that it was excellent and not too light at all. He then proceeded to count the number of cups obtained from half a package. Everyone present had to admit the merits of his observations. The atmosphere remained convivial and extremely relaxed, but the smile vanished from the storekeeper's face for he knew that, behind the joking tone, Amirouche was sending a message calling for strict rigor in his management of scarce supplies. Embezzlement was punishable by death.

Amirouche issued instructions to resupply food stocks whenever possible, from small villages that were not yet suffering from a French embargo. Flour and canned and powdered milk, sent from Tazmalt to the mountain villages, were subject to severe restrictions. Even a bag of semolina loaded on a donkey was cause for stern interrogation at check points that controlled entry to and exit from Tazmalt.

Amirouche then reminded everyone that he had sent a circular to all the heads of the four zones of Wilaya III, to the political commissars, and to the village storekeepers rationing meat consumption. "You know that our livestock is being devastated. We ordered the suspension of ritual sacrifices on the occasion of Eid El Kebir. With this in mind, eating meat is strictly rationed. Two days a week. The days are specified in the circular. Moreover, on meat days, no lamb will be sacrificed for less than a platoon of mujahedeen [35 fighters]."

Then came hearings devoted to the grievances of local residents. Most complained of suffering from harsh poverty, a direct consequence of the "forbidden zones" established by the French Army. The peasants could no longer farm their plots located in a declared no man's land. French Army aircraft attacked anyone who ventured into a forbidden zone, killing peasants as well as their goats, donkeys, and mules. The bitter joke among villagers was that even the goats had learned survival tactics in those parts of the country that had been returned to wilderness by daily bombardments. As soon as they heard the roar of an aircraft engine or the hiss of a cannon shell, the poor beasts lay still under a bush until night fell on the mountain. Goats, in general, were a species endangered by the ravages of war. Fighter pilots did not hesitate to use them, or the donkeys roaming the no man's land called Kabylia, as target practice.

A few peasants begged for help as their wives were on the verge of giving birth and in dire need of nutrition to breastfeed their infants. The help that Amirouche ordered for the poorest farmers was inspired by sympathy for their misfortune. It spoke to the bonds that he had forged with the population over the last three years.

The hearings were open to all and invariably scheduled at the expense of the Colonel's safety. The French blockades of cities and their massive regroupment of the population in camps were hardly new. These tactics were part of a scorched-earth policy against revolutionary forces first implemented more than a century ago following the French invasion of 1830. Etienne Gerard,

Secretary of War under King Louis Philippe, had declared in 1832, "We must resign ourselves to drive way back, even to exterminate, the indigenous population. Desolation, fire, and ruining agriculture are, perhaps, the only ways to firmly establish our dominance."[37] The only item missing from this list of gruesome intentions was genocide.

During each hearing, Amirouche listened in silence, training his piercing eyes on the peasant conveying his plight. I could see what it cost the men in pride to reveal their destitution in public. Amirouche ordered the storekeeper to deliver, as the case may be, a bag of semolina, a gallon of olive oil, or a few cans of sugared milk. Hearings lasted all afternoon. Amirouche systematically conducted these unannounced management controls, meeting with every peasant who wished to see him in each area that we inspected.

At around six o'clock a group of soldiers joined us. The sun was setting behind the mountains and dusk gently descended over Aït Hamdoun. Giving the departure order, Amirouche turned to me, handed me a briefcase stuffed with papers, and ordered, "Take care of this. You're coming with us."

What incredible joy! "I can also carry something heavier," I ventured to say in a voice choked with emotion.

"You're the one who gives orders here?" he interrupted sharply. I immediately stood to attention.

I seized the briefcase with a shaking hand. All the villagers were gathered along the narrow streets to catch a glimpse of Amirouche. Young children saluted militarily by slamming their bare heels. Women whispered timidly, "God bless you my children, my brothers." At the edge of the village, my fellow auxiliaries who were not on guard duty smiled at me and waved a farewell that expressed both envy and the satisfaction of finally seeing me fulfilling my wish of joining the National Liberation Army.

Five hundred yards away, I turned one last time towards Aït Hamdoun, exposed to so much turmoil and yet keeping an unshakable faith. Then I cast a glance towards the lights of Tazmalt with thoughts of sadness for my mother. The new course that my life was suddenly taking depended on the will of God. Mentally, I recited Victor Hugo's thought: "Those who live are those who struggle. A firm design fills their soul and spirit." I was uplifted with a pride that I had never known. The prison camp of St.-Maurice-l'Ardoise, where my father was to be locked up a few months later, would soon learn that the son of one of the detainees was serving his country with the great Amirouche.

Chapter 9

Under the Command of Colonel Amirouche

I saw peasants dry the tears of their wives
who were raped before their eyes
Frantz Fanon,
The Wretched of the Earth

We had hardly walked a mile when we heard a scarcely perceptible sound from a grove of olive trees. Three times the sound repeated: tap, tap, tap. I knew a moment later that it was made by two stones knocked together. Instantly our guide announced "triumph" and a voice, like an echo, answered, "in the struggle."

We followed a rocky mountainous path that overlooked the valley, walking in single file about ten meters apart. We could see the road linking Algiers and Bejaia about two miles down the mountain. Further down the Soummam River, a humble stream in summer, sparkled in the moonlight. Our guide exchanged the password with the watchmen at regular intervals along our route.

After walking for about three hours, the lights of the city of Akbou appeared. The guide stopped to ask directions from the platoon leader. As a few soldiers gathered around him, the voice of Amirouche snapped like a whip, "What kind of soldiers did I get? A single burst of submachine gunfire would wipe you out, clustered as you are!"

Immediately the guerrillas resumed their single-file formation, and the procession continued for another hour. A sentry called to us one last time at the entrance of the village of Iamouren, perched on a hillside. A safe house had been prepared for us, a large, windowless room with a dirt floor on which we spread blankets. A candle dimly lit the room, projecting on the plaster ceiling gigantic shadows of the guerrillas. The platoon leader did not need instructions from Commander Amirouche. It took him only a few minutes to organize the guard around the village. Flat bread, olive oil, and dried figs were served by the shelter manager. But, worn out by the four-hour walk, we barely touched the food. We lay down on the blankets and were soon asleep. The next day, under cover of olive groves and thick bushes, we descended to the village of Ighram.

Along the way, the guide told us that two days earlier, serious fighting had broken out between a company of heavily armed guerrillas just returned from Tunisia and French soldiers. The latter, for the first time in this region, had faced a barrage of gunfire that claimed their vanguard. Their total panic sharply contrasted with their blasé reaction to the buckshot they were used to facing. On that day, the traditional battle cry of the French soldiers, "It's only shotguns. Forward!" was nowhere to be heard.

The French forces were ascending the hill leading to Iamouren village, confident and determined to humiliate the remaining populace: old men, women, and children for the most part. Some of the soldiers even had their arms casually slung over their shoulders. Suddenly bursts of German MG 42 and British machine guns, submachine guns, and semi-automatic rifle fire routed the French platoon. Retreating in disorder, the soldiers began to shoot through windows. Some managed to regroup and, with the support of fighter-bombers, fought until evening. We could see empty brass casings and cigarette cartons strewn on the trail. Our men had certainly died there, spilling their blood fighting the French occupiers. We shared our guide's pride and the revolutionary enthusiasm for the heroic example set by those who died in battle defending their sacred land.

We entered the village Ighram, where a bearded second lieutenant, former sergeant of the French Expeditionary Corps in Indochina, greeted us along with the head of the safe house. There was also an officer dressed in a paratrooper's uniform, an emissary from the Wilaya I Military Command, and a group of guerrillas under the command of a second lieutenant.

The officer briefed Amirouche on the general situation in his region, and the storekeeper provided his accounts of food stocks accumulated before the city of Akbou was virtually cut off by embargo. Then he informed us that someone would go into town to run some errands. I learned later that it was also to get a briefing from either National Liberation Front militants monitoring French troop movements or Francophile Algerians turned informants. Some of us asked for razor blades, newspapers, and almost all demanded DDT powder. Nobody had spare underwear or uniforms, showers were rare, especially in winter, and lice were proliferating.

Amirouche turned to the officer and said, "As soon as razor blades arrive, you get rid of that beard." Beards, symbols of religious fundamentalism or revolutionary communism, were banned in the Wilaya III Military Command. Besides, joked Amirouche, we had to be pampered to the very door of the slaughterhouse because it was important, if we were killed, to be healthy looking and clean.

While waiting for our meal, I concentrated on getting better acquainted with the small group that accompanied Amirouche, of which I was now an integral part. Abdelhamid Mehdi, tall, fair skinned. and powerfully built, and Tayeb Mouri were Amirouche's aides de camp, his primary assistants. Tayeb, strikingly handsome and impassive, was the most reserved of the group. Sliman Laïchour was the courier for Wilaya III. He soon became a close friend

121

and confidante. Unlike Abdelhamid and Tayeb whose education level was elementary, Sliman had some high school education and shared with me some lustful stories typical of our age whenever our search-and-destroy operations allowed it.

But I quickly realized that what I thought was a superiority complex exhibited by Abdelhamid and Tayeb was nothing more than shyness and reserve, mirroring their modest level of literacy. Their demeanor towards me completely changed when they learned that I had been a blacksmith, and was the son of a blacksmith who had joined the North African Star at the age of 22 and then the Movement for the Triumph of Democratic Liberties, a man who was arrested and tortured in May 1945 and November 1954.

They were two or three years older than me, and adopted me immediately. Soon they asked me, as did Amirouche later on, to draft letters, to their parents. I am still deeply stirred when I recall the times that Amirouche quietly whispered almost in my ear, as if he shunned betraying any weakness, "Write to the old one," never using the term mother.

I'd rather not indulge in psychological analysis; however, I am inclined to think that it was my youthful physical appearance that encouraged Amirouche to confide in me his filial attachment to his mother. With an aide of his age, he would probably have refrained from revealing his emotions in a letter. So I would write a few lines for him in large, legible print, beaming with affection as if I were addressing my own mother. Never reading it, Amirouche handed the letter to a messenger bound for Tassaft, Amirouche's native village.

But that night at Ighram, we thought only of our food. Preceded by an exquisite aroma, a large tray of roasted chickens suddenly appeared in the room, carried by Baha, the manager of the safe house. At the sight of the dish, Amirouche flew into a rage as violent as it was unexpected. "Did you get my last circular setting out the days in the week when meat is permitted?" he asked in a harsh voice.

"Yes, Commander Amirouche, Sir," stuttered Baha.

"So you do know that today is not meat day?"

"Yes, Sir,"

"Then," said Amirouche between his teeth, "the next time you break a rule for anyone, you will be executed. Take the dish to the sentinels."

Pale, the tray shaking in his hands, Baha complied.

We all followed with our eyes the golden chickens that Amirouche had snatched from our hungry mouths. It was the only day members of our group cursed their bad luck for not being on guard duty. We had to content ourselves with boiled potatoes, flat bread, and dried figs, accompanied by the delicate aromas left behind by the roasted chickens.

After lunch, perplexed by Amirouche's angry outburst towards Baha, I took Tayeb aside and asked him, "Do you really think Amirouche will order the execution of Baha if he breaks the rule again?"

"No doubt about that," replied Tayeb. "It's the whole credibility of his leadership and his authority that are at stake. Amirouche is an implacably righteous leader. He sets the example; he is the role model for everyone. He constantly repeats that only rigorous moral conduct will sustain our fight till the end. He is so just that sometimes he is unjust."

"What do you mean by that, Tayeb?"

"I'll give you an example," he said. "One day guerrillas had conducted body searches of a few villagers to ensure that everyone complied with the injunction aimed at hurting the colonial economy, to refrain from smoking and chewing tobacco. Those who were found to carry tobacco were severely punished and humiliated by having their mustaches [a traditional symbol of manhood] shaved.

"When they returned from the expedition, one of the guerrillas accidentally dropped a box of chewing tobacco from his belt. Amirouche picked it up and checked its contents. The soldier, petrified, lowered his head, trembling. 'Why,' Amirouche said in a low voice, 'you just spent a few hours humbling peasants in front of their wives and children because they broke the rules. And you yourself indulge in chewing tobacco?' The soldier remained silent. What could he answer? Amirouche instantly ordered his execution[38]. I have tears in my eyes whenever I think of him. "I can't believe," I said, "this disproportion between the fault and the punishment!" "What can I say?" replied Tayeb. "Amirouche was certainly facing the quandary of reconciling justice with emotion and anger. Here in the woods, we have no prisons. For benign disciplinary cases, the soldiers are dispatched to serve in the forbidden zones, depopulated by the regrouping camps, where there is nobody to provide shelter or supplies, where they feed on acorns and wild greens accompanied by almost daily bombardments. For all others, it is either forgiveness or death. But exigencies of justice stretched to their extreme become injustice. Is this too high a price to pay for the credibility of the Revolution?"

In the wake of this exchange with Tayeb, I remained thoughtful. But over the subsequent months, as I grew to know Amirouche, I understood the meaning of his words: "Without justice and moral rigor, no cause can triumph." I was to discover what Tayeb meant: Colonel Amirouche was utterly fair in his dealings, and his unwavering readiness to accept responsibility in success as well as in failure was legendary.

After lunch, we went out into the courtyard where a group of schoolchildren who had just finished class came out, led by their teacher. The latter, although a combatant whose bravery was recognized and praised, had been demobilized and assigned to teaching duties. A rare Arabic scholar, unlike the Aït Hamdoun teacher, he shunned time-consuming patriotic singing and taught the rudiments of the Arabic language to the Berber-speaking children of the region. Amirouche began to joke with them, "I know you dream of being sent to Tunis to continue your education, huh? I would like you to. But you're too young, you could not sustain a march of more than a month and you would risk being captured by French soldiers."

I quickly learned that Amirouche was constantly on the lookout for young students of Arabic or French with a certain potential, dispatching them to Tunis under the protection of guerrillas sent there to carry arms and ammunition. Many perished on the way, usually victims of air raids. Dozens of them were executed by their own Berber brethren in the Wilaya I Military Command; these guerrillas were exacting revenge for measures taken by Amirouche in Wilaya I in early 1957. Those students who survived the trek to Tunis were provided room and board, medical care, and clothing in a student center personally created by Colonel Amirouche. He was the first National Liberation Army leader to begin thinking ahead to the requirements of an independent Algeria beyond the war.

Leaving the young to their dreams, a thoughtful Amirouche, hands behind his back, began to pace up and down the yard, humming a famous song of the Wilaya III, "From Algiers to Tizi Ouzou, my heart cries over this misfortune of colonialism, maker of widows and orphans."

The company that had just arrived from Tunisia loaded with weapons, ammunition, and rockets, ambushing a French Army column on the way, had received orders by special courier to remain in the village. In the evening we joined them. Within the company there were two casualties of the recent battle. One of them had a piece of shrapnel in the eye. Dr. Mustapha Laliam, an ophthalmologist, operated on him, which was probably one of the most painful scenes I witnessed during the war. In the courtyard of the sanctuary, with no anesthesia, Dr. Laliam inserted his scalpel again and again into the eye of the fighter, with four of his

124

companions firmly holding him down. Captain Hamimi Ou Fadel rested his hand on the forehead of the wounded man and whispered encouragement. The soldier clenched his teeth in silence, reacting with convulsions to Dr. Laliam's digging scalpel. The operation lasted over an hour, during which the four companions used all their energy to keep the patient still.

The second wounded soldier had been luckier: a small piece of metal was lodged in his calf. Dr. Laliam operated the same way, with the four "anesthetists" tightly holding the patient. Both patients received a glass of warm milk and their cases were closed.

Each fighter of the company had brought from Tunisia at least two weapons, an MG 42 German machine gun or a British Bren machine gun. The armament was to be distributed to different military zones in the Wilaya. Amirouche ordered me to be the recording secretary of the first formal work meeting that he scheduled. He retrieved from the briefcase I was carrying a school notebook and looked up the list of troops active in each region and the corresponding weaponry. Under his direction, I produced a new list of the weapons and ammunition assigned to each region.

In the courtyard, weapons of all brands and calibers were stacked beside a huge pile of ammunition. The soldiers, forming a circle around this treasure, plunged and plunged again their hands into the cartridges like pirates about to share their spoils of gold coins and precious stones. The exhilaration of the guerrillas was extraordinary. No longer would they be subject to the contempt and even casualness with which the French Army met volleys of buckshot. But, as we will see later, the French soon responded to the new threat. They built, at enormous cost, electrified fences along the Tunisian and Moroccan borders to stem the flow of arms and ammunition.

Bren machine guns were assigned either to experienced veterans of the war in Indochina or to the burlier fighters. Those who had been allocated Sten or Thompson submachine guns, German Mausers, or English 303 rifles were ecstatic. The Italian Statis, on the other hand, were not popular: they often jammed or heated very quickly. A soldier who received a Model 86 rifle of interminable length was subject to taunts from his comrades, "You're all set for the olive harvest. No need for a pole, you have it!"

I anxiously watched the arms distribution and wondered whether I would be included among the beneficiaries. I was. Amirouche, with a broad smile on his face, handed me a Sten submachine gun and two magazines. An indescribable joy lifted me as I fondled the weapon with both hands. Someone briefly explained how to use it, but I barely listened to him. My mind wandered to my father, from whom I had not heard for months. His image, chained like a convict and surrounded by gendarmes, still haunted me. I wondered what I would have done if I had had that gun in my hands when he was escorted to the bathroom in handcuffs by two policemen at the Beni Mansur railroad station.

Along with the submachine gun, I also received a combat uniform identical to those of the French Army. Now I was an armed resistance fighter who only lacked battle hardening, a clash with those contemptible French soldiers who fought us with their aircraft and armored vehicles. My wish would be fulfilled many times over in the months that followed.

The operational scheme and command was a classic one for a guerrilla leader and head of a large Wilaya area such as Amirouche and his companions. He knew he owed his life to God, certainly, but also to a perpetual mobility that made him elusive. A tireless walker with prodigious energy, he subjected us, on average, to eight hours of walking every night. We almost never stayed more than 24 hours in one village or one area. Unlike his predecessor, Mhammedi Saïd—undoubtedly the largest human being in the Wilaya III Military Command and too heavy to sustain a long march—Amirouche inspected each sector in each region during the two months that elapsed between Wilaya councils.

Also unlike his predecessor, who was obsessed by personal security and once wanted a machine gun mounted on his mule, Amirouche's inspections were conducted with no escort. He addressed his troops in his powerful voice, using virtually the same speech with some variation:

Dear brothers, our struggle is just and it will triumph. We have not invaded France, it was the French who, with their deadly arsenal and their great numbers, invaded and occupied our land, trampled our customs, bombed our villages, humiliated our women, terrorized our children. They possess modern aircraft, but we have faith in God and God is on the side of just causes...

Do not harass military posts at night any more. Ammunition is too precious. Spy as long as necessary on French troop movements. Patience must be the first attribute of a mujahed. Go for the small supply convoys or isolated patrols. Prior to the ambush, marshal maximum firepower, semi-automatic rifles,

126

submachine guns, and machine guns. The ambush should never last more than a few minutes. Seize the arms and ammunition of the killed enemies and fold up quickly. Break into small groups and disperse into the bush before the aircraft can intervene. We are expecting no mercy from our enemies. Never forget that the choice is only between independence or death.

The Colonel approached his duty by imposing his will on everything and everyone in his path, but he never demanded of anyone anything he did not demand of himself. He certainly knew how to galvanize Algerian patriots as never before, and perhaps never again.

Amirouche rarely alluded to the disparity between the enormity of the task at hand and the laughable means that could be mustered to execute it. He felt himself united with all his men in total communion, sharing in the common effort with a serene determination to fight to the death. Even after a brutal setback, when he no longer hummed "Cry oh my heart...," he lifted his head and planned the almost impossible and yet inevitable triumph of the struggle.

Proof that Amirouche's oratory and the automatic weapons that had just arrived from Tunis had drastically altered the balance of power soon spread to every corner of Kabylia. After months of inactivity, the fire of the revolutionaries in Wilaya III was kindled once again. For example, a second lieutenant named Lahcène had mounted a brilliant ambush on a supply column between the Horra and Bouzeguène camps. As the region was devoid of vegetation apart from a few stunted olive trees, the officer and his company laid their ambush on both sides of the road in the wee hours of the morning. Camouflaged from head to toe, covered by cut branches, they were hiding almost in plain sight.

The wait was very long and the lieutenant would have ordered the lifting of the ambush had there been a way to retreat without betraying their presence. Besides, he told me afterwards, he kept repeating to himself what Colonel Amirouche had told them, "Patience must be the first attribute defining a mudjahed." The binoculars of French soldiers perched in their watchtowers were constantly scanning roads and trails, where ambushes and landmines were an ever-present danger. The mines were often 105-millimeter cannon shells rigged as improvised explosive devices by the guerrillas.

Late in the afternoon, the spy who watched Bouzeguène signaled the departure of three trucks towards Horra. At once the order to arm the machine guns was given. Minutes later a hail of gunfire immobilized the first truck and the guerrillas turned to the occupants of the other vehicles. Some French soldiers resisted a minute or two, and then a total silence fell on the scene of the carnage. Lahcène ordered two fighters to go down to the trucks to ensure that the silence was not a ruse. A French corporal was found hiding under a truck and taken prisoner. Lahcène and a dozen of his comrades relieved the trucks and the dead soldiers of their weapons and ammunition. Withdrawal was swiftly effected to the protective asylum of a thick forest.

I met the French prisoner, Master Corporal Paul Bonhomme, a few days later in the woods of Akfadou. He was not tied up. Surrounded by guerrillas, he was being questioned, not on troop movements and abuses of the population, but on his home and life in France. He showed no apparent concern about his fate, swearing that he had been drafted and forced to fight in Algeria, and loathed risking his life to defend the rich European settlers who owned the country.

It was a strange experience to hear the guerrillas, most of them formidable warriors, quietly evoking memories of their stays in France as immigrant laborers at the Renault auto plant or the Lorraine coal mines. To be sure, one or two of them would have abused the French soldier and for good reason. They had close relatives upon whom Paul Bonhomme's brothers in arms, if not he himself, had inflicted the worst mistreatment. But Amirouche had issued strict orders not to harm the Frenchman—he was valuable for prisoner exchange.

Of course, the French had long ago decided that the Geneva Conventions on the laws of war did not apply to those they considered rebels and terrorists. A word of explanation is required here. Though perhaps unimaginable today, at the beginning of the Algerian Revolution, every French soldier killed was subjected to an autopsy as if he were the victim of an ordinary murderer. The magistrate sometimes ordered a reenactment of the "crime," that is to say, the scene of the ambush! [39]

Thus one can perhaps understand the contemptuous refusal of the French Army to negotiate an exchange of prisoners with us. As a result, the execution of National Liberation Army Lieutenant El Hocine Salhi in 1958 was followed by the execution, in retaliation, of Lieutenant Olivier Dubos, captured along with 17 others when their camp was overrun in El Hourane on February 4, 1958. In a letter to Lieutenant Dubos' family, Colonel Amirouche explained that this execution followed the assassination of an officer of the ALN "previously tortured by the French Army." [40]

128

An editorial in the French daily Libération [41] stated that "the application in Algeria of the Geneva Conventions would prevent the chain of reprisals."

According to the newspaper l'Humanité [42] six prisoners from El Hourane died of exhaustion during their captivity. All the others said, after being released, that they had seen Amirouche several times, that he spoke to them at length, and that he lent them his pen and notebook so they could write letters to their families. Soldier Raymond Koppel stated that the Colonel did not subject them to any interrogation. "He even said, 'I do not ask you any question: I know as much as you do, probably even more than you do.' He gave us as an example the size of our command staff that we would have been unable to spell out." Koppel said he saw Amirouche three times and "he always certified that as soon as the International Red Cross came to Algeria, we would immediately be released." He and his comrades eventually were, although no exchange took place.

As for Master Corporal Paul Bonhomme, refusing or unable to sustain the march to Tunis where he was being taken for a prisoner exchange or propaganda purposes, he died on the way. I am unable to say under what circumstances. What I do know, having walked the distance myself, is that it was exceedingly difficult to stay alive on this infernal journey to Tunisia.

Paul Bonhomme's story did not end there, however. While putting the last touches to the draft of my book *Akfadou, Un An avec le Colonel Amirouche*, I googled Bonhomme and discovered that his brother was still searching for him in 2009, more than half a century later. I was so deeply touched that I wrote to him describing the circumstances of my meeting with his brother, emphasizing the fact that he had been well treated and that, when I left him, Colonel Amirouche was planning to send him along with other prisoners to Tunis to propose, under the sponsorship of the Red Cross, an exchange of prisoners. I concluded that I was unable to determine by talking to my surviving war companions the fate of Paul Bonhomme. The brother tersely replied that I didn't want to tell him the truth and that Paul's fate had been sealed on the night of the ambush. I responded that, if that had been the case, I would have never written in the first place. The bitterness that pervaded his curt messages explains why he cut short our correspondence.

During the months that followed the arrival of the automatic weapons, the inspection tours of the Wilaya III Military Command, coupled with Amirouche's gifted oratory, revived and inspired military actions unmatched across Algeria. Most were accomplished by elite battalions superbly armed and well seasoned, led by two guerrillas: Azil Abdelkader El Bariki and Mohand Ourabah Chaïb, both eventually killed in battle.

Abdelkader El Bariki earned the reputation of unprecedented ferocity. He never took prisoners after an ambush, instead passing each body previously stripped of its uniform and boots and pumping a bullet into the soldier's head. I was told that the men under his command were seen slicing off the genitals of dead French soldiers and stuffing them into the corpses' mouths. When I expressed my strong disapproval of this barbaric mutilation, Tayeb Mouri silently stared at me and then, in a barely audible tone, uttered these words: "Only those who have been forced to watch a scene worse than death, the rape of their wife, their sister, or their mother, can understand."

For our part, the small group accompanying Amirouche rarely engaged in armed action. But warning alerts, if not operations mounted against us, were our almost daily lot. Colonel Amirouche was not a man to adopt such a low profile as to shun interacting with his people. I discovered quickly that our group paid the price of his popularity and his national stature. His fame prompted the mobilization by the French Army of huge resources, including, beginning in March 1958, the infamous Bleuite Plot, hatched to weaken and destroy the Wilaya III Military Command from within. But more of that in Chapter 11.

The adulation surrounding Amirouche was such that each time we passed through a village, a French informant inevitably found out and quickly signaled our presence to the enemy. In general, in the absence of radio transmissions, the spy led his sheep, goat, donkey, or cow, depending on the number and rank of the guerrillas camping in the area, to a predetermined hill. The French sentinels in their watch towers took care of the rest. Often 24 or 48 hours later, Sikorsky helicopters, followed by T-6 bombers, appeared.

Amirouche was fully aware of the security issues we faced. He was still alive in 1958, four years after he took to the mountains, thanks to trickery, guile, and perpetual movement. Except in the forests of Akfadou where our command post was located, we rarely lingered more than 24 hours in the same location. The number of times a village we had just left was attacked the day after our departure was a clear indication that our visit had been reported. We wondered whether the National Liberation Front turncoats had been manipulated in Algiers by the psychological services of the French Army and then infiltrated the guerrilla ranks.

Occasionally, the French Army resorted to psychological warfare. They spread persistent rumors of imminent search-and-destroy operations, for instance. In the fall of 1957, we fell into their trap and moved from an area rumored to be targeted to a safer place, only to find the same rumor of an impending operation wherever we went. I will always remember those three or four days of forced marches dogged by a nagging threat that never materialized. Exhausted physically and morally, we decided to entrust our fate to God and crouched behind miserable bushes in broad daylight in the wilderness.

The major operations that targeted several villages at once required the mobilization of large reinforcements that could not go unnoticed. French troop movements were scrupulously monitored and reported, allowing the guerrillas either to leave the target area, or to plant improvised explosive devices or set up ambushes on their way back to their garrisons.

To spare the villagers the inevitable retribution that the French Army mercilessly inflicted on them when a guerrilla was caught in their midst, we camped as far away as possible from human habitation. But often, we were caught in a village by a surprise operation mounted without large reinforcements from one of the French camps that crisscrossed Kabylia. The pattern was usually the same. In early morning sentinels warned us of French soldiers heading towards the village, either by opening fire on the soldiers of the vanguard who did not give the password or who did so with a French accent, or by leaving their post and rushing to our shelter to alert us.

We first had to confront aircraft and artillery before even considering fighting the enemy soldiers, who outnumbered us twenty to one. Hence, before the French could complete their deployment and encircle a village, we retreated at full speed from tree to tree, in single file, towards the peaks, ravines, and forests inaccessible to the French infantrymen. The vulnerable bare and low ground and the superior high ground were incessant reminders that, in armed confrontation, topography was fate.

Our group rarely, if ever, exceeded six in number. Amirouche, always on the alert, owed his longevity to extreme mobility combined with the unwavering protection of the population. Peasants foiled traps set by the French, who were aided by informants whose existence was demonstrated almost daily by the operations mounted regularly in the regions that we had just left.

The French Alpine Corps often set ambushes near bridges and known transit areas for guerrillas, but our lookouts near the camps always alerted us in time. Then we would change our route and, as an additional precautionary measure, announce our

131

destination aloud to civilians as we departed. Once we were a few hundred meters away, we moved in the opposite direction.

We paid dearly to discover the tactic French soldiers used to carry out an ambush or plant land mines. Our sentries were on the alert for headlights, but the French jumped or were quietly dropped into the bush by trucks moving without headlights. We were auxiliaries, not guerrillas, when some of my comrades were blown up by a landmine in Ihitoussen. But even if our group had been part of an active combat unit, we would have avoided a firefight since French infantrymen stormed guerrilla positions only when they were convinced that they had been wiped out or considerably "softened."

Fundamental to the rules of guerrilla warfare is that no battle, no skirmish is to be fought unless it can be won. Forgetting this rule, a National Liberation Army officer saw his company of over 100 soldiers wiped out in September 1958 during the massive search-and-destroy operation code-named Brumaire. The sentinel of the company signaled the arrival of several military trucks on the highway not far from the company's encampment. Contravening guerrilla principles which called for breaking up ranks and dispersing in small groups, the company commander elected, with unusual recklessness, to set an ambush. The next day, French air power and artillery decimated the company.[43] Because he naively believed that there would be a ground war between infantry units, Saddam Hussein saw much of his army massacred in Kuwait in 1991 by U.S. aircraft and cruise missiles[44].

The French Army (or the U.S. military in Iraq or any army in the world enjoying air superiority) sends its soldiers into harm's way only after heavy shelling of enemy positions—as we learned regularly from bitter experience. Besides using devastating force, the French Army had recourse to secretiveness, treachery, and surprise. When these were foiled, it was only because vigilance on our side prevented surprise. During the years 1957-1958 we were taken aback by perhaps a dozen operations. I will mention only those in which we recorded casualties, leaving for the end the most dreadful, a deadly ambush we fell into on the border between Algeria and Tunisia on April 26, 1958.

Chapter 10
Search and Destroy

Just kill them.
François Mitterrand,
French Minister of the Interior and later
President, regarding the treatment of Algerian prisoners

———————◆———————

Barely a month after joining the Revolution, Amirouche demonstrated for the first time his leadership qualities. When the leader of his group was killed in action, Amirouche immediately took over, on his own initiative, the command of the region of Aïn El Hammam. When Krim Belkacem, one of the original leaders of the Algerian Revolution and responsible for the organization of the Kabylia command zone, learned that a soldier named Amirouche had, by his own authority, assumed leadership, Krim summoned Amirouche to account for his actions. But upon meeting Amirouche, Krim realized that he was dealing with a "tough, determined, alert, sharp, ruthless" man.[45] To take such a vital initiative in a moment of distress caused by the death of a chief, without waiting for orders, was the action of a born leader.

Without having to say it in so many words, Amirouche conveyed to Krim the belief that a leader must always be held accountable for blunders, but not necessarily always for decisions taken in the best interest of the Revolution. Krim did not need to ask for explanations; it was Amirouche himself who spontaneously provided them. "When our leader was killed, I saw the men distraught, and a bit demoralized... I took charge, waiting for your arrival."[46]

Krim learned that Amirouche not only had taken command of the region but had also recovered weapons, raised money, and recruited and trained guerrilla groups. Amirouche submitted to Krim a handwritten brief laying out his activities, which also contained the list of men recruited and the exact sums collected.

Amirouche showed such exceptional traits of leadership and authority that Krim wanted them implemented on a larger scale. But if he was delighted by the qualities shown by Amirouche, Krim did not express it. He decided to confirm Amirouche in regional responsibilities, but not in his native region; for security reasons, he explained. Thus Amirouche found himself responsible for a vast stretch representing about half the territory of the future Wilaya III Military Command: the Soummam Valley, Bouira, the Bibans, and the eastern Arabic-speaking regions of M'sila and Bordj Bou Arreridj.

The tasks at hand, agreed upon between the two leaders, were gigantic. First and foremost, Amirouche would need to establish links with the neighboring Constantine command zone.

Organizing armed groups was easy since one could recruit from a pool of thousands of volunteers eager to join, but to arm them was a different story. Therefore, recovering weapons, essentially shotguns, from the peasants, and taking weapons from the enemy during ambushes were absolutely imperative.

Another primary mission was to strengthen the National Liberation Front and impose its monopoly of representation of the Algerian cause throughout the whole country as well as the international arena. But that was not easy to achieve due to a rival organization, the Algerian National Movement [47](MNA), established in the Sétif and Guenzet-Bougaâ regions. A tragic irony, according to Amirouche, was that it was far easier to generate loyal support and receive aid in an area deemed neutral than in one where the Nationalist PPA/MTLD was firmly rooted. Eventually Amirouche was able to integrate many MNA supporters into his own units. Yet he also displayed his ruthlessness as a military commander towards MNA officers and political commissars captured during battle.

The meteoric rise of Colonel Amirouche, and the national significance that the Wilaya III Military Command acquired under his leadership, did not escape the watchful eyes of the French Army Special Services. Kabylia is almost a country unto itself within Algeria, Berber speaking with no Arab influence, Muslim but with pagan and Christian practices. Too poor to settle or to intimidate, too autonomous to buy off, Kabylia turned out to be "a focal point...of the rebellion," to quote French General Jean Olié.

Hence the French Army, particularly after General de Gaulle took over in 1958, focused its destructive power against the Wilaya III Military Command located in Kabylia. The French troops' orders were to kill insurgents, while the Specialized Administrative Sections endeavored to convince the Algerian people that the French were friends; the rape of women and bombing of children but unfortunate collateral damage. This proved a hopeless task.

Because his command covered such a vast area and became a force to be reckoned with under Amirouche's leadership, the French Army organized specific actions designed to kill him as well as infiltrate the area. Our small groups was caught in a number of operations which were quite frightening for a teenage guerrilla like me. The first took place in Aït Waâvane. That late summer day in 1957 has remained vivid in my memory. At dusk we left a tiny village where a chance encounter had made my day. One of my classmates for whom I had a boundless affection, Hocine Omar, was serving in the region. But more heartbreaking than I can describe, I also witnessed with a profound distress the

135

sentencing to death of a "Messalist" who, although a patriot, was labeled a traitor because he remained fiercely loyal to Messali Hajj. Many patriots vowed an almost fanatical support to this nationalist leader and folk hero who formed the Algerian People's Party in the 1930s.

Throughout the day, Hocine and I jettisoned the anonymity of underground life, with its false names and assumed pseudonyms, as we fondly recalled our childhood games at school and our platonic love for the only three girls in the classroom, all of whom were French. We exchanged news of our classmates who had joined the insurrection and were still alive or had fallen on the field of honor, the usual formula announcing the death of a companion. I could not imagine, then, that Omar himself would be killed a few months later, as were almost all of my buddies from primary school and the Vocational Center. Among the fallen were so many whose graves will never be found or will forever display the sign, "Combatant known only to God."

The officer in charge of the military precinct presented three Messalist prisoners to Amirouche: a political commissar considered an "old" man about 35 years of age and two youngsters, all in civilian clothes. I will never forget Amirouche's speedy and rough justice, ultimately attributed not so much to his temperament as to the circumstances of a Revolution which I was beginning to think may have been triggered too hastily. Colonel Amirouche listened quietly to his officer's briefing and without any hesitation ordered, "Execute the political commissar and integrate the two youths into our ranks."

The commissar was taken away, and although he knew his fate, he exhibited a haughty coolness and did not plead forgiveness. And for good reason: a massacre ordered by Amirouche's predecessor was still fresh in the commissar's memory six months after it had occurred. If National Liberation Army units could mercilessly slaughter almost all male adult villagers, there was little chance that Amirouche would show magnanimity towards a political commissar who played a decisive role in the recruitment and indoctrination of Messalist militants.

For the first time, I wondered if those who sparked the revolution on November 1, 1954, had not done so prematurely. They could surely have taken the necessary time to reunify the ranks of the nationalist movement that had imploded in the summer of 1954 when the Central Committee of the Nationalist Party rejected the plea of its President Messali Hajj to be granted full powers to reorganize the party. Contesting the authority of the charismatic leader, father of the modern Algerian nationalist movement, was unprecedented; it generated the fracture briefly analyzed in Chapter 6. If the Centralists had postponed their insurrection by only six months, they might have spared the country its horrific war between patriots. Although to question the Algerian founders' choice of time to launch the Revolution is considered sacrilege in Algeria today, I did so in a piece published in *Le Soir d'Algérie* on March 24, 2010. Twenty years after independence, I cautiously tested that assertion on the late Saâd Dahleb, former member of the Movement for the Triumph of Democratic Liberties, former Minister of Information of the Algerian Government in exile, and one of the key negotiators of the 1962 Evian Accords ceasefire. I asked him, "Si Saâd, in Wilaya III, until 1958, we were at war against genuine patriots but who pledged allegiance to Messali and the Algerian Nationalist Movement. Don't you think that triggering the revolution on November 1, 1954, was somewhat premature, without serious regard to reunifying first the ranks of Messalists, Centralists, or others, who were all in favor of armed action?"

Dahleb paused before answering, "You are right. We handed our enemies propaganda fodder. France used it to claim that she could not grant independence to a people killing each other and eventually convincing many of the MNA groups to surrender to the French."

If I dwell on this painful and rather fruitless subject, it is because I still relive the memory of thousands of patriots who, after devoting their lives to the relentless struggle to liberate the country from French occupation, died at the hands of their brothers-in-arms. These were patriots who had experienced torture and abuse at the hands of the French police, some of whom had survived the 1945 massacres.

It is always with deep sorrow that I discuss the fate of another leader, Si Larbi Oulebsir. I was still in grade school when I first met him. He had joined the nationalist party in 1943 at the age of 23 and became a member of the paramilitary Special Organization at its inception in 1947. When he was arrested in 1950, he became a model for nationalist militants: he went on a hunger strike which lasted 27 days. I still remember my father's pride as he cited Oulebsir as a role model whose courage and determination inspired so many activists in my hometown and among the ranks of all patriots.

As a member of the leadership of the MNA, the National Liberation Front's deadly rival, Oulebsir travelled to Tetuan in Morocco to purchase weapons in April 1955. After that trip he disappeared forever, perhaps executed by his brethren from the

National Liberation Front.

I remember a talk about boy scouts that Oulebsir gave to some primary school children, including my brothers and I, in 1950 or 1951. I heard for the first time of Baden Powell, the founder of scouting, and of the Algerian Muslim Scouts, of which we became Cubs. Oulebsir was so proud of us when, after school, he saw us marching in step and shouting "Scout ... Be ... Ready!" One evening, marching and singing a patriotic song, we stumbled into a surprised gendarme. As we went by him, we sensed his hatred. The oldest among us was not yet 13 years old.

Here I was, seven years later in 1957, hearing with a heavy heart the order of execution of a Messalist who, like Si Larbi Oulebsir, had committed no crime except to belong to a rival faction of the nationalist struggle.

The sun was just disappearing on the horizon as the marching order was given. I turned to my friend Hocine, and I will never forget his sad smile and melancholy eyes. I was never to see him again.

The long hike, nonstop through the thick bush of hills and ravines, lasted more than 11 hours. We arrived in a village at daybreak, dazed and exhausted. Extreme physical exertion blunted our instincts and reflexes; we forgot that dawn, when raids often occurred, was the worst time of day to pull off our boots. Hardly five minutes had elapsed after we settled in the safe house when a burst of gunfire pierced the morning silence and brought us back to the brutal reality of war. We lost valuable time retying our bootlaces and buckling our belts. The village was surrounded, and our group of five was in no state to engage the French troops in a hopeless and suicidal battle. The only possibility of escaping death or capture was to climb the cliff against which the village was built. We set out to attempt just that, literally on all fours. But the physical exhaustion was so overwhelming that after a few minutes we gave up.

Tayeb Mouri was the first to express what we all, except of course Amirouche, felt—that he was quitting, surrendering to fate. Tayeb said he would wait for the French, empty at least one magazine of his Thompson submachine gun, and end his life under the heavy fire of a T-6 fighter-bomber. End the war for us, once and for all, was our shared sentiment. I vividly remember how our exhaustion dealt a terrible blow to our morale.

But Colonel Amirouche was cast in a different mold. He instilled in us some of his extraordinary will power by simply tapping us lightly on the shoulder, punctuated by soft urgings of "come on, come on" as he led the way. His physical vigor proved an extraordinary tonic to us. Without him we would have awaited our fate leaning against the rocky wall of the Djurdjura Mountains, washing with the red of our blood those arrogant claims painted in white: "Kabylia, French Land."

Under the Colonel's leadership, it took us nearly two hours to climb the mountain and begin our descent down its southern flank. Fifty-four years later, in 2011, I revisited the cliff. I could not believe that we had managed to climb it. It was practically a vertical wall.

The French soldiers, a few hundred yards below us, behaved with their usual caution. The French knew that when the watch guards of the revolutionaries fired a shot, they were alerting guerrillas who, unlike their sentinels, were armed not with shotguns but with automatic weapons. On this day, our fire would have been all the more lethal because the barrage would come from the top down. Aircraft had to be summoned. The French probably never imagined that we would manage to escape up the cliff. But by the time the warplanes appeared, we had crossed the mountain.

On the other side, the south side of the Djurdjura, existed a paradise. The house of a militant nicknamed Mustache had been turned into a safe shelter in a tiny village built on a hillside. There, an extraordinary reception awaited us, with honey cakes, omelets, buttermilk, figs, grapes, and above all, security.

We had left behind the bare and rocky slopes of Aït Waâvane. Shady groves of olive trees would have shielded us from the firing line of aircraft gunners—but curiously, no aircraft blackened the sky. French soldiers were busy, no doubt, punishing the villagers on the other side who had provided us with food, support, and security. We lived amongst them "like fish in water," and the French Army had no qualms about setting fire to their miserable shacks and displacing millions of people.

A second violent encounter with French troops also haunts my memory. It took place in the village of Azrou on November 8, 1957. We were returning from an inspection of the only hospital in the Wilaya III Military Command, located in the forest of Akfadou. It had rained, and the droplets of water clinging to the few remaining oak leaves twinkled feebly. There was not a breath of wind. The sky was dark with rain clouds, so low that they seemed to brush the treetops. We loved such weather, extending its protective arms above us and keeping the French air force at bay. Near the big tent which served as a hospital, a heartbreaking scene was taking place: two guerrillas, Khelil Amrane and his wife, Jamila Danielle Amrane Minne, were sobbing bitterly.

Colonel Amirouche had decided to transfer to Tunisia all

139

female fighters in his command and had already ordered me to draft the pass that would allow Jamila to walk all the way to Tunisia. Now Jamila and her husband were trying to persuade Amirouche to reconsider and make an exception. I was their age and was myself moved to tears. I discovered that day a new dimension to Amirouche's character. I could not have imagined that he could be so patient and so fatherly.

"Please, Colonel, Sir," pleaded Khelil, "allow her to stay. She can render so many services in the infirmary. Or, let me go with her."

Amirouche showed an exceptional indulgence. On his usually impassive face was a trace of emotion. Certainly, he personally had allowed them to marry a few months earlier and, although unwavering in his decision, he found the right tone, at once considerate and final. He said, in a firm but kindly voice, "Try to understand, this is a general measure that can't be jeopardized by a single exception." Then, his face somber, he proceeded to the hospital inspection.

There the situation was appalling. Amirouche soon realized that a single nurse could not meet the needs of some 30 wounded fighters, tuberculosis patients, and other sick guerrillas, shivering from cold in the inadequate tent that served as a hospital. Even with a nursing diploma, the incomparable Hamid Mezaï, whose self-sacrifice and dedication deserved 100 National Liberaton Army Medals, the highest war distinction, was clearly overwhelmed. Doctors Belhocine and Laliam were forced to travel the whole Wilaya Military Command to attend, on site, to the most serious cases.

As soon as he completed his inspection, Amirouche ordered me to draft a mobilization order to be sent immediately to Dr. A.O. To protect the doctor in case the order fell into the hands of French soldiers, I included death threats if he did not answer the call. Dr. A. was a loyal patriot who regularly supplied us with prescription medicines and medical equipment. Head of a large family, successful and popular in the town of Akbou, he understandably declined our "invitation" to join the armed struggle. When Amirouche learned that the doctor refused to comply, he sentenced him to death and instructed me to draft the execution order. What saved Dr. A. was the bold intervention of Dr. Laliam, who happened to be present. In a soft and shy voice he pleaded, "Colonel Amirouche, sir, I share your anger. The health conditions are catastrophic and Dr. A. should answer the call. But A. is not a traitor. He is collaborating with us in his own way. If he is executed, there will be one more foreign doctor we'll have to hire after independence. I am only voicing my humble opinion: spare his life."

Laliam knew that Amirouche would be sensitive to this argument, as eager as he was to train as many Algerians as possible to take over from the French in an independent Algeria. As mentioned before, he did dispatch to Tunis all young people able to continue their studies to the student center he had created for them.

Amirouche's silent stare conveyed his displeasure at Laliam's plea. But then he ordered me, with a nod, to tear up the execution order. I heaved a sigh of relief that must have been heard throughout the Soummam Valley: Dr. A. was our family doctor, known for his generous dedication to the people of the region.

Thus Dr. Mustapha Laliam saved the life of a colleague who was later elected to the first National Assembly of independent Algeria.

For now, immediately after the inspection and before our departure, we had a frugal but delicious meal of flat bread and canned sardines. It was not a meat day, and I remember that we all thanked God and Amirouche for not including sardines in his circular limiting the consumption of meat to two days per week.

After another long trek, we reached Azrou just as daylight was breaking. Once in our safe house, we had not even unbuckled our heavy bandoliers when we heard the warning gunfire of our sentinels. We moved fast to reach the nearby forest before the French encircled the village—but it was too late. Two hundred meters ahead, French troops were deploying and readying their machine guns.

We were no more than a dozen, so we immediately made an about-face. At once a machine gun began to crackle and bullets whistled past, breaking twigs around us. Amirouche ordered "Scatter!" but his command was absolutely futile. Three of the twelve were mortally hit, and we could do nothing for them. The forest was only about 500 meters away, but to reach it, we had to cross a track where armored vehicles were already lining up. Like most soldiers fighting a war and risking their lives on a daily basis, I was quite religious and began to say my prayers. Then we were literally thunderstruck by what we perceived as divine intervention bordering on a miracle: a thick fog suddenly fell and covered our retreat. The T-6 bombers circling above the tracks were neutralized. Only the powerful roar and hum of tanks and aircraft engines continued to be perceptible. We stayed in the shelter of the forest all day and as usual, as soon as night fell, we were masters of the terrain once again. We cautiously made our way towards the village.

But there was no village any longer. The French soldiers had set it on fire. Huge flames illuminated the trees and the bushes around us. All the villagers had fled or been apprehended. The sole remaining inhabitant was an old woman holding a goat on a leash, who whispered, "God bless you my children." I thought of my own mother, in the warm, cozy comfort of the town of Tazmalt and, at that moment, I sensed that ties of kinship were being redefined more by revolutionary solidarities than blood relationships. I felt so much closer to that old lady and shared with her an everlasting kinship. This book is dedicated to her. [48]

The third sweep in which we were engaged was the most violent and memorable. It was no doubt directly caused by one of the most sensational feats of the officers of the Wilaya III Military Command: their seizure, without bloodshed, of the fortified camp of El Hourane near M'sila, and the capture of Lieutenant Olivier Dubos, the camp commander, along with 17 soldiers on February 4, 1958. This brilliant action, which thrilled guerrillas as well as the civilian population, would never have been possible without the help of one of our moles, Staff Sergeant Mohamed Zernouh, a member of the French Third Spahis Regiment light cavalry.

El Hourane was an outpost equipped with armored vehicles that best suited the flat and barren terrain and required only a small force to fortify. The nearest forest was no less than a five-hour walk. The entire area lived in relative peace because the terrain did not lend itself to guerrilla attacks. Our daring operation began under the initiative of revolutionary leaders in charge of intelligence and communications who established contact with Staff Sergeant Zernouh. After carefully strategizing the plan of attack, the leaders entrusted its execution to an elite battalion commanded by Lieutenant Mohand Ourabah Chaïb. The health officer of the area and his team were present to attend to the eventual wounded. The Region 4 Company was mobilized with the mission of protecting the elite battalion's retreat.

The date of assault was set for the night of February 4, 1958. Inside the outpost, unsuspecting French soldiers had gathered in the dining hall. Sergeant Zernouh, responsible for the guard that night, let one of our three battalion companies into the camp. Once they realized that guerrillas had overrun the post, the French soldiers locked themselves up in the dining hall and opened fire through the door, slightly injuring a second lieutenant.

The guerrillas threatened to burn the besieged troops alive. "We heard the rebels light gas cans," remembered de Gaillande, who was taken prisoner and later released. "They were shouting very loudly that they were going to grill us like rats if we did not surrender... We threw down our weapons and we came down from the attic where we hid, one by one, hands up."[49]

We learned through the press that a forest ranger who happened to be in the camp that day was able to escape by hiding in the chimney flue. Without wasting any time, the guerrillas gathered all the weapons stored in the arsenal, the heavy 12.7 and .30 caliber machine guns mounted on armored cars, and a few 60-millimeter mortars. These they loaded on mules ready for transport. The booty was fabulous. There were 49 French-made MAT submachine guns, 50 Mac pistols, and whole cases of ammunition, grenades, and land mines. The convoy of 35 mules with the French prisoners took off towards the forest of Beni Ouagag around midnight, intending to reach it just before sunrise.

Before leaving the outpost, the guerrillas set on fire anything that could not be taken: facilities, fuel drums, armored vehicles. It was reported that the flames were visible from the city of M'Sila several miles away.

After a day of rest, the convoy resumed its journey at dusk towards the southern flank of the Djurdjura Mountains. The planners had chosen a route that befuddled French forces, who had mobilized a sizable number of troops in search of the prisoners. The convoy headed northeast and finally arrived in the forest of Akfadou, where Colonel Amirouche was waiting at our headquarters.

Following this action, the French Army, probably acting on a tip, launched a combing operation in the region of Ouzellaguene where we had traveled for an inspection, in the wake of the sudden dismantling of the village garrison by the French Army. There a chance encounter cheered my evening: Messaoud Ouchouche, a primary-school friend from Tazmalt, was resting in the village. So were Sargent Mohamed Zernouh, with whom we took pictures, as well as the elite battalion commander Mohand Ourabah Chaïb and his troops, superbly armed with some of the machine guns captured at El Hourane. I still remember my surprise at seeing Lieutenant Chaïb walking carelessly in the village without sporting a *kachabia*, the traditional mantle covering one's weapon and uniform. That was one rule violated. He was also wearing a red cap that could be picked out by any pair of binoculars trained on the village from a nearby camp, a breach of regulation. Brave to the point of recklessness, Chaïb was always ready for battle and looking the part.

The day after our arrival, at around 8 a.m., a T-6 fighter-bomber announced itself with its unnerving engine roar and began circling over the village. Shortly after that, the sentries signaled the

143

arrival of a French Army platoon. In order to avoid triggering T-6 gunfire, the guerrillas of the battalion, one after another, headed towards the French soldiers and set an ambush. They hid behind thin bushes, olive trees, and the low stone walls adjoining fig and olive groves.

Under the direction of Amirouche, our small group scattered and began to climb towards the peaks more densely covered with heath, oak, and olive trees. The T-6 veered towards us and I still remember my whole body tensing and knees weakening when I realized that the butt of my submachine gun, which formed a huge lump under my *kachabia*, would trigger the fire of the fighter-bomber. But then we heard a blast of gunfire on the outskirts of the village, and the T-6 changed course. Our group of five climbed a few hundred meters and sat under the oak trees. Above us rose the bare peaks of the Djurdjura, behind which nestled the village of Aït Zikki. But continuing was out of the question once 105-millimeter artillery shells started to rain down relentlessly.

General George S. Patton once called combat "an orgy of disorder." I wish it were only that. That day in February 1958, from sunrise to sunset, we were subjected to a dreadful bombardment that sprayed shrapnel as well as pieces of rock. A fragment of rock thrown into the air by a powerful blast hit me on the head and I received my first and only war wound, luckily a light one, which caused no more than a bump under my cap.

I cringed and, seeing me paling, Colonel Amirouche, as imperturbable and fatherly as ever, asked me softly, "You are scared, eh?"

Shaking in my boots, I nevertheless answered, "No, Colonel, sir, I am not." I wished that, like Colonel Amirouche, I could view the heavy artillery bombardment as nothing but deafening noise, at worst unpleasant for sensitive ears.

Then B-26 war planes suddenly darkened the skies and began releasing napalm barrels. It was my first encounter with that fiery and destructive jellied gasoline that set ablaze everything around us, even the rocks. Heavy artillery shells exploded closer and closer, as if the gunners knew our exact position and were adjusting their shooting.

Curiously, we did not observe the usual rules of maintaining space between us. The danger was so close and so real that the members of our group of five were practically welded to each other. Each one of us strove to draw from the other the courage to remain dignified and conceal our trembling. I remember looking at the heavens from which divine help, was supposed—was expected—to come. But the only answer to our prayers was more napalm

144

dropped almost on our heads by those birds of the apocalypse, the B-26s.

I felt that my life would end at any second that it was completely behind me. It wasn't even a full life but only a yearning, a sketch yet to take form, and the French Army was going to have no qualms annihilating it. It was packaged and sealed, ready to be shipped to the Almighty. There was in this package so much that was unfinished: wishes never accomplished, dreams of romantic love never fulfilled. I hoped it had been a good life, but neither I nor anyone else could make such a judgment.

A few hundred meters downhill, the bombardment could not silence the fierce battle raging, and automatic weapons did not stop crackling. Flattened to the ground, helpless, breaking the safety rule to keep our faces down, we watched the infernal drums of lethal gas raining down on our land. All day, guns and B-26s pounded our positions relentlessly and dropped their napalm.

Finally night fell and the enormous advantage that French soldiers had on us, their aircraft, was neutralized. At night we were the masters of the land, forcing the French to hole up in their fortified bunkers. Except for a few shells exploding intermittently, silence soon enveloped Ouzellaguene. We cautiously got up, stretched our aching bodies, formed a column, and climbed to the top of the mountain. After two hours, we entered the village of Aït Zikki. As we had not eaten all day, the hot cakes served with olive oil and dried figs were a real treat.

While we were resting, a liaison officer was announced. Out of breath, he asked to see Colonel Amirouche. The officer stood to attention and saluted, then whispered something to the Colonel, whose features twitched suddenly. He took a while to recover, pacing back and forth in the backyard of the house. After a moment, Amirouche called me and in a low voice told me the sad news. "Chaïb was killed. Draft a message to inform the zone leaders. The courier is waiting."

I learned from the courier under what circumstances the battalion commander had met his end. As soon as the alert sounded, he had posted his battalion in ambush along the French troops' trail to protect our group. When the French soldiers appeared, a fusillade mowed down their vanguard, including the handler of the 24-29 heavy machine gun. The other soldiers, as usual, were not going to engage in an O.K. Corral-type gun fight and expose their lives, not if aircraft and artillery could accomplish their task. They fell back in disorder, leaving the machine gun on the dirt track. Chaïb, despite calls for caution from his subordinates, was determined to retrieve the abandoned arm, ideal for ambushes. He cautiously ventured onto the track—but not cautiously enough. A T-6 gunned him down.

It was a day of mourning for all of us. Chaïb was one of the bravest warriors of the Wilaya III Military Command. His courage and exceptional calm in battle, combined with unusual simplicity, had made him a cornerstone of the Algerian resistance. He was but one of so many heroes whose biographies deserve to be brought to life and history but which, alas, never will be.

These operations were decisive in hardening my nerves: I was now battle tested without ever firing a shot. I had resisted the temptation to discharge my submachine gun on one of the B-26s only because I followed strict orders given for good reason. A discharge would have betrayed our position.

To be sure, when a fighter jet began to hover above our heads, an almost daily occurrence, rare was the day when at least one of us did not betray a nervous reaction, particularly in an area devoid of natural protection. One day in a village in a barren area, just as night was falling, our sentinel announced the deployment of French troops outside the village. A T-6 fighter-bomber controlled our movements. A politically appointed second lieutenant, unable to control his quavering voice, asked another second lieutenant, a military man, what was to be done. The latter stared coldly at his colleague and curtly replied, "Well, we are going to attack them!" I will always remember the feeling of pride and admiration at the officer's cool-headed way of conveying to all of us his disdain for imminent danger. It dawned upon me at that moment that bravery, just like panic, was contagious.

In retrospect, I realize that the military officers and NCOs, whose mission was to engage in combat, enjoyed much more authority and prestige than the political or intelligence and communications officers of the same rank. Because Colonel Amirouche excelled in combining the political and military dimensions of command, his authority was spontaneously accepted by every fighter as well as by civilians. But he was an exception. My own experience that evening illustrated the differing reactions of two officers of the same rank. Then, however, the French soldiers did not venture beyond the immediate vicinity of the village. Our sentinels signaled to us that the French set up an ambush to surprise guerrillas coming for supplies, for they were not aware that we were already inside the village.

As soon as night fell, Colonel Amirouche ordered the officer to deploy his platoon on the heights without betraying our presence unless the French soldiers ventured too close to the village. Fearing an operation in the region the day after, Amirouche

146

decided in the middle of the night to cross the icy waters of the Soummam River—this was in early December—and take shelter in a hamlet overlooking the town of Akbou.

There, another chance encounter filled me with joy. As if he had been expecting me, my friend Abdel Hamid Naïli was the first to emerge from the group resting in the safe house and embrace me. "You know," he told me, "when I heard you joined the guerrillas, I decided to do the same and here I am." Three months later he fell in a skirmish with a French Army unit near the town of Akbou where he was born. He was just 18 years old.

Each one of us, including the bravest, candidly admitted to fear of French fighter planes and of the Wilaya I Military Command, which we had just left. That area was stripped of protective vegetation "like the head of Si Mohand Tahar," our bald liaison officer. But if I considered Mother Nature too stingy in terms of protection on the southern bank of the Soummam River, it was because I had not yet seen the Sahara desert where, a few months later, we were to fall into a deadly ambush.

The author, next to Colonel Amirouche, center; behind, third from left, Mohammed Zernouh, the officer who successfully planned the storming of a French Army camp and the capture of a lieutenant and 17 soldiers.

(mid- February 1958)

Chapter 11
Dirty Tricks of the War:
The Blue Bird and Bleuite Plots

[A] revolution is not a dinner party, or writing an essay, or painting a picture, or doing embroidery; it cannot be so refined, so leisurely and gentle, so temperate, kind, courteous, restrained and magnanimous. A revolution is an insurrection, an act of violence by which one class overthrows another.
Mao Zedong

149

When French General and Operational Commander Jean Olié declared on May 11, 1956, that "Kabylia will be a focal point, either of pacification, or of the rebellion," he implicitly rendered homage to Colonel Amirouche, commander on the "rebel" side of his operational zone. Olié's successor in September of that same year, General Jacques Faure, was reportedly so bedeviled by Colonel Amirouche's ability to thwart all attempts at kill or capture that the general framed and hung Amirouche's photograph above his desk.

This French focus on the Wilaya III Military Command and on Amirouche himself, bordering on obsession, explains the relentless seek-and-destroy operations mounted against us. But when these were repeatedly foiled, the French Army resorted to subversion and the organization of counter-guerrilla groups. In more than seven years of war, nowhere in Algeria was psychological warfare put to more lethal use against Algerian insurgents than in Kabylia.

The Bleuite plot, devised to destroy Wilaya III from within, led to the execution of several hundred collaborationist "suspects." Hence, to this day, whenever the name "Colonel Amirouche" is evoked, including by Alistair Horne in *A Savage War of Peace*, it is echoed by the word "Bleuite." I should emphasize that the Bleuite strategy was, in large part, a vicious revenge by the French for a counterinsurgency plot code-named Blue Bird, which turned into a disastrous blowback for the French.

What was Blue Bird? I heard about the plot for the first time on a tour of inspection near Azzeffoun, where the events unfolded. Various officers directly involved volunteered details on this counterinsurgency operation planned by the French Secret Service. The story is recounted by soldiers and officers as one of the most celebrated highlights of the war in the Wilaya III Military Command.

Operation Blue Bird, also known as Force K (for Kabylia), was hatched by Governor-General Jacques Soustelle's office at the end of November 1955, and continued under his successor Robert Lacoste. It was brought to an end only in September 1956. Its objective was to develop an anti-insurgency guerrilla force, under the motto in vogue at the time, "to hunt the wolves of Baluchistan, it is necessary to use the dogs of Baluchistan."

To set up the project, Governor-General Soustelle appealed

first to the Service Action (SA) of the External Documentation and Counterespionage Service (SDECE), which was already smarting from its bad experience with the insurgency in Indochina. That had turned into a fiasco, and the SA declined to get involved. The implementation of the conspiracy was then entrusted to the Documentation Service of the Tenth Military Region, assisted by the Kabyle "dogs of Baluchistan," one of whom, Tahar Achiche, was the kingpin.

Achiche travelled to Azzazga, his home town, to launch the operation. Taking his daily meals in a restaurant, he hinted to the restaurant owner, Ahmed Ouzaied, at plans to set up an armed force to fight against "Krim's bandits, murderers of women and children." But Achiche was not aware that Ouzaied, a former nationalist activist, had known Krim Belkacem since 1947 and had kept contact with him after the insurrection was unleashed. And Krim, as noted in an earlier chapter, was the man first responsible for organizing the military district of Kabylia, and the leader who first spotted Amirouche's exceptional leadership qualities. Encouraging Achiche to believe that he was ready to participate in the plot, Ouzaied informed the regional National Liberation Front leader. The latter, in turn, consulted Krim himself who, without any hesitation, gave the green light to enter into the scheme with Achiche for the organization of "Force K."

The French were recruiting, to begin with, a few dozen trustworthy Algerian volunteers who would constitute the core of a secret army living in the wild, acting as guerrillas and traveling only by night, whose mission would be the destruction of the National Liberation Army units operating in Kabylia. All of them, guaranteed to be "reliable," were chosen by Ouzaied and the regional guerrilla commander. The list was transmitted to Achiche and Operation Blue Bird, a "highly secretive and shadowy enterprise," [50] was launched.

These men managed to trick the French Secret Service into supplying them with more than one thousand modern weapons by convincing them that they were arming a counterinsurgency force. Restaurant owner Ouzaied received dozens of weapons, including French MAT 49 submachine guns, machine guns, and U.S.-made Garand rifles, as well as millions of francs earmarked as military pay, all transported in a van delivering colonial newspapers. The fake counterinsurgents staged mock ambushes, leaving on the battlefield the corpses of traitors or Messalists brought from other regions or summarily executed locally.

In August 1956, it was time to launch Krim's troops, now superbly armed by the French, in renewed attacks. Before rallying

National Liberation Army units permanently, the Blue Bird "counterinsurgents" staged two deadly ambushes against French troops. The first targeted the 151 Infantry Battalion, which lost 35 soldiers. For the second ambush, Force K, supposedly participating in a search-and-destroy operation against the rebels, proposed to go first and form the vanguard. They were supplied with additional arms and ammunition as well as white flares. The vanguard promised that, "as soon as we see the rebels, we'll alert you with a flare and you join us."[51] The Force K "counterinsurgents" carefully laid their trap and drew in the Alpine Corps 151 Battalion, which lost 40 soldiers. Before rallying the National Liberation Army units, Ouzaied and his colleagues revealed the hoax to Achiche and pumped three bullets into his chest.

By the end of Operation Blue Bird, insecurity for French patrols reigned everywhere, furnishing explosive proof that a classic army had been held in check by ragtag guerrillas. Their "dogs of Baluchistan" strategy, napalm bombings, and resettlement encampments had proven powerless to subdue or wipe out resistance to occupation. French leaders utterly failed to recognize the limits of power, show political vision, and exercise intelligent statecraft.

The failure of Blue Bird was kept secret for many years. Because Operation Blue Bird resulted in arming several Wilaya III companies with modern weapons, we can understand why the conspiracy of silence still plays to this day regarding Force K. On the French side, the absolute secrecy and the omerta code of silence surrounding the stinging blowback were so pervasive that historians Henri Alleg and especially Yves Courrière[52] encountered enormous difficulties in reconstructing the plot, even after speaking with former senior aides to Governors-General Soustelle and Lacoste, or with the Secret Service of the French Army.

After the failure of Blue Bird, the French Army had no choice but to resort to a more insidious plot named "Bleuite." In sharp contrast, French tongues untied and showered praise upon the Bleuite instigators, who did manage to introduce suspicion, incite tortures, and provoke executions on a large scale in the Wilaya III and IV Military Commands. The French Secret Services were able to put in play one of the most devastating tricks of subversive warfare, in part because they had mastered the techniques of falsification of documents and forging seals. Taking advantage of a submissive civil administration, the Secret Services had been granted special powers by a law introduced by Prime Minister Guy Mollet. A majority of the French Parliament, including the Communist party, approved the law on March 12, 1956. The law surrendered, for all intents and purposes, civilian powers of the police and courts to the French Army.

More importantly, as soon as French paratroopers arrested Saâdi Yacef, the commander-in-chief of the Autonomous Zone of Algiers (ZAA) and the leader of the Battle of Algiers on September 24, 1957, the Zone passed under the total control and command of Captain Paul-Alain Léger, a subversive warfare specialist. Two days before Yacef's arrest, a letter that I personally drafted sent by Colonel Amirouche to the Zone leader and reproduced by Captain Léger in his memoirs[53], proves beyond any doubt that mail, arms, or funds dispatched from Wilaya III went directly into the captain's hands. A measure of corroboration for at least the latter claim is provided by Alister Horne's allegation that "Captain Léger found himself, in effect, virtually controlling the FLN [National Liberation Front] apparatus attempting to re-establish itself in Algiers." [54]

When Captain Léger boasted of receiving Czechoslovakian submachine guns from Amirouche, he was probably telling the truth: I remember very well when we sent them to the ZAA for the simple reason that I was surprised Amirouche could be so generous, despite the acute arms shortage plaguing Wilaya III.

For us, in the interior, danger signals flashed with the sudden and shocking arrest of a highly esteemed officer, Lieutenant Hocine Salhi, in January 1958. Following a general staff meeting, Amirouche had nominated Salhi as political assistant to the Zone 4 commander, Captain Ahcène Mahiouz. I remember Salhi's slender and impeccably handsome figure when he bid us good-bye and, with a guide, left Akfadou, the no man's land where our headquarters were located. Two days later the news of his capture hit us like lightning. That a lone officer with a guide was apprehended by surprise was not infrequent. But capturing a lieutenant along with half a dozen of his staff members, without a shot being fired, was unprecedented. The arrest was the warning shot alerting Amirouche that we had been infiltrated; Salhi's capture unleashed suspicion within our ranks, along with "enhanced" interrogations, torture, and executions.

I would know exactly what happened only 50 years later from an unlikely source, the memoirs of Captain Léger himself, and from a war buddy who endured atrocious abuse and torture at the hands of his comrades-in-arms. It is not easy to recount the poignant narratives of those combatants who, after wrongly arousing suspicion, endured so much in the flesh and in the soul before dying under torture. Even though hundreds of them were vindicated long after their executions, the dishonor brought to their families still reverberates to this day. I had to lie to so many fathers after the war, assuring them that their sons had died in battle when I knew they had been executed as suspects.

That the Bleuite Plot was masterminded by a mere captain, a specialist of psychological warfare, is one of the peculiarities of the war that needs further examination. To shed light on the psychological warfare battle lost by Wilaya III in 1958, it is essential to briefly summarize the circumstances and the context that facilitated its design and its successful implementation.

On January 28, 1956, Ramdane Abane and Larbi Ben M'hidi, two prominent FLN leaders, ordered a general strike in Algiers. Proclaimed to coincide with U.N. debates on the "Algerian question," the general strike "provided a unique opportunity for the French paratroopers-turned-cops to dismantle the secretive, compartmentized networks of terrorist groups."[55]

Thus was triggered an irreversible cycle marked by the systemic use of torture, abuse, and urban warfare pitting the militants against the Tenth Paratroopers Division commanded by General Jacques Massu. A flagrant misnomer, the "Battle of Algiers" was made famous in Gillo Pontecorvo's 1967 film. An integral part of the Battle of Algiers, torture marked an "episode where [it] did produce a net tactical gain for the victors" but was far from being as "rare" as historian Alistair Horne claimed.[56]

The dismantling of the FLN organization in Algiers led to the capture of a large number of militants, and through such tactics as torture, brainwashing, and blackmail, Captain Léger persuaded a number of these captives to collaborate with him. They were dressed in blue overalls, the uniform characteristic of the *Harkis,* or Algerian collaborators with the French—hence the term bleuite, or blueness. They collaborated with the French and infiltrated groups in Algiers or in National Liberation Army units in the interior.

"Convinced," wrote Léger, "that nothing tangible can be achieved without the support of Muslims... I thought that the underground action of turncoat rebels reinjected into the system was the best way to curb terrorism."[57] The Intelligence and Exploitation Group (GRE) Léger created under Colonel Godard's command took advantage of the "sensational flair"[58] of Captain Chabanne, an intelligence officer of the Third Paratrooper Regiment who kept secret the arrest of Hassan Ghendriche, in charge of the eastern military subdivision of Algiers. Handed over to Captain Léger, Ghendriche agreed—after enhanced interrogation, interspersed with blackmail, such as threatening to rape his sister and mother while he was watching—to work for so-called "law-enforcement" authorities.

Ghendriche was installed in a studio on Tangiers Street where he continued, under Léger's command, to communicate with Yacef Saâdi using the pseudonym of Safi (the Pure). Shortly before his arrest on September 24, 1957, Yacef appointed Ghendriche—and in effect, Captain Léger himself—military commander of the ZAA. After Yacef's arrest, Ghendriche took over as commander-in-chief of the ZAA. From that moment on, Léger did not need to falsify documents or forge seals. It was with an authentic pass from the commander-in-chief himself that Léger traveled with a group of his indigenous "Bleus" to Zone 4, where he captured Lieutenant Salhi and his staff, including Boualam Hedroug, the Zone Secretary, who personally confirmed to me Léger's account.

One of the first freedom fighters to be suspected of being a Bleu was none other than one of my closest war friends, Mohand Chougar. His gripping testimony provides a personal insight into this tragic conflict and throws additional light on the leadership qualities exhibited under duress by Colonel Amirouche, who never ceased conveying to his troops the same simple message: "For four years, we outwitted the French Army; ingenuity and cunning have carried us this far and will carry us further to independence, irrespective of the French Army's criminal tricks."

Mohand Chougar was the epitome of what was expected of a revolutionary under dire circumstances. In 1982, for the first time since the Revolution, we met during a chance encounter in Marseille. I had accomplished my mission in Damascus representing Algeria at the Arab Iron and Steel Union, and at a United Nations Industrial Development Organisation Conference held in New Delhi in 1982 and presided over by Prime Minister Indira Gandhi. I was driving from Damascus to Marseille when an urgent meeting in Algiers forced me to leave my car in France and fly to Algiers. At the Air Algérie airline counter, the face of the agent who issued my ticket looked so familiar that I struck up a conversation with him.

"I drove all the way from Damascus to Marseille," I said.

"What itinerary did you take?" he asked.

"Syria, Turkey, Greece, Yugoslavia, Italy, France."

"Yugoslavia," said Mohand, lowering his voice to a whisper. "That's where I was treated for my war wounds."

"Which military command?" I inquired.

"Wilaya III," he replied.

"Tell me, during the war did you ever meet Colonel Amirouche's private secretary?"

"Hamou?" he asked. "Of course I did. And I still don't know whether he's alive or was killed with Colonel Amirouche."

"He's alive, all right," I said. "He is in front of you."

He stared at me for a split second (I was sporting a beard), and though handicapped because a burst of submachine gun had severely damaged his kidneys, he jumped from behind the counter to embrace me.

As soon as we began to talk about the war, a cloud of sadness darkened his face, which was marked by the terrible memories of ordeals that I did not know about as yet.

"Ah, it's something to find you again after so many years... It's something ..." I was deeply touched by these simple words coming from his heart.

"One day," he said, "I'll tell you about what I witnessed and the atrocious tortures I suffered at the hands of my own brothers-in-arms while the Bleuite plot was unfolding."

That day, and the discovery of a rare and noble soul, was to come about 17 years later. In 1999 I traveled to Albi, France, where Mohand Chougar was undergoing kidney dialysis, and recorded his spellbinding testimony.

"The Bleuite plot was uncovered in April – May 1958," began Mohand.

"In fact," I corrected, "we had already exposed some traitors infiltrated from Algiers, before I left on a mission to Tunis in March 1958."

"I didn't know. Personally," Mohand continued, "I was arrested in late August. Following an order issued by the head of the Region, Amar O., the mujahed B. woke me up with a light tap on my boot. I thought it was my turn for guard duty.

'Forgive me, brother,' he said, 'the Organization is tying you up.'

"And he bound me with a cord. Amar O. was himself arrested shortly after. He died under torture. As for B. who tied me up, he was summoned to the Command Post and decided to surrender instead to the French Army. He was killed in an ambush by an National Liberation Army unit. After I was tied up, I was taken to Bounaâmane, in Akfadou, where I was tortured for 29 days."

"To make you confess what?" I asked.

"The first question was, 'how did you contact Colonel Godard?' "

"How were you tortured?"

"With sticks from a pomegranate tree, attached to a pulley. Shirtless. Every time I was struck, it was as if my body caught fire. After three minutes, I blacked out. At my side there was a mujahed tortured to death. He was known as K-Moh. He was crying 'If I

156

were a traitor, how come I never disclosed to the French that the El Hourane armament was hidden in my house?' He was screaming till he died under torture.

"Brave warriors such as K-Moh," Mohand told me in a trembling voice, "staring unflinchingly at their brothers-in-arms turned executioners, had little regard for their life that was about to be ended. Their shattered honor alone mattered. They exhaled a single plea: 'Companions, if any one of you were to survive, take this message to my family. K-Moh is not a traitor, K-Moh is the victim of a terrible blunder.'

Mohand Chougar's voice choked into a whisper. "I've never had the opportunity to meet someone from his village to convey this message. Maybe I didn't have the courage to seek such an opportunity. There was another combatant who became almost totally blind under torture. Clenching his teeth, he called on Captain Ahcène (chief of Zone 4, the grand inquisitor of the Bleuite), 'How can you tolerate such injustice? Order my execution and let's get this over with. I am in too much pain!'

"Captain Ahcène grabbed his cane and struck his knees.

'If you claim you have been suffering for 20 days,' the captain said, 'Algeria has been in pain for more than a century.'

Mohand said, "The tortured mujahed kept quiet. He had been so tormented"—here the poor man's voice broke down again—"I really don't want to recall these atrocious moments. He had become virtually blind and his eyes were infested with maggots. He was found dead in the morning after a day or two. Another one tore my heart apart and broke my soul. It was M., a noncommissioned officer who died before my eyes.

"The Psychological Services of the French Army had spread rumors of an imminent search-and-destroy operation that never materialized. Nevertheless, orders were issued to evacuate the area immediately. But M. was terribly weakened by torture. He would make an effort to walk, but would quickly fall on his knees and beg Y., 'Cut my throat, brother. I just can't.' Y., in response, hit him hard in the ribs with a dagger handle, shouting, 'Stand up, you traitor!'

'Don't you call me traitor! I'm not a traitor,' M. uttered through gritted teeth. He made an effort to get up and walk two or three hundred yards before collapsing totally exhausted, saying 'I can't, I just can't walk any longer.'

"So Y. grabbed a knife and cut his throat. Before my eyes. When I saw that, I felt very dizzy, my heart started to race, an unbearable wave of fear swept through my whole body. I was still tied up. A few yards further on, I sensed that I had peed in my pants."

157

Listening to Mohand, my body tensed to control my own emotions, but my mind wandered to Y., whom I knew very well and who is still alive. More than once later on, I took his picture out of my war photo album to study the expression in his eyes or in his face to determine if some particular feature betrayed a predisposition to torture and murder. His face seemed congenitally incapable of smiling, but his rather pleasant, almost handsome features revealed nothing. I could hardly believe that he had become an "accredited" executioner, taking it upon himself, without orders, to end the life of a freedom fighter.

"Continue, Mohand," I said, after a moment.

"I wish I could forget this nightmare," mumbled Mohand. "Those who woke up in the morning discovered that four or five suspects had died from abuse. One day, Colonel Amirouche appeared. Everybody rose, except me. I had not recognized him or I was too weak to pay attention. He stared at me and I didn't blink.

'And this soldier,' he asked Captain Ahcène, 'has he made a statement?'

'Not yet, Colonel, Sir,' replied the captain, 'but I am personally in charge of his case.' Amirouche still looked at me quizzically. Seeing that I was so young yet not intimidated, he had perhaps begun to ask himself whether he shouldn't step back a while—which he did a few weeks later. But at the moment, he kept silent.

"A few days later, still in September 1958, Lamara Hamel [a general staff member] came to see me: 'Between you and me,' he whispered in my ear, 'tell me the truth. I have not laid a hand on you, I did not subject you to any brutal treatment. You are accused of having contacts with Colonel Godard.'

'I can't believe this,' I shouted. 'I've never heard that name. I've heard about all kinds of officers of the French Army, Bigeard, Massu, Ducourneau, Lacheroy, never Godard.'

"Visibly shaken by the sincerity of my answer, he took me to Captain Ahcène.

'You are going to die,' said Ahcène.

'We will all die one day or the other.' I replied.

'Since you're going to die,' continued Ahcène, 'after your death, I will pursue the investigation. If it turns out that you're a traitor, each Independence Day, I will drop a cartload of shit on your grave. If you are innocent, at every celebration of independence, I will lay a bouquet of flowers on your grave.'

"It was then that I exploded with anger towards Ahcène, said Mohand, raising his voice. 'If I am a traitor, your brother-in-law, your sister's husband is a traitor as well. We were raised

158

together, we attended the same school and we were scouts in the same squad, we lived together in France, we both chose to join the National Liberation Front and not the Algerian National Movement, we went underground at the same time and he is my closest friend. If I am a traitor, he is also a traitor.'

Captain Ahcène, caught totally off guard, scrutinized my face and I stared back defiantly. I just couldn't take it any longer. Then, without adding a word, he turned on his heels and left.

"The commander of an elite battalion had captured eight Harkis in an ambush near Kherrata. In another ambush, two policemen and a prison warden were kidnapped along with their wives. The spouses were placed on mules and were directed towards Larbaa Naith Yirathen. The mules knew their way. Ammi M'barek, who was guarding the prisoners, suddenly had the shock of his life: one of the Harkis was his own brother-in-law, his sister's husband. He called out to him; 'I warned you not to side with the French.'

'The Caïd [Algerian administrator appointed by the French] has bamboozled us', replied the Harki.

'And now?'

"Ammi M'barek, naturally, was terribly embarrassed to have a traitor as a brother-in-law. You remember how we hated Harkis even more intensely than Foreign Legionnaires. You should have seen the torture inflicted on the prisoners. With them, there were also Messalists taken prisoners. Bellounis, the Messalist general, had taken to the bush again and was killed in a clash with French Army units along with two of his daughters. With the chaos that reigned inside the Algerian National Movement, many chose to surrender to the National Liberation Front. Amirouche pardoned the youngsters but not the others. With National Liberation Front NCOs and other Bleu suspects, there were, by my side, a total of 35 prisoners. One day it was announced that they would be taken to the infirmary. 'Taken to the infirmary after first tying them up?' I wondered to myself. I was the only one left alone—along with the young Messalists granted amnesty by Amirouche. They were teenagers. Amirouche, because of the shortage of armament, had ordered their release.

"Suddenly an atrocious chill ran through my spine: Y. began to whet a butcher's knife. When he found that it was sharp enough, he turned to Captain Ahcène and, pointing the knife in my direction, asked: 'This soldier from your village, what do I do with him?'

'Leave him alone.' Captain Ahcène saved me. Otherwise, I would have met my fate, like the others. Thirty-five were slain by

159

Y. and the commando-executioners. A large trench was dug and they were buried in a mass grave.

"Too many innocent mujahedeen were executed. Towards the end, even Colonel Amirouche admitted his terrible mistake. In October 1958, five months before his departure to Tunis, he brought us all together. Companies, battalions, officers, NCOs, soldiers, there were thousands of us.

'My dear brothers, many people voice allegations that the ALN [National Liberation Army] engages in unjust actions. I want to tell you that the ALN does not commit any injustices, but we do commit errors. Throughout history, there has not been a war in which cases of tragic errors have not been documented.' Then Amirouche raised his voice and bitterly added, 'But it is better to lose by mistake a thousand, ten thousand mujahedeen, rather than lose Algeria. People say we commit injustices. Again, we do not commit injustices, we commit mistakes. They did not die of an injustice, they were victims of an error.'

"Amirouche told us that it was better to sacrifice suspects who may be innocent than to have real enemies behind our backs in battle. This was almost word for word, the speech he delivered just before moving the Command Post as a precautionary measure."

Mohand Chougar paused a moment before resuming. "I recall that you, Hamou, told me that Amirouche had reason to suspect that the ALN was infiltrated since every time that you spend some time in a village, it was targeted by a search-and-destroy operation the next day and forced you never to spend more than 24 hours in the same place."

"It's true," I said. "But because we were rarely targeted by those operations in woodland sanctuaries, completely isolated, until the capture of Lieutenant Salhi, we thought it was the civilians who had traitors in their midst."

"Yes, I do know that Salhi was captured without a fight and that he was executed by the French Army, but I do not know under what circumstances," said Mohand.

"Neither do I, really," I replied. "I still remember his slim and elegant gait when he was nominated to Zone 4. When the news of his capture reached us, Amirouche was bewildered for a long time, mulling over the possible culprits for this betrayal, because it was clear that Salhi had been given away. Capturing an officer along with half-a-dozen of his aides, without a single shot being fired, was unheard of."

"I read somewhere," Mohand continued, "there were 8,400 informants on the eve of November 1, 1954. So..."

"Continue your story, Mohand."

"I will, only because you're insisting. I wish I could forget about it all. A former Parisian immigrant worker," continued Mohand, emotion once more choking his voice, "Staff Officer T., tortured to death, began to rave and shout, 'Hey, Jeannine, a steak, French fries, and a salad. And don't forget a carafe of house wine.' He died on September 20, 1958, the day after the proclamation of the Provisional Government of the Algerian Republic in Cairo. For this occasion we were given a bit of meat, but he could not eat. The next day he was found dead. For my part, I think my vehement reference to Captain Ahcène's brother-in-law being a traitor if I was apparently did the trick. The torture stopped immediately and I was exonerated."

I recorded Mohand's riveting story in Albi, France. He spoke haltingly, in broken sentences, in the intonations of a man outraged by so many incomprehensible injustices, actions we never expected from those for whom we had been ready to give our lives. His rage alternated with the plaintive pitch of a teenager on the verge of sobbing. Mohand's testimony speaks for itself without the need for further analysis, except to clarify one crucial fact: Ahcène Mahiouz was about to order Mohand Chougar's execution and resume the investigation of his case after independence, which can be explained but hardly justified by the exceptional circumstances of this guerrilla war, the overwhelming pressure of the enemy, and the fact that there were no prisons and no possibility of dispatching suspects to Tunisia. At no time did Mohand's testimony convey bitterness, censure, or condemnation of Colonel Amirouche, who allowed such a treatment of suspects. On January 26, 2001, Mohand passed away.

How many combatants were executed by their own brothers-in-arms is a question that is unlikely ever to be answered. In his memoirs, the French instigator of the Bleuite Plot, Captain Léger, wrote proudly of his accomplishment. But just before he died in 1999, he confessed to his wife that he was tortured by his conscience for having caused the deaths of hundreds of innocent Algerians[59]. He was, however, merely doing the job for which he was trained.

The technological gap between the guerrilla's shotgun and the B-26 fighter-bomber mirrored the disparity in the two sides' respective mastery of the techniques of subversive warfare. On our side, we had little military training and still less experience with any psychological tactics worthy of the name. Our tricks, such as the wiliness with which we turned Operation Blue Bird into a stinging blowback for the French Army, as well as our sacrifices, occasionally offset our limitations and shortcomings. But just as often, we acted like greenhorns. At the end of 1957, the superb German MG 42 and British Bren machine guns we received, transported from Tunisia by valiant mujahedeen laden like mules, made the Alpine Corps Units more careful during their patrols. Thereafter, the French Army used rumormongers to spread alerts of imminent search-and-destroy operations in each region where we happened to be on an inspection mission.

This insidious misinformation sometimes forced us, as we have seen, to wander from one region to another until, exhausted, we opted for combat against French troops regardless of their numbers and firepower—but they never showed up. As saboteurs, we dug and dug again the same trench on a dirt road to prevent its use by military convoys for reinforcements or supplies until a landmine blew some of us to pieces.

No doubt, the first two years of the war had been characterized for us by inexperience and, all too often, by ineptitude. A long seasoning was required and was ultimately achieved at a very high price. Sadly, by the time we had begun learning from our mistakes, roughly three years after the outbreak of the war, our country's borders were sealed by the French and virtually no arms, and more important, no ammunition could reach us. The huge disparity in knowledge of subversive warfare and in the sophistication of the weapons explains why there is no common measure between the respective death tolls of the National Liberation Army and the French Army: one for seven, according to French statistics.[60]

But the damage inflicted directly or indirectly to the French economy, to France's honor and prestige, was immeasurable. Stuck in the Algerian quagmire, France was reduced to contemplating, powerless, the rise of West German domination, while the French themselves persisted in pursuing a hopeless war. Everyone noted what a splendid army France had, well-drilled in Indochina and copiously supplied by NATO—yet no one, not even General de Gaulle, could lead it to decisive victory.

The Algerian War ended the career of many French political and party leaders, saw six Prime Ministers voted out of power, destroyed the Fourth Republic, led to a "constitutional" coup d'état, threatened the Fifth Republic with a military landing in April 1961 and a fascist regime, and led France to the edge of civil war. By organizing the coup in Algiers on May 13, 1958, and bringing General de Gaulle back to power, the army made a dramatic splash into French politics, in the manner of a banana republic. Such action had not been seen since the December 2, 1851 coup, staged by Napoleon III, established the Second Empire.

Chapter 12
Life in the Bush

[T]hey massacred thousands of compatriots who dared say no to the
occupier and who had brandished no other weapons
than flags unfurled under gunfire.
Colonel Amirouche
addressing the troops

The life of a guerrilla is varied and full of surprises, not just the dangers to which we were exposed, but also the quality of hospitality we were offered, the regional cuisines we sampled, and even the linguistic differences that I would not have expected after traveling no more than 50 miles. I discovered the explanation, right there, for the preservation of Berber dialects: geographical isolation. While in the plains or the urban areas, ethnic Berbers refer to themselves as "Arabs"; Berbers in the Atlas Mountains of Algeria and Morocco or the nomadic Tuaregs in the Sahara Desert have maintained their language, culture, and traditions. In Kabylia in the north, protests against the government onslaught on Berber identity are, today, taking on separatist overtones among the young.

After just a few months in the countryside, I acquired a new vocabulary in the Tamazight dialect: *aqrour* for *aqshish* (child), a*dhil* for *thizourine* (grapes), and *ousingh ani* for *ousingh ara* (I do not know).

We rarely ate meat, largely because of the order restricting meat consumption to twice a week. And because we were such a small group of five, we were not allowed to slaughter a lamb even on a meat day. Butchers had never existed in the mountain villages, due, among other factors, to a bizarre cultural tradition of disdain for the trade. Chickens were an endangered species due to the high esteem, absolutely deserved, in which they were held by the lieutenant we nicknamed "the hen lover," Abdelhafid Amokrane.

When we ventured further south, we delighted in chili peppers, tomatoes generously prepared with olive oil, honey cakes, and fresh figs or grapes according to the season. The sourdough cakes and cracked wheat cooked in zucchini flower broth of Aït Zikki were specialties I relished. Pesh pesh, the enormous fried donuts of Semaoune, were a real treat we slowly savored once safely hidden in the forest nearby. They were especially delicious when enjoyed with a rare cup of black coffee. At Borghas, by contrast, declared no man's land by the French Army, we often had nothing to eat except a small piece of flat bread with salad, or rather wild herbs. In Vounaâmane where the command post of the Wilaya Military Command was located, barley cakes and olive oil were in fair supply. But the cakes kneaded with more bran than flour never satisfied us, and scatological jokes were commonplace.

It was not until we arrived in Wilaya I territory, in the Aurès-Nememchas region, that we could stuff ourselves with meat and couscous seasoned with a thick, greasy sauce. But this region, partly controlled by the lethal dissidents of a rival guerrilla group, did not much excite our appetite when we crossed it in April 1958, on a grueling journey to Tunisia. At Vounaâmane on the coast, exceptional security and peace prevailed, largely making up for the dietary rations to which we were limited. Although French warships frequently fired artillery shells, they would harmlessly explode several hundred meters from our command post.

In areas that had not been emptied of their population, where we sometimes had the opportunity to see girls our age, we fell in love several times a day. But we also knew the terrible penalty in case of a suspected affair: death. One girl of rare beauty would follow my companion Tayeb Mouri and me to a creek at the edge of a grove near the command post. Admittedly, she followed Tayeb more than me, for Tayeb's handsome countenance and manly figure, readily apparent in his photographs, were enough to turn the head of any girl. But too many repressed desires throbbed inside us, and to avoid temptation we put an end to our bucolic walks along the creek.

The toughest tribulations for all those who served under Colonel Amirouche's command were undoubtedly the nightly forced marches. We had to be in exceptional physical condition to keep pace. The sick or injured, condemned to immobilization, lived in fear of being surrounded and captured by occupation forces. Dread of summary execution was not part of our nightmares, but we were haunted by the knowledge that no guerrilla taken alive escaped appalling abuse and torture. Furthermore, we all knew that anyone not wounded who was captured alive inevitably drew disgrace and dishonor. Many a captured prisoner went through the indignity of being paraded through a village on a leash like a dog, then forced to give a radio address urging his comrades to quit their hopeless fight and surrender.

I remember a day when I was struck by the Asian flu. I was so weak that walking for seven or eight hours was out of the question. Nor could I stay behind in the village of Taslent, an area devoid of vegetation surrounded by French military camps. Arezki Ighil Ali, a powerful fellow with Popeye arms but exquisite gentleness, carried me for nearly three hours.

We rarely stayed more than 24 hours in a safe house, or even in the same village, because the security of a leader of Amirouche's caliber required permanent mobility. A tireless walker, he subjected us to a breakneck pace. Hard on himself as well as on his troops, his Wilaya Military Command was a model of organization that achieved a rare symbiosis between the guerrilla and the populace. It was usual for a village that we had just left to fall victim of an punitive French operation the next day.

It was as if our own death, like our shadows, followed us step by step. Our existence was a miracle graciously renewed every day. Each time we survived an operation, we gave thanks to our Creator who kept us on our beloved land and kindled our faith and determination.

We were undoubtedly living on borrowed time, but it was not the fear of death that made us march incredible distances in 24 hours: it was simply not in Colonel Amirouche's nature to go incognito through any region. In each village we visited, he listened to the grievances of the humblest peasant. He felt united in a common effort with all the people as he was one of them, sharing their hopes and dreams as well as their hardships. He refused to admit the disparity between the enormity of the goal of liberation and the smallness of our means. In our merciless struggle, Colonel Amirouche reminded us at every moment, always with the same ardor and the same serenity, not to expect leniency or any lessening of our enemies' efforts to wipe us out. His popularity was such that word of his whereabouts eventually caught the ear of a traitor who was quick to signal our presence to the French. French operations in Wilaya III were all the more easy to assemble as Kabylia was a focal point of the rebellion and, unlike the rest of Algeria, was crisscrossed by hundreds of French military camps equipped with watchtowers. Kabylia's topography, its large population, its proximity to Algiers, and especially its importance under the command of Colonel Amirouche, made it a choice target for destruction.

During his inspection tours, Amirouche addressed the troops without notes, in perfect Kabyle. His speeches left a mark on his listeners' minds and awakened from their torpor guerrillas who had felt leaderless for months.

The previous head of Wilaya III, Colonel Saïd Mohamedi, alias Si Nacer, had been summoned to Tunisia just as Amirouche was returning from that country, where he helped organize the supply of arms and set up the student center that housed hundreds of young Algerians with the potential to take over from the French after independence. The heavyset Si Nacer was not a man to subject himself to the daily walks of several hours needed to harangue the fighters and give a boost to their morale. Among ranking officers of Wilaya III, Si Nacer had the reputation of being a bunker man, safe in underground shelters. A paragon of pretention, he often appeared in an incongruous Wehrmacht steel helmet, having parachuted in 1943 in Tunisia as a German agent. Captured and sentenced to life imprisonment, he was paroled in 1952 and joined the Revolution almost as soon as it started.

Amirouche, by contrast, was tall and lean and endowed with incredible energy that even illness, a fever, and a severe attack of the mumps in the winter of 1957 could not alter. When we arrived at a destination, he gathered the troops and appealed to them using the same themes with some variations. It is said that good generals do not usually have good powers of expression, but Colonel Amirouche certainly did. He always began by flattering the pride and *nif* (honor) that swelled the chest of every fighter. Here is one of his most rousing speeches:

> For over a century, the colonial troops have been occupying our country, plundering its riches, seizing its lands, humiliating its people. We can break but we'll never fold. We were defeated in 1830. They thought it was over. We rose again in 1871. We were broken once more and again, seeing that we would never recognize a superior bravery, they thought we would instead submit to the superiority of their weapons or of their numbers. They are still and will be forever mistaken. More recently, barely a decade ago, in 1945, they massacred thousands of compatriots who dared say no to the occupier and who had brandished no other weapons than flags unfurled under gunfire.

> But only God is all-powerful. And this time, we will win because our cause is just and God is with the righteous. For three years, the French Army has been trying, with means never used before, to break our will and make us surrender to theirs. What have they accomplished with their B-26s, their T-6s, and napalm bombing? What have they achieved by razing our villages and terrorizing our women and children?

> Stage your attacks at a time of your choice when they least expect it. Scatter like sparrows when they show up in considerable numbers. Do not harass any more camps at night. Munitions have become increasingly scarce and valuable. Do not waste a single bullet. Mount carefully your ambushes, with the goal of recovering weapons and ammunition. The measure of success in such encounters is *never the number of French soldiers killed, but the number*

167

of weapons and munitions taken from the enemy. You know the flow of weapons and ammo from Tunisia is increasingly problematic.

But by the beginning of 1958, with us his closest companions but never in his speeches, Colonel Amirouche was already showing some bitterness mingled with anger against the army stationed for the most part in Tunisia along the Algerian border, which could not even prevent the French from erecting electrified fences and planting millions of land mines that cut off the National Liberation Army in Algeria from its main source of arms and materiel. Made up of recruits from the Algerian side of the border for the most part, and staffed by Algerian officers of the French Army who deserted in 1958, that army led by Colonel Houari Boumediene took over after independence.

This is why Colonel Amirouche emphasized in each of his addresses to the mujahedeen the crucial objective of recovering weapons and ammunition in every attack. In early 1958, I drafted, on the basis of his guidelines, a circular addressed to the heads of the Wilaya III Command in which he warned that "any officer who set an ambush, without recovering arms and ammunition, would be automatically demoted."

Amirouche's addresses to the troops were immediately and highly effective. Wilaya III was reenergized and ambushes were mounted in the areas where the Colonel had spoken. General staff meetings in all four of the zones in Wilaya III were normally held every two months, the time required to conduct a tour of inspection. In two months we were able to tour, on foot, the whole of Wilaya III, nearly the size of the state of Connecticut.

Following this inspection, a meeting was held at the command post in Bou Naamane. The staff meeting included the Colonel, his immediate subordinates, the three majors, the military, political, and intelligence and communications commanders, the four captains, zone leaders, and officers. Topics of discussion included activity reports, namely attacks against the enemy to acquire arms and ammunition; propaganda activities by the political commissars; the state of food supply and stocks; fundraising and budget; material and moral support provided to the population, particularly to a family whose breadwinner was killed in action or captured; intelligence work and mobilization especially at the resettlement camps; and the crucial coordination between different areas of operation.

The forbidden zones created by the French Army by emptying the countryside and the mountains of its inhabitants were war crimes. The French followed Mao Zedong's principle that a guerrilla lives among the people like a fish in water. Just as fish are asphyxiated if they are deprived of their natural element of water, a massive displacement of the population would kill the guerrillas.

The green hills at the edge of the vast forest sanctuaries where we found shelter were now depopulated, for their inhabitants had been forced at gunpoint to settle in barbed-wire encampments which "looked horribly like concentration camps"[61] and were closely monitored by the French Army. Describing conditions in one such camp, a journalist wrote in 1958, "Crammed together in unbroken wretchedness, 15 to a tent since 1957, this human flotsam lies tangled in an indescribable state..."[62] But it was Michel Rocard, future French Prime Minister, who officially unveiled for the first time, on February 17, 1959, the dramatic consequences of this strategy. In a report to the French Government, spelled out in the following chapter, he vented his outrage.

Because France is a permanent member of the U. N. Security Council, and because Guy Mollet, then Prime Minister, was not the obscure leader of an internationally powerless Middle Eastern or Balkan country, none of the perpetrators of this war crime have ever been prosecuted before the International Criminal Tribunal. Readers must therefore judge for themselves.

Letter drafted by the author, dated September 22, 1957, signed by the head of Wilaya III, Amirouche, and sent to the commander of the Autonomous Zone of Algiers (ZAA), Yacef Saâdi, and ending in Captain Léger's hands since Léger became, in effect, the new commander of the ZAA following the arrest of Yacef on September 24, 1957.

Chapter 13
The Regrouping Camps [63] and
Colonel Amirouche's Response

If you had known, good people of drowsy France, if you had known what? That in your name, people have been tortured for seven years, and that for over a century, attempts to stifle the voice of a people, here deported on their own land, there imprisoned in that country the name of which once meant freedom and the symbol of which is now for Algerians the Fresnes or Barbarossa prisons...?

Andre Mandouze,
quoted in *Le Monde Diplomatique*, July-August 2001

Eminent French personalities denounced this crime against humanity; they constituted the core of humanists who redeemed France's honor. In June 1957, the famous ethnologist Germaine Tillion traveled to Algeria with an international commission to visit the colonial camps and prisons. What she discovered was shocking. "What is happening before my eyes is obvious: there is, now, in 1957, practices that were those of Nazism. Nazism that I hated and I fought with all my heart…," [64]she wrote. When French politician and Socialist Party member Michel Rocard arrived in Algeria in September 1958, almost five months after General de Gaulle had taken over, he had already distinguished himself by his courageous stands against the war and for Algeria's independence. He even denounced in a report submitted to his party the genocide and atrocities committed by the occupation forces. His clandestine mission was to investigate the "regrouping camps," the French Army's euphemism for concentration camps.

Second Lieutenant Bugnicourt, his friend who greeted him in Algiers, painted a startling and horrific picture of the situation: the French Army, in utter secrecy as far as the international community was concerned, was in the process of undertaking a mass displacement that would reach the staggering figure of two million people in 1962, [65] close to 20 percent of the country's total population. Hundreds of thousands of Algerians, mostly peasants, were torn from their native villages to prevent the National Liberation Front from establishing itself among the population and to allow relentless napalm bombings. Once they lost their crops and livestock, many of these poor people starved to death. The French had decided that, since all of Algeria was on the side of the National Liberation Army, every Algerian man and woman was an "insurgent." They could all be targeted without any qualms as soon as they grew out of childhood.

Sometimes, said Bugnicourt to the incredulous Rocard, the villagers were given only eight days' notice. Unable to take anything with them, they were transported by truck to the camps and crammed into hastily built barracks. Sometimes they were put in tents as far as possible from "rebel" strongholds to languish with their wives and children in the greatest destitution. What Rocard discovered revolted him: overall, a million people in 1958—including a great number of women and children—were

172

"concentrated in unspeakable conditions," though for Rocard, this was hardly "a surprise: I knew that Guy Mollet [Prime Minister until June 1957] was a bastard."[66]

And for good reason! Guy Mollet first called the conflict a "stupid and hopeless war." And we were all hoping, when we read the news at the time, that he would negotiate with the National Liberation Front and put an end to the killing. But Mollet reneged on his promise after the extremist supporters of "French Algeria" pelted him with ripe tomatoes in Algiers on February 6, 1956. When Mollet travelled to Algiers to install General Georges Catroux in his duties as Minister-Resident, he was greeted with fury—red-tomato fury—by the Pied Noir French opposed to the appointment of Catroux, whom they considered too liberal. It was Mollet's government that presided over the hijacking by the French Air force of the Moroccan Airliner transporting three leaders of the Algerian Revolution, Aït Ahmed, Ben Bella, and Khider, on October 22, 1956. They were incarcerated until the end of the war.

In the camp located in Ouarsenis, Michel Rocard counted 600 children out of a total of 1,100 regrouped. While he visited, a two-year old child died before his eyes, the third in four days. As there was no money to feed the displaced, they died of starvation. Rocard estimated at 200,000 the number of internees who died of hunger. Driving his own car, an old 403 Peugeot, Rocard traveled the countryside in a radius of 200 miles from Algiers. Around Blida, Tiaret, Chlef, and Sétif, he encountered what he described as appalling conditions of confinement. He argued in his report that "the genocide could not be described as systematic and deliberate" and that "the camp leaders were not Nazis," but the candid and brutal use of the very term "genocide" considerably weakens his argument. On February 17, 1959, Michel Rocard submitted his report to the Prime Minister. Although President de Gaulle was naturally aware of the report once it was published in the daily *France Observateur,* no serious action was taken to end this human-engineered disaster, grounds for prosecution for war crimes.

Questioned in Parliament, the Prime Minister under de Gaulle, Michel Debré, rather than pledge to put an end to the humanitarian catastrophe, claimed instead that the report was "Communist-inspired." France was embarrassed by accusations of mistreatment of "its own people" in front of the fourteenth session of the U.N. General Assembly on July 14, 1959. The outcry was so loud that the government was forced to release 100 million francs (about $5 million) just to keep alive one-third of the rural population crammed into camps.

Dead silence surrounded many of the villages, bereft of human signs of life, that we crossed, stirring a poignant sadness in our hearts. The crying of a child in the middle of the night in a village that had been spared deportation grabbed us by the throat, always eliciting the same response. "Do not cry, child, thou shalt live in dignity and freedom. As for us—if we die, God will grant us mercy."

There were two ways to spare teenagers, at least, the rigor and humiliation of the regrouping camps if not outright death. One way was to recruit them, to give them a chance to live proudly or die fighting. However, weapons were still in short supply. My case of not being able to join the regular National Liberation Army for several frustrating months, despite all my attempts, illustrates how serious was the deplorable shortage of arms and, beginning in 1958, ammunition.

The second way to save young people was championed by Colonel Amirouche, whose vision of an independent Algeria included the preparation and training of leaders. He ordered the head of each of the zones in Wilaya III to draw up a list of young people whose educational background or potential warranted their routing to Tunis for further education. They went under the protection of guerrilla convoys traveling to Tunisia to fetch arms and ammunition, and those who survived filled, after independence, thousands of civilian as well as military positions.

Amirouche, as we have seen, had already established facilities for students of Wilaya III during his stay in Tunis at the beginning of 1957. The repression against teenagers was as fierce and relentless in neighboring Military Command (Wilaya IV), but the response there was of a different nature. In early 1958, a convoy of young people, supervised by some guerrillas, crossed Wilaya III en route to Tunisia to fetch weapons. The oldest among them was only 12 years old. We all expressed our astonishment, for in 1958, it had become virtually impossible for even small and seasoned guerrillas to cross the electrified fences, minefields, and artillery barrages of the French. Colonel Amirouche pointed that out to the leader of the convoy.

"Colonel, Sir," the officer replied sharply, "these kids have a better chance of survival by marching 40 days or more to the border, walking through minefields while cutting 5,000 volt cables, than by remaining in their villages waiting for the executioners of the French Army."

It was rare indeed that we encountered a resistance fighter who did not have a family member, often a teenager, killed during a search operation. The young, their lives snuffed out in the prime of life, inflated French statistics of rebels killed or captured and tortured to death to disclose information that the French officers already had. Seldom has history so clearly shown the folly and ineptness of using bombings and indiscriminate killings. Against all odds, we were out to stop them. Just causes, we were convinced more by faith than by history, always triumphed. We were all fairly religious and certain that most of our martyrs ascended to heaven, but no passion for eternity inspired us.

In fact, as noted earlier, we had adopted a motto expressing the secular essence of our struggle: "It's because we love life that we accept to die." Our maxim paralleled a famous hadith (saying) of the Prophet Mohammed: "Work for this world as if you were immortal and work for the next world as if you were to die tomorrow." But we all realized that nations were also mortal. Many of us had seen Western movies and knew that American Indians were victims of a documented genocide and that whole nations could vanish into nothingness and the unrelenting indifference of history.

Left A. Mehdi, Colonel Amirouche's aide de camp,
and Moh Arezki, the greatest comedian of Wilaya III;
killed in action in 1959.

Chapter 14
Mission to Tunis:
Special Envoy of the Wilaya III
Military Command

We are not permitted to choose the frame of our destiny.
But what we put into it is ours.
Dag Hammarskjold,
former Secretary General of the United Nations

Colonel Amirouche owed his longevity, as we have seen, to his extreme mobility as well as his extraordinary popularity which turned, with rare exceptions, every man or woman of the Wilaya III Military Command into a guard constantly alert to any suspicious movement of French troops. The populace reported enemy activity, particularly at nightfall when the Alpine Corps soldiers laid their ambushes.

During the blessed year I was Colonel Amirouche's companion and private secretary, I never saw his aides-de-camp Tayeb Mouri or Abdel Hamid Mehdi, incorrectly labeled his bodyguards, stand guard at the entrance to the safe house where we rested. I cannot help but point out, by contrast, that the leaders of the bunker governments that have successively ruled Algeria since independence are forced to hug walls and travel in armored cars, invariably selecting their secret service agents and bodyguards from their own tribe, if not from their own family.

In areas where tribal rivalries were still alive, where families had provided soldiers to the French Army, Colonel Amirouche resorted to the simple ruse already described: summoning a guide, announcing our destination aloud and, half a mile away, heading in an opposite direction. Often the village we declared as our destination was targeted by a French bombing operation the next day.

Colonel Amirouche took about two months to inspect all of the Wilaya III territory, from east to west, north to south. This inspection was then followed by a meeting of the Wilaya Council, which took place in the command post in Akfadou at Tahar Amirouchen's, Amirouche's trusted and highly competent aide. During these meetings, Amirouche's powerful and intimidating voice could be even heard from outside. I remember an officer who once confided to me after the meeting that he was "more afraid of Amirouche than of a T-6 bomber."

The last Wilaya meeting I attended in March 1958 was marked by a dramatic incident. We were gathered in the shelter when we were suddenly alerted by gunfire: a soldier armed with a shotgun, seized with a fit of madness, opened fire on his comrades. Two of them were killed instantly, the other escaped. The gunman then barricaded himself in the room but met his fate in a way that illustrated for me once more how summary revolutionary justice could be. A fighter ascended to the roof, removed a tile, and threw

178

in a grenade that tore apart the poor mentally ill soldier.

On a happier note, that March 1958 meeting brought the opportunity to chat at length with Major Mohand Oul Hadj Akli. When he learned where I came from and who my father was, he clasped my shoulder affectionately and told me that he knew my father very well. "He is an old nationalist activist, a true patriot. I know he had a narrow escape in May '45."

"Yes," I replied proudly. "He joined the North African Star in Paris in 1926."

"And what became of him?"

"Well," I answered, "he was arrested on November 3, 1954, and sentenced to 15 months in jail and 5 years of house arrest. He was released a year later, thanks to a brilliant lawyer. He was declared *persona non grata* in Tazmalt. So he fled to Ihitoussen. When he was informed that the police was again searching for him in Tazmalt, he decided to leave for France."

"How old is he?" asked the Major.

"Fifty-four years old."

"He went through a lot but he surely stands more of a chance to see Algeria free and independent than you or me."

This was true. The French Army killed many of us. According to the daily *L'Aurore* of September 26, 1958, "Between May 15 and September 20, 1958, 13,500 *fellaghas* (bandits) were 'put out of state to harm,' or more than 106 per day." In these statistics, it is appropriate to include, of course, "collateral damage," a euphemism referring to civilians guilty of being the water that sheltered the guerrilla fish and hence subject to massacre. In 1958, it was rare to meet a resistance fighter who had joined the fighting in 1956. To encounter one who had joined in 1955 was rarer still. Almost no 1954 volunteers survived that long—the life expectancy of a mujahed was usually no more than two years.

We stayed almost a week at the March 1958 Wilaya meeting and, as we guerrillas put it when we felt completely safe, we bathed in independence. The humor of sharp-tongued Sergeant Moh Arezki amused us all, particularly Amirouche who constantly sought his company. Moh was full of life, impervious to anxiety even when the French Navy bombarded us. Often, his whipping boy was none other than Lieutenant Abdelhafid Amokrane. Nicknamed "the hen lover," Abdelhafid, according to Moh, was known as a devourer of chickens even beyond the boundaries of Wilaya III. "Watch him, don't you see in him the eloquent countenance of someone who is digesting? Get closer to him, and you will hear clearly out of his belly the clucking of all the hens he gulped."

Moh sometimes entered into competition with Mustapha

179

Hakimi, a highly educated officer who had joined us from Wilaya I, whose valor Colonel Amirouche had immediately recognized when the two men met in Tunis in early 1957. "I hear you're a dissident of the Aurès-Nememchas. You're coming with me. You'll serve in Wilaya III and continue in that rebel role of yours among other Berbers like you."

Hakimi's humor equally and ferociously targeted the hapless chicken lover. "Abdelhafid," Hakimi told us, "was resting in the refuge of Tiniri in Zone I with Captain Hamimi Ou Fadhel," the Zone chief whose bravery in battle was legendary. "Endowed with a perfect knowledge of his area, Hamimi proposed, for safety reasons, not to linger in Tiniri and push towards Moka. But the cuisine was much richer in Tiniri and Abdelhafid declined. Suddenly artillery shells started to rain down on Tiniri and Abdelhafid scampered in his socks. Captain Hamimi calmly put on his boots and ammunition belt and joined Abdelhafid half a mile away. Derisively, looking at Abdelhafid's torn socks, he said to him: 'I warned you Abdelhafid, I warned you, didn't I?'

The convivial atmosphere in which we temporarily basked created the flimsy illusion that the war was far away. In our imaginations, independence would first and foremost signal the end of the infernal daily marches, the end of the nerve-wracking roar of aircraft graciously procured by NATO to France. There was no French military camp nearby from which an operation could be improvised.

We were resting on the edge of a dense, nearly impenetrable forest, where boars didn't interrupt their naps even when we walked within a meter of their den. But the top of the hill on which our command post stood had been declared a no man's land by the French. Their observation aircraft often flew over our heads, their warships often disrupted the quiet of the area, but at least we did not suffer the ravages of the B-26s and their infernal cargoes of napalm.

During this time I had the privilege to meet or see again nearly all the officers of Wilaya III. Laughter filled the woods, temporarily bringing life to the no man's land. Sergeant Moh Arezki, with his extraordinary sense of humor, had his job cut for him. Inside the command post, only the rattle of a typewriter broke the peace and quiet.

When the time came to leave the command post and resume our inspections, Colonel Amirouche took me aside and said, "I have appointed you to be part of the mission which will leave immediately for Tunis. Abdel Hamid [an aide-de-camp] will lead it. Mohand Tahar [Louaifi, the liaison officer of the Wilaya] ,

Sliman [Laichour, courier], and young Hamini [Gharsa,] will also be members of the group."

I was so stunned that I just opened my mouth and kept silent.

"You don't look excited," remarked my chief.

There was unmistakably a touch of coldness in his voice and I quickly replied, "On the contrary, Colonel, Sir. I'm ready to go."

"Good." He then joined captains Abdellah and H'mimi chatting nearby.

It took me a long time to digest the news. I knew that this mission was probably the hardest and the most dangerous that a guerrilla could possibly undertake. The forced march to the Tunisian border would last several weeks through unfamiliar territory and meant crossing Wilaya I where "dissidents"[67] had slaughtered in their sleep an entire company of Wilaya III soldiers after hosting them. Then we would have to cross the Morice and Challe electrified fences and the minefields along the Tunisian border. On the other hand, the prospect of being part of such a crucial assignment was cause for great pride.

In early March 1958, our week-long period of relaxation, marked by its atmosphere of solidarity, conviviality, and good humor, came to an end. Reports and letters had been typed and were ready to be routed to Tunis. The meetings were completed and reports labeled "Armed Actions," "Troop and People's Morale," "Logistical and Financial Report," were readied for dispatch to the Committee for Coordination and Execution, which was in reality the future Provisional Government of the Algerian Republic stationed in Tunis. A green knapsack was stuffed with the documents, a huge sum of money, and a letter to be handed only to Krim Belkacem, one of the leaders of the revolution, himself. A pass was prepared by the secretariat of the Wilaya, translated below.

Front and National Liberation Army
Wilaya III
Laissez-Passer (Pass)
The mujahed Hamou, on mission to Tunisia, is authorized to travel through the Wilayas III, I and II. All ALN officials are requested to facilitate his journey and to provide aid and assistance by all means in case of difficulties.
National Liberation Army, March 15, 1958
Commander Amirouche [He was head of the Wilaya but was not yet officially nominated colonel.]

Then followed a handwritten addition: "Officials at the border are requested to facilitate the passage to Tunis and to the Coordination and Executive Committee. The carrier of this pass is a special envoy of Wilaya III." Below was affixed the seal of Wilaya III and the signature in Arabic and French of the head of the Wilaya.

The moment to leave the area came and, with it, the pang caused by the belief that, for some of us, this would be the last Wilaya council that we would attend. Nobody could foretell which one of us would be recalled by the Almighty in the days and months ahead. Liaison officers were selected to act as guides and, as usual, we took to the road as soon as dark fell. Amirouche resumed his inspections, heading east in the direction of the Tunisian border. But he was more anxious and more withdrawn than usual. He no longer sought the company of natural comedians such as Moh Arezki, and we no longer heard him humming his favorite patriotic song: "Sil dzaïr ar Thizi Ouzou…" (From Algiers to Tizi Ouzou, my heart cries...)

The staff meeting that had just concluded was mostly devoted to the consequences of the closure of borders with the completion of the second electrified line, the Challe fence. Doubling the 460-kilometer-long Morice Line, which ran along the Tunisian border, it was barbed, electrified with 5,000 volts, mined, and monitored day and night, as we were soon to discover. The last circular letter the Colonel ordered me to draft made it imperative to acquire arms from ambushes of French troops, acknowledged that the military situation was not very bright and that, consequently, the morale of the population had taken a tremendous hit. In 1958 the people bled, humiliated every day by a French Army frustrated and powerless to root out the rebellion. The peasants talked little about liberation and cared little about political objectives, the thirst for revenge taking precedence over all other considerations. The extraordinary jubilation of the people that greeted each deadly guerrilla ambush expressed their burning hatred of the French soldiers which swept aside, at least momentarily, all aspirations for freedom or independence.

With large-scale French operations combing the bush and the countryside, the National Liberation Army was impaired—but the echo of our revolution was beginning to reverberate internationally.

In fact, the weakening of the interior by French troops was largely offset in the international arena thanks to Algeria's brilliant diplomats. Even the massacre of Messalists in Beni Ilmane[68],

182

though amplified by French propaganda, was turned in favor of the Algerian cause by M'hammed Yazid.

Just as the administration of George W. Bush, after the invasion of Iraq unleashed sectarian violence, claimed that U.S. troops could not leave Iraq as long as Shiites and Sunnis were at each other's throats, the French government declared that it was out of the question "to grant independence to people who are killing each other in a fratricidal struggle." Both U.S. and French leaders validated the parody in Daniel Defoe's *Robinson Crusoe* where that English castaway, a good Christian, slaughtered "savage cannibals" to prevent them from devouring each other and thus from violating Christian Scripture. Algerian diplomats were not going to fold before French propaganda.

In a stroke of genius during a press conference, M'hammed Yazid accused the French Army of perpetrating the killings in the region of Beni Ilmane. "If the international community is not convinced," he cried, "we demand a U.N.-appointed international committee of inquiry to be dispatched to Algeria to investigate the massacre." France considered the war in Algeria an "internal affair," a mere "restoration of order" in three "French provinces," and rejected the Algerian diplomat's proposal. After Algeria was denied access to an impartial commission of investigation, international opinion concluded that the French had something to hide and substantiated the charge that the French Army had indeed been responsible for the Beni Ilmane massacres.

At the meeting of the National Council of the Algerian Revolution (CNRA) in Tripoli in 1960, Colonel Ben Tobbal, former head of Wilaya II, derided "these arm-chair diplomats roaming five-star hotels." M'hammed Yazid, head of the Algerian Permanent Mission to the U.N., famously replied:"You military guys do everything you can to expose the butt of the Revolution [referring to the massacre of Beni Ilmane] and we diplomats spend our time pulling down its skirt to hide it."

To give further weight to the action of the Algerian diplomats, the Coordination and Execution Committee planned to proclaim a provisional government. In fact, a few weeks before our departure, a letter came from Tunis, channeled through the usual pedestrian courier. Colonel Amirouche asked me to read it to him in the dim light of a kerosene lamp. It originated from Krim Belkacem in person and informed Amirouche of the Coordination and Execution Committee's intention to declare a government in exile. Consultations with friendly Arab and Muslim as well Eastern European governments were underway to assess the chances of their granting recognition.

183

Meanwhile, resentment of the mujahedeen against the idle troops stationed in Tunisian and Moroccan sanctuaries was becoming more and more intense. We could not understand the ease with which the French Army could close the eastern border by erecting two successive electrified fences with no serious attempt to sabotage them by the 30,000-strong Algerian army.

In the knapsack that we were carrying was a letter from Amirouche that did not mince words, accusing the Border Army sitting in Tunisia of ineptitude. I recall that we often discussed the problems caused by the Morice and Challe fences, and some of us did not hesitate to level accusations of treason against the staff of the Border Army, pointing a finger at the deserters from the French Army who staffed it.

Most of us entertained prejudices that were not groundless against the French Army deserters. In so doing, we overlooked sacrifices of all kinds, in terms of economic and social status, made by the deserters, including those who actively participated in search-and-destroy operations staged against us until the eve of the ceasefire. There was a difference between Algerian soldiers who had deserted from the French Army as soon as the first shots of the revolution were fired, and those who had joined us only after four or six years of hostilities. This confusion failed to underscore the huge disparity between the first group, forcefully drafted into the French Army; and the second, who enlisted and are referred to as DAF (Déserteurs de l'Armée Française) to this day. I was soon to meet some of the latter in the Tunisian sanctuary, and none of them reflected revolutionary spirit and dedication.

Colonel Amirouche accompanied us to the confines of the Wilaya III Military Command. We spent the night in Zenouna, a small village near Bordj Bou Arreridj. We took pictures and the film joined the millions of French francs and the documents in the green knapsack. Then the time to part came, without any solemnity or expression of emotion, though with the pang that came from the conviction that, in all likelihood, we would not meet again. We were each handed a large sum of money, some $40, the largest amount I had ever had in my possession. Our farewells were brief and simple, marked by the imbalance between the finality of goodbye and the briefness of these last moments of fraternal communion lived together.

Colonel Amirouche offered no valedictory advice. He shook hands with us and quietly launched his brief and eternal injunction, impossible to translate: *zaoureth*. (He meant by that, "be worthy of my trust; be vigilant; do not be lured by life in Tunis, come back soon.") With that single word he instilled in each one of us a sliver of his prodigious energy. He left us in the care of our guide and mentor, Mohand Tahar Louaifi, who had seen it all. He had already undertaken the trip twice and survived in dire circumstances. Only once, he told us, a stray bullet, shot by a French soldier shaking in his boots, had scratched him and left a whitish scar across his forehead.

Lieutenant Tahar Amirouchen, Colonel Amirouche's trusted aid.
(early March 1958)

The author, left, with Tayeb Mouri, one of the colonel's aide de camp. Killed in battle with Amirouche on March 28, 1959. Picture taken in Zenouna in March 1958, one day before bidding good bye and heading to Tunisia.

Chapter 15
En Route to Tunisia: The Long March

No, the safe house is not too far. You see that star shining out there on the horizon? It's right under it.
Berber guide

Hiking from northern Algeria to southern Tunisia, sleeping practically in the snow in the Aurès Mountains, crowded literally on top of one another in a bunker dug in the middle of a plain near N'gaous, bypassing the southernmost electrified fences and the vast minefields, falling into a deadly ambush near the border, crossing it between armored cars equipped with powerful searchlights: that 42-day march remains etched in my memory as the most grueling trial I went through during the war.

We carried the precious green knapsack in turn. We four mujahedeen and a boy in our charge began our journey heading east, then southeast, always at dusk, interrupting our brisk walk only at dawn. Each stage was evaluated by the approximate number of walking hours. At each stop, a new guide was assigned to us. When, utterly exhausted, we asked if the next shelter was still far, the guide invariably replied, "No, not at all."

I recall one night in the Wilaya I Military Command when we failed to secure a guide who was familiar with the area. With no map, and equipped only with a phosphorescent compass, we were lost in the middle of the night. We knocked at the door of a shack that was clearly inhabited. Yet despite our persistent appeals to "open the door, we are guerrillas," no one answered. So many times the French soldiers, accompanied by traitors, usually Harkis posing as mujahedeen, trapped our poor gullible peasants. But Abdelhamid Mehdi did not hesitate: he kicked the door of the shack open. Shrill cries of children and a woman rose from the hut along with the protests of the man of the house. "Why, why?"

"Don't be afraid, and shut up! We are mujahedeen. We just need a guide!"

Leaving his fearful family behind, we commandeered the services of the man of the house. Finally, after several hours, we found another civilian to guide us. I hoped we had put enough distance between us and any French soldiers our first reluctant guide may have alerted to our presence.

During our long walk, we experienced some tense moments with the inevitable T-6 bombers hovering over us, and outright fear when we crossed the area suspected to harbor the Wilaya I dissidents who had revolted against the disciplinary actions ordered by Colonel Amirouche. By contrast, we basked in a feeling of almost complete security in the wooded hills and snowcapped Aurès range. Referring to the immense cedar forests covering these mountains, a Lebanese friend of mine told me that it was the Aurès and not Lebanon that should be labeled "Land of the Cedars." It took us several days to cross the majestic beauty of this mountain range.

On several moonless winter nights, we were forced to hold each other's hands to avoid losing our guide or falling into a ravine. I will always remember one cold night we spent shivering after a very long journey. It had snowed and the wind had piled drifts even under the cedar trees. We managed to sweep away the snow, huddle together, and try to find sleep. But our thin mantles were powerless to protect us from the bitter cold. To keep warm, we had recourse to physical exercise. After a bout of movement, we would manage to sleep for only a few minutes before the intense cold woke us up, and we had to exercise once more.

The next day, bright sunshine lit up the magnificent mountains and valleys of the Aurès, and, a rare occurrence, we could undertake our next stage in broad daylight. As we were about to cross a clearing, an incredible spectacle left us speechless: a herd of wild horses grazing in a meadow. As soon as they caught sight of us, they ran off at full speed. For years afterwards, I was unsure if I had dreamed it—was it a western movie that had resurfaced from my subconscious? Before writing these lines, I confirmed with my only surviving companion of that march, Sliman Laïchour, that we had indeed witnessed that fantastic sight in the Aurès.

That day when we were bathing in sunshine and enthralled by the wilderness, we were led to a group of officers and fighters who greeted us genially, but who did not inspire trust and confidence. After all, we did not know exactly which part of the Aurès was controlled by Wilaya I dissidents. We did know that a full company from Wilaya III had been welcomed with brotherly warmth only to be slaughtered in their sleep—all 142 of them!

The common identity of race and descent, of language, religion, and history, of collective pride and colonial humiliation, had been swept aside by a burning hatred that ended the life of so many innocent young men. We could not understand what political aim or lust for revenge could be satisfied by cutting their throats. But the fraternal welcome that we received was genuine and concealed no treacherous intention. We took pictures and were surprised to find that, in Wilaya I, smoking was not prohibited. One young fighter noticed my companion Laïchour's watch and offered him his own in exchange. Laïchour was reluctant: his watch was a gift and a souvenir that he was reluctant to part with.

"Gift or not," retorted the fighter, "that watch of yours will

189

end up on the wrist of a French soldier. Seriously, you really think you will cross the border and arrive alive in Tunisia?" Laïchour, in very slow motion, took off his watch and gloomily handed it to the teenage mujahed.

Of course, in the wilderness surrounding Mount Chélia, declared a forbidden zone by the French Army, there was no safe house, no civilians to provide us with food, shelter, and rest. But curiously, there were sheep, apparently raised by the guerrillas. So a lamb was sacrificed, butchered and shared among us. We were able to enjoy the rarity of grilled meat, fresh and tough as it was, with no bread nor salt. But we were starving, and none of us complained.

The conditions were to change drastically two or three days later when we arrived in a place of plenty and abundance but were, at the same time, subjected to our first real scare since we left our home zone of Wilaya III. The guide directed us to a shelter south of Batna, where a cluster of guerrillas was waiting for us. A beautiful hand-woven Berber carpet was spread in the room. The excessively warm welcome we received made us wary. It was exactly the way that the previous Wilaya III company had been greeted before being killed.

Furthermore, while our uniforms, as well as those of previous mujahedeen who had offered us accommodations under the cedars of Mount Chélia, were an identical olive green pattern, those of our new hosts were very light brown, almost white, without the usual stripes indicating rank. All of them wore a turban of the same color. They were beardless. In the midst of other Berbers, it was out of the question for our group to communicate among ourselves in the Berber language. We needed only a sign discreetly exchanged which meant "Beware!" We sat near the exit door, two on each side, keeping our belts, guns, and grenades at our fingertips. A huge wooden bowl filled with couscous and red sauce, with chunks of meat the size of the Mount Chélia, the likes of which I had not seen since 1954, were served. It was the first and last lavish meal we enjoyed before arriving in Tunis. Satisfied beyond words, I whispered to Laïchour, "This may be our last meal, but after such a feast, it's okay if they cut our throats."

"That's not funny," growled Laïchour.

Noticing that like most Shawi Berbers, they spoke Arabic among themselves when non-Shawis were listening, I tried the few words of Arabic I had learned, pointing to my belly to express our gratitude for their hospitality. But our vigilance did not relent. After tea flavored with fresh mint, the leader of our hosts asked, "Is there anyone in your group who can read French?" I raised my hand. He took out of his pocket a sheet of paper and handed it to me to translate.

It was a Special Pass delivered by the French Specialized Administrative Sections, authorizing the bearer to travel anywhere, unhindered, day or night. When the leader learned what it was, he said through clenched teeth, "traitor." Turning to me, he said "Hamou, we now have proof that the man who was carrying this pass is a traitor and will be executed immediately. Would you mind writing a few words that will be pinned on his dead body?" And, without any qualms, I drafted the message that the executioners were to leave on the traitor's corpse: "Thus, traitors die." Signed, National Liberation Front.

I must admit that it was only at that rather macabre moment that our small group began to relax. We were now almost certain that we had not wandered into a nest of dissidents. We spent the night in comfort on the thick Berber carpet.

The next two stages were going to be particularly grueling as we had to cross a wide expanse of flat land on horseback. Thirty civilians leaving for Tunis joined us, all clad in immaculate white robes and led by a staff sergeant nicknamed Mustache. Despite our arduous journey, our group was in far better physical condition than the fighters of Wilaya I, who were for the most part, heavy smokers. But we were poor horseback riders, which Laïchour and I immediately proved by falling off the horse that we shared.

Fortunately, we were not injured—it would have been a terrible blow to our pride to be put on the disabled list by a tumble from an aging nag.

Mustache, who took charge of our group of 35, might have been small in size, but he was driven by exceptional energy. "Faster, faster," he urged us, and he set the example by taking the lead of our column, galloping. When we were caught by daybreak in the middle of this vast plain, we abandoned our horses, but kept a mule to carry a wounded fighter.

We spent one day in a three-meter-deep forage shelter in the middle of the plain, crammed in with our legs tucked up. To answer a call of nature, we had to climb out of the hole and pray that no pair of binoculars was trained on us. But if we thought this was one of the most testing moments of our journey, we had not seen anything yet.

The author, standing, first from left in the Aures Mountain with officers of Wilaya I. Fourth and fifth are Abdelhamid Mehdi and Slimane Laichour members of our commando. Crouched, first from left, is Louaifi Mohand Tahar and fourth from left, Hamimi Gharsa, the youngest member of our commando (16 years-old).

Chapter 16
Deadly Ambush on the Tunisian Border

If you charge hard enough at death, it will get out of your way.
General George Patton

◆

It took us a week to cross the Aurès Mountains, mainly due to a wide detour we were forced to make to avoid the unfamiliar region supposedly controlled by the dissidents. It became clear during the discussions we had with officers of Wilaya I that it was out of the question to attempt a passage from the north, cutting the electrified wires and risking stepping on land mines, especially since our group had expanded.

The Mustache band assigned to bring weapons from Tunisia consisted of adult civilians dressed, as I said, in white and wearing white turbans easy to spot even in the dark. This group had increased our number to 35. The mule carrying the wounded occasionally served as a mount to anyone exhausted who needed to take some rest. In these cases, the injured man gladly accepted to share his mule and take a passenger behind him, or ceded it outright to briefly stretch his legs.

We had already left the heights for a while. The sense of discomfort that we felt in the highlands southeast of the Aurès was probably comparable to that of a fish out of water. We had passed El Jebel Abiod from the south, and our intention was to subvert the southernmost electrified lines and minefields. We walked for over eight hours towards Mount Boudjellal, a mound rather than a mountain, expecting to reach at dawn. It was the last hill with two or three bushes of interest before we plunged into the desert and attempted to cross the border.

We were already walking on sand, which slowed our progress. When we saw a column of trucks with their lights on appear and disappear on the horizon, we hardly paid any attention. The ruse of the Alpine Corps soldiers, who jumped from moving trucks at night to plant bombs in ditches in Ihitoussen, was buried too deep in my memory to trigger a warning system. We were exhausted, sleepwalking like automatons, one leg at a time, and our alarm systems were totally numb.

Except for the muffled, regular, monotonous sound of the mule's hooves on sand, a total stillness filled the night. Laïchour and I had custody of the knapsack and the wounded fighter had invited us to take a rest on the mule. I was whispering in Laïchour's ear, "Poor thing, if it is not shot by a T-6 on the way to Tunisia, it will surely be on the way back," when suddenly the crackle of automatic weapons pierced the silence and a hail of bullets rained upon us. I do not know if the mule received a burst or if it was the

194

result of acquired reflexes after being shot at so many times, but it collapsed under us and Laïchour and I found ourselves biting sand and losing our precious knapsack.

I am still surprised today by the coolness we showed under gunfire. Tracer bullets continued to whine past our ears, pinning us to the ground and tossing sand in our eyes—but that was the least of our concerns. "The bag, the bag," Laïchour and I both thought, barely restraining ourselves from howling the words out loud. It took several interminable seconds of feverishly scrabbling in the dark, fighting an almost insurmountable panic, to find it. I managed to recover my cap in the same way. All the while, red tracers arced across the desert while the stutter of a machine gun kept us flat on our faces. I could hear the moaning of our wounded comrades around me, but for the moment there was nothing I could do to help them.

Suddenly the gunfire ceased. We knew from documents seized from the bodies of ambushed French soldiers that they were forbidden to leave their positions before daybreak. Muttering our names, we managed to seek each other out under the cover of the predawn darkness. After a few minutes the remnants of our little group was again reassembled, along with our precious cargo. The French would take a minute or two to reload, and as the silence persisted, we crept a few dozen meters before we stood up and assessed the situation.

We counted our ranks. Out of the original 35 we were no more than a dozen survivors. In the dark desert night, we were unable to determine from the moaning we heard how many of our companions were killed or wounded. Sergeant Mustache and our guide, so vital in that wide stretch of arid desert, were among the missing. Our phosphorescent compass could tell us where to head but, at 3:30 in the morning, we had less than two hours before sunrise—and we knew that the French soldiers knew it, too. Once it was light enough, they had only to follow our footprints in the sand.

In Wilaya III territory, when we happened to cross dusty or sandy tracks, we used a simple stratagem: either the last in line dragged a branch behind us to obscure our footprints or we crossed the track backwards. This was a ruse used by Jugurtha and his warriors as early as the second century B.C.E. against Roman occupiers, and by the Emir Abdelkader almost 2,000 years later against the French. In the Sahara, however, this stratagem would not work; and in any case, we no more than an hour to find, as far as possible from the ambush site, scrub or rocks in which to hide from the enemy. It was desert on all sides, limitless and uninterrupted in its expanse as far as the eye could see. Since beginning to head east from the Kabyle mountains, never before had we felt so vulnerable and so close to the Lord—and to the superbly armed French soldiers determined to dispatch us to Him. When we suddenly heard a dog barking, breaking the terrible reign of silence, I thought immediately that it might be a divine intervention that could decide our fate.

In Wilaya III, crisscrossed by dozens of military camps, we had killed virtually all of these poor animals guilty of betraying our arrivals at night in the villages. We headed towards the barking and after a quarter of an hour the shadow of a nomad's tent appeared in the middle of nowhere. We surrounded it and a man, awakened by his furious dog tied to a pole, came out of the tent. It did not take us more than a few seconds to explain our plight in the vain hope that he would find us a safe haven.

"My brothers, it is almost daylight. You only have two options: Mount Boudjellal, sprinting, you can reach it in half an hour. Or my tent." There were only a few seconds of hesitation. The only advantage offered by the mound was the possibility to die fighting, our ridiculous handguns in hand. The first place that the French troops were going to thoroughly comb in less than an hour would surely be Mount Boudjellal. Si Mohand Tahar Louaifi, without consulting us, opted for the tent. After all, he had traveled that route before and he was the courier of Wilaya III.

Furthermore, although naturally suspicious, we thought that the Algerian nomad, was unlikely to betray us to the French. He invited us into his tent which he shared with his spouse. It proved large enough to spare his wife the lustful glances we were still capable of, even though we were toughened by war and in dire circumstances. The first glitters of dawn began to flood the desert; we wondered if we would see the sunset.

We sat on a thick carpet but none of us took off his boots. The traditional curd and dates were served to us and we enjoyed them as if they were our last meal. Our host then went away for a moment to "place a lookout on a nearby bump," he said. We stared at each other without a word, all thinking the same thing: perhaps our host was going out to negotiate our skin. But it did not happen, and I thought that if the Revolution had penetrated even into these farthest reaches of our country, it definitely signaled the death of French Algeria.

Hardly an hour passed before we heard the roar of the large banana-shaped helicopters used to transport troops. Through the opening of the tent, we could see them circling above Mount Boudjellal. Almost immediately after, the cursed T-6 began to skim the nomad camp. As the crow flies, Mount Boudjellal was less than a mile from the tent and it was clear it was infested by French troops landing from the dreaded bananas.

But it was too early to congratulate Si Mohand Tahar, who intuitively anticipated the troop landings on Boudjellal. The T-6 swung towards our tent and we could almost see the whites of the pilot's eyes. Equipped with a siren that sounded when it dived towards its target, the aircraft may have been designed, like the notorious German Stuka during World War II, as a psychological weapon against both guerrilla fighters and civilians. It was simply impossible to get used to the characteristic roar of the T-6 and although we had experienced it dozens of times, it put our nerves on edge each time.

Si Mohand Tahar, the most seasoned of us all and, at 35 years considered an old man, was quick to realize that we were very nervous as it became more and more difficult to conceal it. Turning to us, he said, in the most serious tone that he could muster, "Huh, looking at you, you are obviously trying to lay eggs!"

We burst out laughing and the unbearable nervous tension that gripped us vanished as if by magic. Courage and coolness, just like fear or panic, are undeniably contagious. Si Mohand Tahar confessed to me later in the safety of a Tunisian café that he was "laying eggs" too, but that humor compensated for his inner doubts and provided the mask of confidence that a trusted leader should wear.

We did not need to graduate from a war college to know that the French soldiers would quickly realize, on the basis of our footprints, how small our group was. We expected their appearance any moment, perhaps even with their weapons slung carelessly over their shoulders. We checked the magazines of our handguns and introduced a cartridge in the chamber and then, mechanically, I passed my finger through the ring of my grenade. If it came to a gunfight, it was with grenades rather than handguns that we could make a stand, and would ensure that we would not be captured alive, the fear and shame of all guerrillas. Perhaps we could even take with us some of our enemies, properly dropping them off to roast in Hell where they belonged, we were convinced, as rapists and war criminals.

It was way past noon, and the sound of helicopter engines and the T-6 circling above our heads had not subsided. But no soldier appeared, nor did the sentinel that our host had posted a hundred yards away. We were quite frustrated with the whiteness of our lookout's robe, but we had no time to attend to it. At the very moment that our host was serving some hot semolina cakes, the watchman appeared, breathless and frantic, and began to cry—these were his exact words—"My brothers, you are dead! French soldiers, soldiers!"

We got up hurriedly and feverishly left the tent. But before going out, and 50 years later I'm still surprised, I had the reflex to pick up a large piece of a cake and stash it away in the deep pocket of my trousers. Had I finished "laying eggs"?

Outside, there was no vegetation, not the slightest hole, not the slightest crevice, which could provide cover for us. But there were a few miserable grayish rocks against which we desperately tried to melt by curling up into balls the size of hedgehogs. Almost immediately, the announced column of soldiers appeared. Never in Wilaya III, even with bullets flying and artillery shells or napalm drums exploding nearby, did we feel so close to death. Mortal danger was our daily companion, following us like our shadow, but trees, a ravine, a thick fog, or a wooded ridge had always secured a stay of execution and preserved the breath of life.

There in the desert we were absolutely naked, about to be delivered to a merciless massacre. We had learned that we should never take counsel of our fears. Yet fear possessed us—not of death, not of flinching under fire, but of failure in our mission with the certainty that in case gunfire erupted, we would never have the time to destroy the precious contents of our knapsack. We readied ourselves to honor our leader, Colonel Amirouche, and not suffer the utter disgrace of being captured alive.

From the bottom of my chest where I had buried my head, I could behold the soldiers' silhouettes, the color of green crickets, appear one after the other. They marched in a single file without haste, like employees ahead of schedule, dragging their boots on the sand. The soldiers were bent, as if they were looking for misplaced items, their right arm swinging, casually holding a rifle or a submachine gun. We knew they were scanning the sand for footprints, and when they arrived at our level, it took a superhuman effort to control our nerves and not shoot first or unpin our grenades, which would have signaled the end of the road for us. The soldiers went silently by, a few yards from us, eyes still trained on the sand, and headed towards the nomad encampment.

We knew from experience that many French draftees, particularly the ideologically left-leaning ones, shunned flushing out guerrillas hidden behind a bush or a rock, knowing full well that they would be the first to be shot. Was it the case, on that day, on April 26, 1958? I will probably never find out.

Whatever it was, they passed so close to us that the sound of their footsteps seemed deafening, and if our numbers had

198

remained at 35 and not reduced to a dozen, our chances of escaping carnage or capture absolutely infinitesimal. We were soon to have an additional illustration of how a small group has better survival chances than a band of 35 when we had to cross the border—running behind an armored vehicle.

High-ranked officers of the General Staff: Second from left Colonel Mohand Oulhaj, Amirouche's successor at Military Command #3. Third from left, the notorious Captain Hacene Mahiouz, the "grand inquisitor" during the Bleuite Plot. (Early March 1958)

The author carrying the precious knapsack containing a huge sum of money and secret documents. Photo taken the morning after we crossed the
Tunisian border on April 26,1958 signaling the end of a harrowing 42 day march.

Chapter 17
A Hero's Welcome

The West won the world not by the superiority of its ideas or values or religion but rather by its superiority in applying organized violence. Westerners often forget this fact, non-Westerners never do.
Samuel P. Huntington

We waited several hours, silent and virtually motionless, human balls stuck against the rocks under the maddening roar of helicopters and the lone fighter-bomber. Daylight seemed to stretch into infinity and dusk took forever to descend. When the protective darkness began to hug us and revive our fortunes, we were masters of the terrain once more—or so we thought. The man who had hosted us emerged from the shadows.

"Your time hasn't come yet," he murmured. We returned to the cold and hardened cake and, while restoring some of our strength, requested a guide. He arrived dressed in white like most of the civilians of the Wilaya I Military Command. I speculated that the ambush must have decimated our group because of their white robes perceptible even in the darkness of early morning. We thanked our host, bid goodbye, and immediately took off in the direction of the Tunisian border.

After two hours of brisk walking we began to hear, reverberating in the silence of the night, the muffled sound of powerful engines. Then we saw them: a column of half-tracks and armored cars was patrolling the border that we had to cross. The sight plunged some of us into total consternation.

"Oh no," I howled silently to myself. "Walk for over 40 days to bypass the electrified fences and the landmines only to face a barrier of armored cars? Avoid Scylla and fall into Charybdis!" is how I would depict our predicament today. At the sight of the armored vehicles equipped with heavy machine guns and powerful searchlights, we immediately threw ourselves to the ground. The floodlights swept the surroundings. The roar of the armored cars' engines was so deafening that we did not need to lower our voices as we discussed what to do. One of the civilians suggested retracing our steps and giving up. But a consensus was quickly established among us: turning back was out of the question. We would rather die than accept defeat, pitifully walking again that infernal route in the opposite direction to acknowledge our failure.

Lying face down on the sand, we observed the armored cars going back and forth and carefully recorded the jerky and uneven sweep of the floodlights. The interval between the vehicles was kept incredibly small. There was only one way to cross between two armored cars: wait for the arrival at our level of one and run very close behind it, praying that its occupants would not look back and that those inside the vehicle behind it would not see our shadows profiled on the sand.

The guide said that he had no business to conduct in Tunisia and declined to follow us. But when Abdelhamid Mehdi, who had taken command of our group with the disappearance of Sergeant Mustache, drew his pistol, the guide had no choice but to change his mind. We required his presence as we were naturally distrustful and unsure whether he had informed the French soldiers of our plans, in which case an ambush could await us on the other side of the border.

At a signal from Mehdi, one after another, at intervals dictated by the frequency of the searchlights, we ran almost glued to the back of an armored car and crossed the sand track in a few strides. We went face down at the very moment the searchlight swept the desert. Miraculously, within seconds we were all on the other side. We took forever, through excessive caution, to clear the zone swept by the lights. At 35 strong, we probably would never have crossed unharmed.

After ten minutes, animated with new life, we were temporarily safe. But the legal border, a dry riverbed, was still quite far. We walked close to four hours before reaching it. When we crossed the official border on April 27, 1958, it was exactly 12:20 a.m. by my watch.

I will never forget the jubilation that overwhelmed us all. We had just been reborn—if a child were born at the age of 20, he would experience the same feeling as I did at that moment. We had made it to Tunisian territory, to a free country. Our companions from the Aurès lit cigarettes without taking the slightest precaution, with the casualness that only absolute confidence can warrant.

Our newly found security proved to be an extraordinary tonic. We resumed our march northward with increased energy and, by sunrise, the small town of Feriana appeared nestled in a valley. On the Algerian side of the border, we were to discover, the French Air Force had not abandoned pursuit. We learned, after arriving in Tunis, why the French Army did not exercise the right of hot pursuit and stage an incursion into Tunisian territory. The French bombing on February 8, 1958, of Sakiet Sidi Youcef, a Tunisian border village where a unit of Algerian fighters had established its quarters, had provoked an international outcry. A school was hit and more than 70 people, mostly civilians, were killed and some 130 others wounded. Foreign journalists were taken to the site of the bombing. For all intents and purposes, the bombing accelerated further the internationalization of the conflict, generating a crisis within the French government which ultimately brought General de Gaulle to power three months later.

As the crow flies, Feriana seemed very close, but in fact it was nearly 32 kilometers from the border. Along the way, walking in the open in bright sunshine, I began for the first time in years to enjoy the splendor of a spring landscape with the thousands of poppies and daisies that dotted the fields. When we entered the city early in the afternoon, bearded, dirty, and underfed, floating in our uniforms, the inhabitants, many of them Algerian refugees or recent immigrants, extended to us an extraordinarily warm welcome that I will never forget.

We asked for directions to the office of the National Liberation Front, and at every step, in addition to touching formulas such as "We're thankful to God you made it safely," invitations to tea, coffee, or lunch accompanied us. Everyone wanted to inquire about the situation "inside," the state of our health, and the circumstances of our border crossing. In retrospect, I found it strange—and fortunate—that the Tunisian police or the national guard did not stop us to establish our identity and check the precious contents of the knapsack I was carrying (see photo on cover). Once at headquarters, our reception was naturally more than brotherly. We exhibited our passes signed by Colonel Amirouche with the seal of Wilaya III, explaining to the office manager that we were on a special mission to the Committee for Coordination and Execution.

"A car will take you to Tunis tomorrow. For now take a rest. Thank God, you are safe in a brotherly country, free and independent."

The manager gave instructions and a few minutes later we found ourselves in a Turkish bath. We took our first steam bath and shower in about 45 days, removing an impressive layer of grime from our bodies. Lice had taken up residence in our sweaters and shirts in such great numbers that we had given up capturing and executing them. (A comrade who was not lacking a sense of humor had one day captured a large louse, stared briefly at it, gave it a warning, and put it back inside his shirt.) Immediately after the steam bath, we were served our first real meal since we crossed the Aurès: fried eggs and grilled lamb chops. Mohand Tahar, always deadpan, did not spoil our appetite when he remarked, "We're not laying eggs in tents any more. We are enjoying them fried."

We laughed heartily and, while eating, asked him many questions about Tunisia. "You know," he told us, "the Tunisians are not a species of Algerians. They are different from us. They are a great people, but not rough mountaineers like us. They are very hospitable, but they are more tightfisted than we are. They invite

204

you to a restaurant, but they only pay for their meal. They are more sophisticated but less forthright than we are."

Then Mohand Tahar told us a story about an Algerian and a Tunisian. The Tunisian said, "You Algerians are a fearless people, generous and hospitable, but you have something ..."

"What thing, what thing?" shouted the Algerian. "That one, your aggressive tone," the Tunisian calmly replied.

We ate without hurrying and retired to "bed," that is to say, we each had a blanket in a room made available to us. We slept, for the first time in ages, a dreamless sleep—even Laïchour, who had once seen so many dead fighters shredded by bombs that he frequently awoke us when he relived the nightmare.

The next morning, at daybreak, we bid farewell to our companions from Wilaya I and left for Tunis in a Citroen. We were assigned a room in a impressive villa in the suburb of Megrine, and almost immediately Krim Belkacem appeared in person. He affectionately embraced us, and I confess that I suddenly felt important. Standing before us was the most outstanding figure of the revolution at that time, the legendary Djurdjura Lion as he was called, the only revolutionary leader to have already been a guerrilla seven years before the outbreak of the war. We were quite relieved to turn over the green knapsack and its precious contents.

Krim knew that it contained, among other things, a report on the morale of the troops as well as the population. However, after inquiring about the conditions under which we had crossed the border and accomplished our mission, he insisted on a thorough briefing on the spirits of the population as a whole and the degree of confidence combatants still held towards the leadership in Tunis. We did not fail to confirm verbally what Colonel Amirouche stated in a letter addressed personally to Krim, that the electrified fences were seriously stifling the armed struggle and the wrath of the mujahedeen towards the Border Army was increasing. Krim listened with a stony-faced expression, clenching his teeth as we bitterly briefed him on the slumping morale pervading fighting units and civilians alike.

For about a week we were treated like heroes who had braved many dangers to accomplish our mission. The huge amount of money that we had managed to bring definitely helped our standing. What a time we had! We relearned the love of sunshine, enjoying cloudless days of streaming light. After the first few days, we no longer awoke with a start at dawn, wondering where we were. We practically lived with the great men of the revolution, shared their meals, listened with reverent silence to the conversations of Krim Belkacem, Ben Tobbal, Ferhat Abbas, and Mouloud Iddir. I noticed with great pride the authority and awe that Krim inspired: when he spoke during meals, for example, other conversations stopped and all eyes converged on him like those of students towards their master.

My deepest regret today is that I was too young to appreciate the historical significance of the moments I was living with one of our country's greatest leaders. I wish I could have recorded for posterity the conversations between these men who have left an indelible mark on Algeria's history. But I did not pay as much attention as perhaps I should have—now that our mission was accomplished, I was soon going back to the Algeria with my comrades in arms.

We donned civilian clothes left behind by militants arriving from Europe and, dressed in ill-fitting jackets and pants, set out to discover the Tunisian capital. One of those militants, Tahar Hamroun originally of Ihitoussen, proclaimed loudly his determination to cross into Algeria and join the armed struggle. He bid goodbye and left with me his immigrant worker's suit. I hastened to alter it and started wearing it. But Tahar chickened out after one week and put me in a bit of a spot when he returned and reclaimed his outfit.

In Tunis we roamed Habib Bourguiba Avenue, frequenting the Maghreb Café and, with more eagerness, the neighborhoods of ill repute of Bab Souika and Bab Djedid. We also took our film to be processed. Soon, our photos and Colonel Amirouche's were displayed in the shop window of the photographer, who began to sell them without authorization and at a hefty price, to the Algerian community in Tunis and, no doubt unknowingly, to French secret agents.

We stayed with the big boys about eight days, during which our discussions were confined to the effect of the shortage of armaments and munitions not only on the morale of the guerrillas and the population, but also on their loyalty towards the political leadership based in Tunis. Alone one day with Major Iddir, the highest-ranking officer to desert from the French Army, I hinted at the anger and frustration that had taken hold of us all, beginning with Colonel Amirouche. The ineptitude of the Border Army, as we labeled them, was exemplified by its inability to prevent the erection of the electrified fences. The major took me aside and, taking on a conspiratorial air, revealed to me something that continues to puzzle me to this day. "I can confide to you now that I have devised a plan to destroy most of the Morice Line in one night. I submitted this plan to the appropriate persons. No action has been undertaken. My plan is buried somewhere in a drawer."

The implication could not be clearer: a plan to sabotage the Morice fence, designed by a commander who had earned his stripes in the French Army, had been shelved.

After a week's rest, Krim determined that we had recovered from our long march. We were ordered to move into a small apartment in Tunis that an Algerian businessman, long established in Tunis, had graciously made available to the National Liberation Front.

I decided to take a break from Tunis and make a trip to the Zitoune border camp. There I was incredibly pleased to see again soldiers and officers from the Wilaya III Military Command. They were all waiting for orders that never came to breach the Morice fence and return to the battlefield. The camp was crammed with weapons and ammunition. This very arsenal was used after independence to usurp power and even to commit the supreme infamy—killing guerrillas who dared resist the new, indigenous, invaders.

But for the moment, I basked in the true fraternity and comradeship of my companions but, by contrast, was thrown off by the demeanor of some of the officers who had just deserted from the French Army—four years after the outbreak of the war. There was no love lost between them and the guerrillas, especially those who had joined the struggle in 1954 or 1955. Although the National Liberation Army had been organized into battalions, companies, and platoons, the deserters, as if they were still serving in the French Army, referred to them as "ragtag armed bands."

Some of these officers, displaying their condescending attitude and never showing any deference or camaraderie, took pleasure in maintaining their distance from their underlings, as befits modern armies. They walked between the tents, their uniforms perfectly pressed, with a never-used hand gun hanging from their belt. Watching them with disdain, I remember thinking that a few drums of napalm dropped on their heads would surely humble them. I took photos with the peasant guerrillas, most of them living on borrowed time, ready to return to combat as soon as they received the order.

Our group was soon to disperse. Our guide and courier, Mohand Tahar Louaifi, had a driver's license, very rare at the time; he was assigned the dangerous mission of transporting arms from Marsa Matrouh in Egypt to Tunis. Slimane Laïchour was sent to Yugoslavia to learn printing techniques. He was to supervise the printing of banknotes after independence. I was saddened and couldn't hold back my bitter feelings when Abdelhamid Mehdi was sent back to the Zitoune border camp after only ten days off in

Tunis. There he was to await his marching orders to carry mail back to Wilaya III. The Morice Line and the land mines were perhaps an insurmountable obstacle for many officers and guerrillas languishing at Zitoune, but not for the likes of Abdelhamid Mehdi.

For my part, I confess that I was completely disoriented. Although Tunis was not Cairo or Calcutta, the city triggered unease in the mountaineer that I had always been. Worse, the bourgeois life that our officials led in Tunis shattered some of my illusions. I was 20 years old and perhaps a little naïve, but fancy suits and shiny cars were an insult to starving Algerians and guerrillas hunted down in their own land. Resolving that I did not belong in Tunisia, I drafted a message to Colonel Amirouche requesting permission to return to the war zone, which my dear companion Abdelhamid Mehdi took with him. Awaiting a response, I made myself available to Major Si Saïd Yazourene, who offered me the position of manager of the student center of Wilaya III.

I accepted the position without much enthusiasm. I managed what could be called a boarding house, providing not only room and board but also clothing and medical care. In theory the student center served only students of Wilaya III but actually admitted many young war refugees. This center, as noted previously, was established by Colonel Amirouche in early 1957. Those who criticize Amirouche and accuse him of being anti-intellectual ignore the foresight that led him to establish this student center entirely financed by Wilaya III funds. No other head of a Wilaya military command, to my knowledge, undertook such a visionary initiative.

With a monthly budget of about $100,000 (in today's dollars), I organized food supplies and strove to respond to the diverse needs of a few hundred students who besieged me with their problems, ranging from toothaches to book purchases. I reviewed invoices and ordered payment of bills. It was during one of these checks that my attention was attracted by an altered number smelling of forgery.

I went to the store that issued the invoice where, after consulting his register, the store owner confirmed my suspicion— the bill had been altered after delivery to the student center. I was indignant beyond words that an Algerian would stoop to embezzlement in the midst of revolution, and particularly embarrassed in front of the Tunisian storekeeper. At first, I was tempted to report the dishonest assistant at the student center who had committed the forgery, but aware that he had a family and fearing that he would be sent to the infamous underground prisons located at the Tunisian border, I decided to fire him and try to

208

forget about it.

This incident increased my discomfort, and my disgust made my task as a manager increasingly grim. I had fulfilled this function for exactly 40 days when a courier from Wilaya III arrived in Tunis. With him came a letter from Amirouche which stunned me: he announced that he was coming to Tunis to "settle accounts with Krim Belkacem." Shaken beyond words, I read and reread the letter with trembling hands, telling myself that it couldn't be. It seemed impossible for Amirouche to be that angry with Krim for failing in his mission of organizing the supply of arms and ammunition to Wilaya III. Utterly dazed, I did not, at first, pay attention to the orders that were given to me: Amirouche informed me that he had received my message requesting permission to return to combat. "It's out of the question," he wrote. "My orders: go back to school!"

Over the years, I have struggled to find an explanation for the spite Amirouche expressed towards Krim. Had he learned of Ramdane Abane's assassination[69] and concluded that, without Krim's consent, nobody would have dared to touch a hair on Abane's head? Colonel Amirouche had already demonstrated that he transcended considerations of regional and ethnic origins and of kinship when he accomplished in Wilaya I the mission entrusted to him by the leaders of the revolution.

I was inclined towards another interpretation: Krim was the Armed Forces Minister in the provisional government. As such, Amirouche considered him directly accountable for allowing the Morice and Challe Lines to stand, and for the inaction of 30,000 Algerian soldiers in their Tunisian sanctuary. These policies were stifling the guerrillas of Wilaya III. I was surprised to learn, years later, that the French journalist, historian, and biographer Yves Courrières agreed with my interpretation when he wrote, "We remember that Amirouche was heading to Tunis to indict members of the [Provisional Government] for their failure to send arms and ammunition when he and El Haoues [the head of Wilaya VI] were killed in battle by French troops."[70]

But to return to my more immediate problem: the Colonel had ordered me to go back to school. Where? And in what grade? Amirouche knew perfectly well my level of schooling. One day, laughing, he even called to me, "Hey, blacksmith!" That's how I learned that he had ordered an inquiry into my background. My formal education amounted, in all, to a primary school certificate and two years at a vocational institute. Hours spent operating machine tools, learning carpentry, forging metal at the blacksmith shop, and designing spare parts on the drawing board, were by no means adequate preparation for admission to high school.

Admittedly, we were taught some basic algebra and geometry, but the curriculum was quite different from high-school programs: for example, we did not study foreign languages or classical Arabic, compulsory subjects in secondary education in Tunisia. Even if I qualified, how could I be admitted to high school at the age of almost 21? In mulling over these questions, I met three people, named below, who were to provide decisive help, without whom I would never have accomplished the feat of earning my French baccalaureat diploma in three years instead of the usual six or seven. The first person who came to my help was an Algerian refugee who was studying at the famous Sadikia College. When I explained my problem, he declared himself willing to provide advice and guidance.

"At your age, he said, "there is no other alternative but to prepare for an entrance examination to ninth grade." I thought bitterly that, not long ago, I was too young to join the armed struggle. And now, I was too old to go back to school.

Then I went to see Commander Yazourène to hand him my resignation.

"Major, sir, Amirouche ordered me to go back to school. If you authorize me, that's what I will try to do."

"That's a commendable idea, my son. For us the elderly, it's too late. We have not had the chance to go very far in our schooling. Go right ahead. And don't you worry. We're here to help you. I will give the necessary instructions to Si Lounes," my successor as manager of the student center.

A few days after my resignation, a young mujahed who lived with us showed disrespect to a female neighbor whose Italian parents complained to the apartment owner. The landlord seized on this pretext to inform us that he was expecting relatives from Constantine and that we had to vacate the premises. Thus, I moved to the student center that I had been managing on Andalusians Street. I found myself sharing a tiny room with two other guerrillas who had just arrived from the bush, Nacer Saâda and Abdel Kader Haddi. With the invaluable help of my Algerian refugee friend and encouragement from other Algerian students, I studied tirelessly throughout the summer of 1958.

In September I took, without much hope, the ninth-grade entrance examination in a school in La Goulette, a suburb of Tunis. To my surprise, I passed the exam. While I was attending the school, Commander Yazourène gave instructions that I was to be hosted as a day-boarder in a Tunisian tavern, of which I have exquisite memories. However, I did not linger very long in the suburbs. Having served in combat with the famous Colonel Amirouche helped me. A member of Krim's cabinet intervened with the Tunisian Ministry of Education to obtain my transfer to a more prestigious institution, the Alaoui High School. I resolved to justify the trust that had been invested in me and studied assiduously—but I did not need the additional motivation. All I had to do to summon the energy and drive to succeed was to think of my companions, particularly Amirouche, struggling to carry on the burden of armed resistance. Unfortunately, in the middle of the school year 1958-1959, the brutal and tragic death of my chief almost put an end to my fledgling school career.

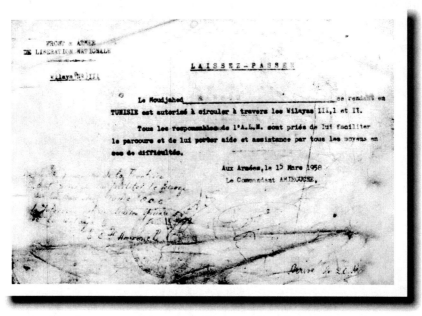

The pass bearing my name, and the mention "special courier of the Military Command # 3," signed by Amirouche who was head of Wilaya III but not yet officially nominated.

Chapter 18
The Death of Colonel Amirouche

Between de Gaulle and me, the finger of God
will designate the winner.
Colonel Amirouche,
quoted in the daily *Combat*, March 31, 1959

In war death was our constant companion and followed us wherever we went. Although we often invoked destiny, we knew that the intractable law of probabilities played against those who were exposed so often to mortal danger. As noted earlier, it was exceedingly rare in 1958 to meet a resistance fighter who joined in 1954 or even 1955, for the life expectancy of a mujahed rarely exceeded two years.

I do not know why we imagined Colonel Amirouche to be invulnerable, so indestructible that I refused to consider as final the news that stabbed us in the heart: Amirouche was killed on March 28, 1959. When his death was confirmed in the press, I passed through successive states of mind, from utter devastation to hope inspired by skepticism about the generally dubious claims by French media, and, when finally the brutal reality could no longer be denied, to a boundless despair.

The French Army had previously announced on many occasions that they had killed Colonel Amirouche. So when I heard the news that last time, I hastened to buy the local newspaper and there, at the newspaper kiosk, nearly fainted. The photo, published on the front page, was indeed of the body of Amirouche. His eyes were wide open. His black mustache and broken front tooth gave him a ferocious expression even in death. I noticed on his neck what appeared to be grenade or rocket shrapnel. In a dispatch dated March 30, 1959, the special envoy of Agence France Press (AFP) paid unusual tribute to Colonel Amirouche, stressing that he "put up a long and fierce resistance at the bottom of a cliff and was killed by grenades." The French daily *L'Aurore* of September 26, 1959, rendered indirect homage to Amirouche when it reported that "The [French] government examines the situation created by the death of Amirouche."

The armed forces that had been deployed against Amirouche under the command of Colonel Girard, assisted by Colonel Ducasse and Lieutenant-Colonel Watel, could not have been improvised quickly with the means of communication available at the time. That fact tends to support the hypothesis of treason. The French forces included the first and fifth battalion of infantrymen, the 584th Bataillon du Train (equipment and logistics), and the Sixth Parachute Regiment supported by units of the Air Force—in all, some 2,500 troops.

The French news service reported that 55 guerrillas were

killed and 17 captured, but was silent on the French losses. "For him [Amirouche]," commented the AFP report dated March 30, 1959, "remains the killing of the legend that surrounded him." But neither the French Army nor any of his detractors have managed to kill his legend.

When I read that my Colonel's body was exposed to be seen by all, I imagined the joy of the French soldiers and officers around his corpse and I was seized with a dizzying frenzy. Blinded by unbearable pain and a fierce hatred, I found myself dreaming of possessing an atomic bomb and dropping it, with absolutely no qualms, on the city of Paris. [71]

A few hours later I met Major Iddir, who doubted the statements of the French authorities. "French hoax is customary," he said.

"No, sir, there is no doubt that Amirouche is dead," I said in a faltering voice.

Suddenly I did not want to see any of those soldiers sheltering in Tunisia and left Iddir standing open-mouthed at the Casbah. Nor did I want to go to school any more. I didn't feel like studying and the future of Algeria was suddenly completely irrelevant. Instead of heading to the boarding house, I began to wander aimlessly through the streets of Tunis. A movie theatre featuring the film *Viva Zapata* caught my eye. I remembered that our high school French teacher, Monsieur Brunswic, had recommended the movie, the story of a Mexican revolutionary peasant who struggled for a cause identical to ours. But on entering the theatre, I was far from expecting the extraordinarily calming effect that the film would produce on me.

When Zapata was riddled with bullets in a trap mounted in circumstances almost identical to those leading to Amirouche's death, the tears of Mexican peasants prompted this response from Zapata's close companion: "No, Zapata did not die. You cannot kill Zapata. Zapata is these eternal and proud mountains, this land soaked with his blood, it's his voice you hear in that moaning wind that gently rocks the trees, Zapata is in all of us where he will live forever."

But the man lying dead on the ground, was he Zapata? No, Zapata fled on his famous white horse to the mountains, as Mexican Indian songs still claim to this day. Zapata cannot die, no one can kill Zapata! And Zapata, like Amirouche in death, inspired such beautiful poems:

215

On the roadside
I found a white lily
I wore it as an offering
And laid it on Zapata's grave.

I left the theater transfigured. The film produced the same effect as the thick fog that God had twice spread above us like a cloak, shielding us from aircraft and certain death. At a moment when I was emotionally annihilated, God drew me to this movie theater and gave me the strength to lift my chin and carry on the struggle.

A few weeks later, when I read the leaflet glorifying the heroic death of Colonels Amirouche and El Haoues, I noted the same themes as those in the film.

On that fateful day of March 28, in a battle between Amirouche's and El Haoues's 40 companions and 2,500 French troops at Djebel Thameur, the two colonels were killed. It was a heroic struggle. Dark was falling, on a night of Ramadan.

They now rest in this Algerian land they loved so passionately.

Soon the dastardly enemy propaganda apparatus was set in motion. In utter contempt for the laws of war, in violation of basic principles of universal morality, they displayed their remains.

But at the same time, the whole of Algeria is proudly and fervently collected at a time when Colonels Amirouche and El Haoues joined in legend Abane, Ben M'hidi, Ben Boulaïd, Zighout Youcef, Mohand Ou Rabah Chaïb and all the great heroes of the Revolution.

Algerians!

Amirouche and El Haoues have left us, but more than ever they participate in the grand epic of Algeria at war.

Already, their fraternal shadows are soaring over the mountains of Kabylia, and paths of the Sahara desert.

Already they lie behind every bush, every mountain peak,

on all dunes, on all paths, in every city, in every village, in every hamlet.

Already, they live on in the hearts of each and every Algerian.

Already the people tell and amplify their sublime sacrifice...[72]
Long live eternal Algeria.

To be sure, a great sorrow continued to gnaw at me, but it was lessened by a kind of revelation. At that age I was a fervent believer that Amirouche was welcomed into Heaven as a martyr. Still, even the certainty that Amirouche was hosted in Paradise did not console me for his death. This was undoubtedly what was tearfully expressed by a certain mujahed, struggling to come to grips with the loss. An ardent believer himself, he muttered that it mattered little that Amirouche was in heaven and that he was indifferent to the independence of the country without Colonel Amirouche. When these comments were reported to Colonel Mohammedi, he forgot that he was dealing with a combatant of the all-volunteer National Liberation Army and not with a German soldier and committed the unforgivable outrage of slapping the mujahed instead of wiping away his tears. When this incident was reported to me a day or two after Amirouche's death, the little esteem I may still have harbored for that officer vanished forever.

But the degree of religious fervor is often proportional to the imminence of mortal danger. More than once, evoking Paradise after escaping a search-and-destroy operation, there were mujahedeen among us who jokingly observed that it was a pity that nobody had come back after death to tell us more about the special place reserved by God for martyrs.

It was almost 11 p.m. and in the narrow streets adjoining Habib Bourguiba Avenue, some eateries where I often bought myself a soft egg and capers wrapped in fried dough, were still open. But that night, a night of mourning and penance, I skipped dinner. With no desire to return to the Student Center, I again wandered aimlessly through the streets. My steps took me to Belvedere Forest. The spring air was warm and the surrounding darkness opaque, except for fireflies fluttering in the undergrowth. The trees appeared strangely like human forms. I saw in them, reincarnated, all my companions coming to keep me company and offer comfort. A large tree, slightly stooped, was Amirouche himself. Next to him, to the right, was Mohand Ourabah Chaïb, felled by a T-6 rocket. A little further, slender arms pointing at an imaginary enemy, was Abdel Kader Azil El Bariki. Facing me up close, shy and peaceful, Hocine Omar; the dim light piercing the dark foliage was his beautiful smile always tinged with a touch of melancholy. There by my side, extending its two branches towards me, was my friend Abdelhamid Naïli, who had joined the insurrection "for me."

Sitting against an oak tree, I tried to imagine the effect of Amirouche's death on the morale of my fellow fighters in Wilaya III. Their spirits were already seriously affected by the scarcity of ammunition, leaving only faith, itself staggering, to sustain and lead the resistance to the occupation. In the minds of many of these guerrillas, I knew right away, there would be no doubt that Amirouche and El Haoues had been betrayed. They were heading to Tunis to demand explanations from military officials who watched, imperturbable and seemingly indifferent, the French Army onslaught on a guerilla resistance virtually deprived of means to resist.

Did Amirouche, en route to Tunis to "settle accounts," constitute a threat to some of our military leaders? Was there a mole in the operational command? I began to think of the conspiratorial tone that Major Iddir adopted to reveal that his plan to destroy the Morice fence had been shelved once for all. Admittedly, the region where Amirouche and El Haoues and many others met their fate remained the last refuge of the perfidious Messalist traitors of the rival Algerian National Movement. It was after decimating their ranks in Guenzet in the eastern part of Wilaya III that Amirouche had acquired the reputation of a ruthless guerrilla leader. The survivors had fled to the Beni Ilmane region adjoining Djebel Thameur, where the two colonels were killed. Coincidentally, this area was not subject to French Army incursion and, at the time, we did not understand why. It was only after the war that we had the explanation. Governor General Jacques Soustelle and his henchmen who specialized in psychological warfare had planned to organize a counter-guerrilla force with the Messalists. In Indochina where the tactic had been employed experimentally, it did not prevent the crushing French defeat at Dien Bien Phu in 1954. The colonial army had learned nothing.

As if sensing what was looming ahead, Amirouche, in a surprise attack, had wiped out the Messalist troops. The survivors fled to the south, where they could benefit from the protection of the French Air Force. This was the desert region of the Wilaya VI Military Zone, the stronghold of El Haoues, the Wilaya leader. Was El Haoues also a victim of his own popularity? Like Amirouche, he was not afraid to mingle with the peasants, undermining his own security.

I remained in the forest for a long time. The French B-26 bombers spilling their drums of napalm and heavy artillery shells were now far away. Did I have the right to experience freedom and independence in a country so extraordinarily hospitable, enjoying full security instead of the mujahedeen who were entitled to such gifts before me, only because I was a student? Was it a form of natural selection that Algerians were doubly penalized, first as illiterate and second as bound to martyrdom before the elites? Was it a blasphemy to think that God should not have recalled to Him, so prematurely, Colonel Amirouche? His people idolized him and needed him at a crucial time when their faith wavered under widespread abuse, bombardment, and torture, with no end in sight.

Finally, I wondered, who cares whether God exists or not if for Him we do not exist? I did not remember where I had read this sentiment and although my faith strongly disapproved of it, it grabbed my thoughts as I pondered the lawless world order where a powerful country could invade, occupy, humiliate, rape, and massacre with total impunity while, as Mohand Tahar Louaifi put it, "God is looking the other way."

I spent the rest of the night in the Belvedere Forest. Dawn was breaking and only the darkest corners of the wood still harbored a few active fireflies. I waited to hear the distant call to prayer before I got up, stretched my legs, and slowly headed to the mosque. After a particularly impassioned prayer, I went to a nearby café, ordered coffee, and took stock of my situation. The fire lit by reckless if not unconscionable militants had caught and the blaze had spread for the first time in more than a century to all of Algeria, burning, in its mad rush, frail and tender shrubs as well as long-dead oaks. No army in the world could now smother it. Colonel Amirouche may be dead, but nobody could kill his memory or his example. I thought of Zapata again. Under the spell of sudden inspiration, I pulled a small notebook from my pocket and began to write the first lines of a poem that I completed nearly 50 years later:

No, Amirouche Is Not Dead

He lives in every home and unborn child
In his homeland now liberated from these troops,
In crystal-clear streams flowing down the valley
Overwhelming the rubble and digging new alleys,
Pressed to fertilize this tormented land,
Burnt by the sun and so bloodthirsty.

Colonel Amirouche in the center resting his arm on the author's shoulder
(September 1957).

Chapter 19
Beginning High School at Age 21

*"All our dreams can come true if
we have the courage to pursue them."*

◆

Walt Disney.

Those few verses jotted down in a notebook in the hubbub of a smoky Tunisian café gave me the serenity necessary to consider the future. Colonel Amirouche had entrusted us with a mission, and we had accomplished it. Colonel Amirouche ordered me to go back to school, and I resolved to marshal all my energy and willpower to fulfill my new mission.

At the Amirouche Center my living conditions were far from ideal. I shared a room with my fellow guerrillas Nacer Saâda and Hadi Abdelkader. Deeply skeptical about my abilities and anguished by a fear of failure, I asked the cook to awaken me at four in the morning, when I began to study frantically until it was time to head to the high school. If my roommates were unhappy to be disturbed by the bare bulb which lit our room in the middle of the night, they did not show it. Battle hardened as they were, they had lived in much worse conditions and would not complain for so little an inconvenience. During the whole year that we shared this tiny room, we were forced to do our homework on our knees and climb over the beds to move from one corner to another. Yet they showed a patience and understanding that only fellow mujahedeen can show towards one another.

In class I was uncomfortable with my fellow students, most of them five or six years younger than I, but I compensated for my discomfort with a maturity, class participation, and attendance that impressed students and professors alike. One of the latter, in particular, the French professor Etienne Brunswic, took me under his wing after I wrote a term paper on a topic that could not be more timely: "Describe an event of your childhood that left a deep imprint on your memory."

It took me no time at all to choose my subject. In ten furiously written pages, I described the invasion of our village by French soldiers, who stormed our house like rabid hyenas when I was seven years old. Unleashing my emotion and barely containing my bitterness and hatred, I described the savage blows dealt to my father helpless on the ground, the comings and goings of the Moroccan Tabor fetching the water that would revive him when he fainted from the pain, and the relentless questioning of the French officer: "Where are the other weapons hidden?" That paper received the best mark in the class and prompted Monsieur Brunswic to show a keen interest in my studies, inquiring regularly about my grades in my other classes. He was the second person whose advice and assistance turned out to be crucial. I completed my first high-school year with a Diploma of the First Cycle, topped with the Prize of Excellence and several other first-place awards.

My success had three immediate consequences: it drew the attention of Belaïd Abdessélam, an official of the Algerian Government in Exile, who closely monitored the students. Collaborating with him was a brilliant lawyer, Arezki Bouzida, who pleaded my cause at the Tunisian Ministry of Education and got my application accepted as a high-school "intern" with free room and board. And finally Monsieur Brunswic decided that I should skip the second year.

"You know, Hamou, the second year introduces very little new material compared with the first. You can study during the summer holidays. Are you ready to sacrifice your vacation?"

I smiled sadly but did not articulate my thoughts—I was an ascetic revolutionary, shunning absolutely any pleasure, any relaxation, as long as France continued to sow death and desolation in my country. Amirouche's tragic death came to my mind. The massacre of so many of my companions was still a painful memory.

"Vacation, Monsieur Brunswic, is the least of my concerns. Subjects like chemistry and geometry are."

"Fine, I thought so. I'll introduce you to someone who will tutor you during the summer and I will draft a recommendation for you to take an entrance examination to the higher grade. Send your application immediately to the principal and stress that you fell behind in your schooling because of the war."

A few days later, in mid-June 1959, as I was still basking in my stunning first-year success, Brunswic introduced me to his former high-school mate Alexis Stern, a stateless man of Hungarian origin whom the French teacher was hosting. Stern was the third person whose help, combined with a wonderful sense of humor, carried me through the subjects most difficult for me to pass: math, physics, and chemistry.

I learned that Alexis' parents had perished in the Holocaust. After World War II, he was granted asylum in France. A leftist Marxist, when the French Army drafted him to be sent to Algeria, he opted for desertion and joined other French intellectuals who were adamantly opposed to the Algerian war in Tunis. Alexis lived in a small apartment of which he was the custodian while the owner, Claudine Pacha, a high-school teacher, was spending her three-month vacation in France. Needless to say, when Alexis suggested that I share his apartment while he was tutoring me, I gratefully accepted on the spot. I had not been looking forward to taking a commuter train several times a day to go to the lessons that Alexis was so graciously offering me. He was himself attending Tunis University, majoring in math, and found it easy to help me not only with my math, physics, and chemistry, but also with French literature and English.

For the first time since I left Tazmalt, I had a room of my own with near-perfect study conditions, especially compared to the Amirouche Center. With the modest allowance I received from Yazourène Si Saïd, I contributed to the cost of food, which rarely included meat or seafood. But Claudine had left a stockpile of supplies in her apartment and invited us to draw from it as needed. To explain this cautionary accumulation of foodstuffs, we must remember the very precarious situation of the French living in Tunisia. Reactions of the Tunisian population against the French after the bombing of the border village of Sakiet Sidi Youcef in February 1958 were hostile. Bizerte, a naval base on the Tunisian coast, was under French occupation, and Tunisians as well as Algerians bitterly resented the arrogance of uniformed French soldiers strutting the streets of their cities. In fact, Alexis and I ventured outside during daylight hours as little as possible: with his blond hair he could be mistaken for a Frenchman and antagonize Tunisians.

We prepared our meals together in a congenial atmosphere heightened by Alexis' exceptional sense of humor. Like many a Marxist, he had in his repertoire countless jokes deriding Communists that made me laugh between daunting math and chemistry lessons. One of his stories that could apply to some of our contemporary political regimes involved three Soviet citizens who found themselves in the same cell of an overcrowded prison. "Why did Stalin order your incarceration, Comrade?" asked the first.

"Well, I was *against* Popovich, Comrades," said the second.

"I was *for* Popovich," said the third.

The first, with a sad smile said, "I *am* Popovich, Comrades."

We spent almost three studious months together, alternating chemistry with math, math with English, English with Western classical music to which I was introduced for the first time. So my ears gradually became accustomed to Vivaldi's "The Four Seasons" as I read the French poets Ronsard and du Bellay, Stravinsky's "Petrushka" as I struggled with algebra, and Borodin's "Polovtsian Dances" as I memorized the periodic table.

Before Professor Brunswic left on vacation, he assigned a reading list of sixteenth-century French literature. I delighted in the discovery of Francois du Bellay and Pierre de Ronsard, particularly Ronsard's *Sonnets pour Hélène*, which I can still recite 50 years later.

224

When you are very old, at evening, by the fire,
Spinning wool by candlelight and winding it in skeins,
You will say in wonderment as you recite my lines:
Ronsard admired me in the days when I was fair.

If I felt my willpower slacken, it was enough for me to think about my comrades in the interior left virtually defenseless. Immediately my determination to succeed was rekindled and new energy was instilled in me.

When September 1959 arrived and with it the fateful day of the exam that would allow me to skip the second year of high school, I was ready. I was hardly surprised a few days later to learn from Brunswic that I was admitted to the higher grade. Claudine's vacation was coming to an end, which signaled my return to the Amirouche Center's boarding facilities. With my war companions Haddi Abdel Kader and Saâda Nacer, we were informed that we were all three recipients of scholarships in Bulgaria, where the French baccalaureat degree was not required for university admission. Hadi and Saâda accepted the awards without hesitation. Housing conditions at the Center were terrible and the level of instruction far from adequate to satisfy the rigorous requirements of the baccalaureat exam.

That had been one of Colonel Amirouche's grievances against the Government in Exile: that it gave the Center no budget to improve the material conditions of students. The congenial fraternity which reigned among us, at first unshakable, began to wear thin in the den where we were packed. One day, for a mere drop of oil dropped by mistake on a paper due the next day, Saâda and I settled the matter with a fist fight.

I myself would have been greatly tempted by the Bulgarian adventure but for Professor Brunswic's objections and the scholarship from the Tunisian Ministry of Education. Brunswic argued that if I were to study abroad, it had to be in a "great country such as the U.S.S.R. or the United States. There," he said, "even if you flunk out, which would surprise me very much, you will have learned at least one very important language, and just by living in a great country, you learn a multitude of useful things to run a country. Your country."

"My country is being devastated, ravaged, and my people massacred..." I began.

"It will be independent, don't you worry," he said.

"With General de Gaulle returned to power by the extremists of French Algeria?"

"Yes, with de Gaulle. If he hasn't already grasped it, he will

225

soon realize that granting independence to Tunisia and Morocco and not to Algeria was absurdly surrealistic. But that's not the only reason. De Gaulle is obsessed with the grandeur of France. He never swallowed the humiliation of being ignored at the Yalta and Potsdam Conferences in 1945, when Churchill, Truman, and Stalin decided the fate of Europe without him."

De Gaulle was well aware, Brunswic explained, that while France fractured itself and ruins its economy in an anachronistic conflict, West Germany was emerging as the dominant economic power in Europe.

"That's why he presides over the most abominable military operations against a defenseless people?" I asked bitterly.

"De Gaulle is a soldier," said my teacher. "He wants to put his generals up against the wall. He is telling them, 'You claim that it is the politicians and not the military who have lost the war in Indochina and permitted the humiliation of Suez in 1956; you are convinced that you can do better than in Indochina, crush the Algerian rebellion, and end the insurgency? Go right ahead. I will provide all the means you will request; you have a free hand in Algeria.'

"Their inevitable failure will leave him a free rein to negotiate with the rebels. And then he will say, 'It is my turn to try something else.'"

I felt immense respect for Monsieur Brunswic and was very fortunate, at the age of 21, to benefit from his vast knowledge outside of French class. In fact, since elementary school and Monsieur Avril, the teacher who had sacrificed his weekends for us to ensure that we were awarded our primary school certificates, and Monsieur Aubert at the Vocational Center, who said to me "if I were you I would join the rebels," I had not yet met a French citizen who could contradict, if only for a fleeting moment, the negative images so deeply planted in my mind of the French as torturers, rapists, and indiscriminate bombers.

"Well, Monsieur Brunswic, I hope you're right about de Gaulle and his army. As for this scholarship. . ."

"Forget about it," said my professor. "You'll be offered room and board at Alaoui High School. You'll benefit from excellent conditions to focus and study hard. In two years you will be awarded the baccalaureat and then you will go wherever you want, but with a résumé. I hope it will be to a great country."

My comrades-in-arms, Haddi and Saâda, left for Bulgaria without me, and there they obtained, respectively, diplomas in civil engineering and architecture. As for me, the relative comfort graciously provided by the Tunisian government offered ideal study conditions. If I felt discouraged or demoralized, I would pull from my wallet Colonel Amirouche's picture, his arm affectionately resting on my shoulder, and it was enough to trigger a new energy and willpower.

I completed my first two years with honors and, a year later, earned my baccalaureat degree. In three years, inspired by the constant presence around me of the spirits of my chief and my dead companions, achieved what most students, following a normal course of study, accomplished in five or six years. The Algerian Provisional Government officials monitoring the students, unaware that I had slept hardly six hours a day and used a profusion of drugs to keep awake, concluded I was a genius. Where else would they send me but to an American university?

The author, standing, first from right. Crouching, second from right, the youngest member of our commando, Hamimi Gharsa. (fall 1957)

Chapter 20
Farewell to My Comrades in Arms

Life is like a game of cards. The hand that is dealt you represents determinism; the way you play it is free will.
Jawaharlal Nehru

E arning the prized baccalaureat degree was a source of unspeakable pride and joy. I was the first high-school graduate to do so from Ihitoussen and perhaps even Tazmalt. Now the former blacksmith I had been could even attend university! Yet this prospect was not devoid of anxiety. Would I be worthy of the challenge? I had achieved in three years what was normally accomplished in six, but did I not have serious gaps in my learning?

When I was asked to fill out a scholarship application specifying not only the subject I wanted to major in, but also the country where I wanted to study, I did not hesitate. I filled out the form without consulting anyone, indicating by order of preference three countries: the U.S.S.R., U.S.A., and Switzerland, and chose medicine as my preferred field.

I think it was the hospital tent in the woods where the wounded and the tuberculosis patients received rudimentary care from an overwhelmed young nurse that determined my choice of medicine. The conditions there had been so unsanitary, so inadequate, the lack of supplies so dramatic, that our family doctor from Tazmalt had refused to obey the order to join the guerrillas even under threat of death.

In high school I had developed a special liking for biology and had selected from the outset experimental sciences as my concentration for the baccalaureat. It was then that I became acquainted with Belaïd Abdessélam. In charge of student orientation, he had other ideas that determined a part of my life and destiny. He unilaterally decided to send me to the United States to study economics. The criteria that determined the host country and field of studies were often arbitrary, but perhaps understandable: after all, we were at war, still mobilized. "Discipline being the main strength of armed forces," as the deserters from the French Army were fond of superciliously quoting, I had to follow orders. In general, Abdessélam dispatched mature students and war veterans to Western countries, which he viewed as highly developed although sources of Satanic temptation. He sent the younger undergraduates to the countries of the Eastern bloc, the Middle East, or to the less prestigious Lumumba University in Moscow. The mujahed B.R., after failing the high-school entrance exam three or four times, was sent to a military school in the Middle East and eventually rose to be a colonel in the post-independence

230

Algerian Army. Mohand Goumeziane, on the other hand, aide-de-camp and secretary to a colonel and a high-school graduate, was sent to the Naval Academy of Alexandria. He stayed there only a few weeks before deserting and returning to Tunis.

"I have not joined the resistance to tap one-two, one-two all day long," he grumbled to me upon his return. He narrowly escaped disciplinary sanctions for desertion at the Tunisian border bunker prison. Eventually, he was sent to Czechoslovakia where he earned a degree in petrochemical engineering.

Sharif Oubouzar, another student and resistance fighter sent to the same Naval Academy, reacted exactly like Goumeziane to the military exercises that an ex-guerrilla could only find ridiculous. But Oubouzar had a different fate after deserting and returning to Tunisia. I met him at the border camp and we took pictures just before he crossed the Morice Line and returned to combat. He was killed in battle in the region of Draâ El Mizan in 1959.

As I awaited my departure, I discovered by pure chance that the manager assigned to monitor the students had established a system that grossly discriminated between high-school graduates who were dispatched by the National Liberation Front from France to Tunis because they were wanted by the French police, and guerrilla-graduates like me. The first group, who stayed in luxury hotels, were paid a monthly stipend five or six times higher than the one I was granted. When I learned this, I called on the manager, and I did not mince words. He stammered an embarrassed explanation, apologized, and immediately upgraded my status to the same level as the Swiss, French, and other Algerian students who, for the most part, hadn't even heeded the student strike order issued by the revolutionary leadership in 1956. Thus, during the long months of waiting for my departure to the United States, I lived comfortably with my monthly stipend of 25 Tunisian dinars, which in 1961 enabled me to rent a small studio for only 5 dinars per month.

Thanks to my brother Zouhir, still a student at the Ecole Supérieure de Commerce in Reims, I had fairly regular news of my father. He was doing as well as he could under the conditions at the St.-Maurice-l'Ardoise prison camp and could even receive letters and packages, at least until he was transferred to the ill-famed Berrouaghia prison in Algeria later that year. So I hastened to reassure my father about my own situation, cheer him up with the news about my baccalaureat, and send him, not packages of tasteless cookies as in Bejaia Civil Prison, but works by Emile Zola and a biography of the Prophet Mohammed.

Incarcerated until independence, he was able to read and

educate himself, activities he had never before had the time to indulge in. The most leisure he had been able to permit himself in Tazmalt, throughout the long summer days of the off-season, was to read every single page of the daily *Alger Républicain*. He duly translated most of it to some peasants, always the same, who were attracted neither by dominoes or card games in the cafés of Tazmalt. Enthroned on a seat carved out of a tree trunk in the shade of the giant eucalyptus in front of his shop, he had done his best to educate his illiterate companions.

My younger brother Lahcène, a high-school student in Bejaia on strike since 1956, had heeded Zouhir's advice and joined my father in Paris to resume his studies. But when our father was arrested in 1960, Lahcène, at my suggestion, joined the National Liberation Front and was able to get a scholarship to Albania, where he earned a degree in agronomy. Very few Algerian agricultural engineers have contributed to research and application as much as has Lahcène, who became Director General of the Agricultural Institute of Research and Development.

Meanwhile, so I could have my meals at the university cafeteria, I enrolled in the Faculty of Sciences of Tunis and the Bourguiba School to take English classes. I soon became acquainted with four other students who were part of the U.S. group. We reflected a microcosm of Algerian society: Madjid Ainouz and I were Kabyle, Ben Drissou and Ben Youcef were Mozabite Berbers, and Mohamed Kebir was Arab.

Of course, with our country still at war, we did not display our differences when we arrived in the United States. We were Algerians and nothing else, and our religious sentiments remained private. Unlike in our homeland, exceptional tolerance and mutual understanding prevailed among us. After all, we were still inspired by the principles spelled out in Algeria's Declaration of Independence of November 1, 1954, that ensured preservation of all fundamental freedoms, without distinction of race or religion.

Those who prayed regularly did not rebuke those who did not, and those who ate only halal meat prepared according to the Koran did not preach strict adherence to religious injunctions. This was unfortunately not the case with other newcomers from various backgrounds who arrived in the U.S. after us. Arabic- and French-educated Algerian students were soon to face each other in tense confrontations on ideological issues during Student Association meetings; these conflicts foretold the 10 years of bloodshed pitting secularists against Islamists that tore Algeria apart some 40 years later. Hence, at a meeting of the Algerian Student Union in December 1962 in Ann Arbor, Michigan, secular-leftists on the one hand and Islamists/Baathists on the other exchanged sharp words, bordering on insults, as they still do today in my current home, San Diego.[73]

But back in Tunis during that summer and fall of 1961, I devoted myself to broadening my horizons not only through my Hungarian friend and tutor Alexis, but also thanks to two professors, Jean-Pierre Darmon and Lucette Valensi, both Tunisian Jews. The latter, a distinguished historian by the age of 23, had been my history and geography professor at Alaoui High School. Through her I met Darmon, also a professor of history at the renowned Sadiki College. He immediately became a close friend, essentially because, like Alexis, he refused to answer the draft order and serve in the French Army. In his letter of insubordination addressed to the Commander of the Military Garrison at Carcassonne and published in the Tunisian press, Darmon wrote:

> I am being drafted to serve under the French colors... I will not obey... I will not come to Carcassonne to serve under your command... I am French by birth ... but only because of French colonial policy, which since the late 19th century had facilitated the naturalization of Jews in North Africa... Neither of my great-grandparents was French... I was born in Tunisia to a family whose installation in Tunisia goes back on the paternal side to the 17th century and, on my mother's side, precedes the Arab arrival [7th century] and goes back to ancient times... In this sense, I'm not French but Tunisian... Now I am being summoned to serve under the banners of an army which has been engaged in a bloody war against a North-African people for eight years... The war in Algeria is the result of more than a century of humiliations for which France is responsible... Then we saw one of the greatest world powers marshal its enormous military and financial potential to crush a small nation... This is a major crime. That is why, Sir, I would feel it as an intolerable impurity being integrated into the French Army.

A passage in his letter intrigued me: "...on my mother's side precedes the Arab arrival and goes back to ancient times." I had no difficulty in obtaining from Darmon a summary of North African history.

"You know," he said, "it is possible that we are from the same strain, you and me, the Berber strain."

When I laughed, he continued, "Hear me out before laughing. The Phoenicians settled in North Africa at about 1200 BCE. They came from the Levant or what we know today as Syria,

Lebanon, Jordan, Israel, and Palestine. The only monotheistic religion at the time was Judaism. Is it through the Phoenicians that Judaism was introduced in North Africa? Before the arrival of Christianity among us, the Berber tribes had converted to Judaism or remained pagan, and some remained so until the arrival of Islam in North Africa in the seventh century."

I learned a lot that day. While I had always thought that French Jews had come to North Africa in the colonial army vans, I discovered that in Algeria it was the Crémieux Decree of 1870 that forcibly granted French citizenship to Algerian Jews, some of whom were probably, like me and every human being who believes in evolution, the cousins of African primates. Jean-Pierre Darmon and Lucette Valensi brought major events in our history to my attention, and a few days before our departure to the United States, Darmon gave me a best-seller, *Algeria, Past and Present*, by Yves Lacoste and André Nouschy.

The days and weeks leading up to my departure were devoted to dealing with visa problems at the United States Embassy and improving my English at the Bourguiba School. In addition, I renewed contacts with my fellow guerrillas in Tunis and the Zitoune border camp, contacts that had been suspended while I was preparing for final exams. I also began to follow more closely current political events.

From the war zone and the Wilaya III command, groups were still managing to cross the border, often after hardships that I myself had not endured, such as being forced to drink their own urine in the Sahara desert. Curiously, those who attempted to cross from Tunisia back into Algeria rarely succeeded. While a few fell victim to land mines, most sheepishly returned, stating that it was impossible. They were then subjected to merciless sarcasm from the mujahedeen who had succeeded in crossing and were still alive to testify to that fact. A common taunt proclaimed, "Approaching an electric fence, he saw a snake and quickly split... towards Habib Bourguiba Avenue."

Among the last fighters of Wilaya III to cross the border in both directions, I will mention only two, the courier Ouaghzen and Azil Abdelkader "El Bariki." Ouaghzen, endowed with a fabulous wit, addressed everyone, Tunisian and Algerian alike, in Kabyle, the only language he spoke. Whether they understood or not made no difference to him. El Bariki, one of the most famous warriors of the Wilaya III Military Command, was a special envoy to the Provisional Government of the Algerian Republic in the fall of 1959. I met him several times in Tunis at the Ministry of War or at the Zitoune camp, and I soon realized that one of his tasks was to

234

provide Krim Belkacem with explanations relating to the Bleuite treachery. More crucial, Al Bariki served as spokesman for the bitterness and anger that gripped every freedom fighter, anger directed against the Border Army's inertia regarding the supply of ammunition. When I spoke to him for the last time, asking about officers and NCOs of whom I had fond memories, Al Bariki answered in his soft voice, "he's been killed"—as he himself was later.

Finally I asked a question to which I knew the answer, but wanted to hear it from a born warrior. "What's the weapons and ammunition situation?"

"What do you want me to say? It is as you left it." He remained silent for a moment and then added curtly, "They have been criminally negligent, those border people, and the French Army knows it very well."

Al Bariki did not incriminate anyone in particular, but the use of the arcane formula "those border people" clearly indicated to whom he was referring. I knew him well enough to remember that he showed little respect for noncombatant civilians. For him, the Border Army was just civilians pretending to be mujahedeen in their impeccably pressed uniforms, commanded by officers some of whom had never ventured a foot into Algeria. He remained silent before adding harshly, "But that dog, de Gaulle, is beginning to get it."

He was referring to the General's speech of November 10, 1959, one year after the October 23, 1958, speech about the *Paix des Braves* (Peace of the Brave), inviting the insurgents to "check their weapons in the locker room" and "brandish white flags." De Gaulle's words sparked hearty laughter in Tunis. "Where are we going to find white flags with the persistent shortage of detergent?"

Al Bariki was not literate in French and asked me to explain to him what this speech of de Gaulle's was all about. So I summarized de Gaulle's words: "If the leaders of the insurrection are ready to discuss with the French authorities the conditions to end the fighting, they can do so... I repeat, those conditions would be honorable... They would take proper account of the courage displayed in armed combat."[74]

When I told him that de Gaulle recognized us as combatants and no longer called us outlaws or terrorists, Al Bariki nodded and repeated, "He is finally starting to get it."

"Are you staying or going back?" I asked him.

"What do you want me to do here?" he replied with a short laugh. "My mission here is finished. I'll cross the fences or die at the border."

235

I was never to see him again. He managed to cross the border and rejoin his post as the chief of an elite battalion, and was killed fighting in the land where he was born. Colonel Amirouche had already recognized his valor when he awarded Azil Abdel Kader Al Bariki the highest distinction of the war, the Medal of the Resistance. As I write these lines, I feel sad and helpless that I have neither the ability nor the time to devote an entire book to each of these great warriors of the Algerian resistance.

Among the mujahedeen closest to me to whom I wanted to bid goodbye, there were first of all Brahim Berkani and Menad Mokrane, both assigned to the Algerian National Labor Union. Then there were Lieutenant Hamimi and Commander Si Saïd Yazourène. Si Saïd had showed me much paternal affection at the Wilaya III Command Post before his departure to Tunis a few months before my own. Surprised by my appearance of extreme youth, he had approached me and asked about my native village and my father's profession, dismissing for a moment the rule that imposed strict anonymity and the use of assumed names. I remember his nod of approval when I mentioned Tazmalt. "It's a region of patriots," he said.

Si Mohand Oul Hajj, Political Commander at the time, joined us. "I know his father," he said "He is a blacksmith but he is self-educated. And he is one of the oldest activists in the region."

The Sage, as Si Mohand Oul Hajj, the new Wilaya III leader, was nicknamed, was the exact opposite of Amirouche. Just as the latter exhibited indomitable energy and showed, on occasion, utter ruthlessness towards traitors, Messalists or Harkis, the Sage projected an image of kindness heightened by his calm and gentle voice.

As for Saïd Yazourène, Amirouche's other assistant and Commander in charge of Intelligence and Liaison, he was a straight-shooting peasant whose sense of humor, sometimes at the expense of Colonel Ouamrane who was rumored to be gay, always delighted us. When I joined him in Tunis, Yazourène not only showed great trust by appointing me as Director of the Student Center, but he also demonstrated a paternal attention that encouraged me to go to high school at the age of 21. When I informed him that I would soon leave for the United States, he made a prescient remark. "Algeria's independence will find you there. We all agree to pursue this goal and we have maintained a semblance of unity. But after independence..." He left the sentence unfinished. "Dedicate yourself to your studies and forget about the rest."

Of course, every Algerian in Tunis was aware of the crisis

236

that was pitting the Army Chief of Staff Houari Boumediene against the Government in Exile in 1961.[75]

It was obvious to Yazourène that this episode did not bode well for the unity of the nation after the inevitable defeat of the French. Bidding me goodbye, he used the same Kabyle word as had Amirouche prior to our long march to Tunisia: "*Ezwar!*" The word encompassed many meanings at once—never surrender to temptation; be worthy of my trust; be a man.

Before my departure from Tunisia I hitched a ride to the Zitoune border camp to bid goodbye to Lieutenant Ziata Hamimi, for whom I had great respect. I had met him for the first time at the beginning of 1958 during a tour of inspection, and we immediately hit it off. Virtually illiterate, Hamimi articulated his native Tamazight language in a classical tone, with a wealth of vocabulary and images I had never before heard. That day, as we were dreaming of Algeria's independence, I uttered a phrase that he reminded me of ten years later in his café in Algiers: "You know, Si Hamimi, we did not take up arms for the sole purpose of replacing a blue, white, and red rag with a green, white, and red one." I was referring, of course, to the colors of the French and Algerian flags, respectively.

I remembered one day as a guerrilla when the sky was low and dark clouds loomed overhead, too overcast for the fearsome fighter-bombers to venture out. Enjoying our brief security, we took off our boots and relaxed as we imagined how a free Algeria would look. Like Colonel Amirouche, we envisioned it as being generous towards its children, establishing justice and social equality through the kind of solidarity that our leader had already begun to build in Wilaya III. With the unquenchable thirst for modern weapons that gripped our poorly equipped band, we dreamed of an independent Algeria armed to the teeth to deter any attempt to attack it again. Amirouche believed that if we survived, it would be out of the question to hand over our weapons and go home. We had first to ensure, he insisted, that power was held by true patriots exclusively serving the interests of the people. We wondered if, after independence, those of us who managed to survive would leave our rocky ridges and dense forests before assessing the quality of leadership taking over the country.

Although none of us believed that he could elude the French Army sweeps forever, each one of us was trying to imagine his role and place in a free Algeria. Our dreams, however, lacked breadth and perspective and were limited by our cultural backgroud and lack of education. We were determined to defeat, by any means, a mediocre enemy lacking vision and devoid of intelligent foresight, but apart from a vague image of Algeria ridding itself of occupation and substituting indigenous peasants for European settlers, no coherent ideology, no long-range development strategy animated the mujahedeens' ranks or the revolutionary leadership.

Like all revolutionaries, we were convinced that the destructive act of expelling the colonial power by any means at our disposal was an instantly creative act, delivering social harmony to the nation and guaranteeing universal justice and equality. It was not until the Charter of Tripoli adopted in June 1962 by the National Council of the Algerian Revolution, nearly three months after the end of the war, that the rough fundamentals of socialist ideology were formulated. The demagogic National Charter of 1976 rhetorically proclaimed this conception of the Algerian State as "irreversible."

At the end of fall 1961, we were finally summoned to the U.S. Consulate and informed that our fellowship applications had been accepted. Our departure was scheduled for early February 1962. Tunisian passports were delivered to my four companions, but surprisingly I was the only one to receive a Moroccan passport.

Si Lounès, my successor as Director of the Student Center, accompanied me to a store to buy me a new wardrobe. "You're going to America, mind you! You've got to be presentable," he said. That experience brought back memories from seven years before, when my father took me to a shop in Algiers to purchase the mandatory clothing demanded by the vocational center.

One final time, I took a shuttle bus to the Zitoune camp to enjoy a last lesson in classical Tamazight from Lieutenant Hamimi.

"So, you're surrendering, are you?

"Absolutely," I replied. "I prefer to surrender to the Americans, than to the French."

"Tell them that their napalm and B-26s are top quality, but the French MAS 49 performs better than the U.S. Garand." Hamimi had been seriously burnt by napalm.

"I will let them know. What else?"

"Tell me," he asked, "how long is your flight to the U.S. going to take?"

"How would I know, I've never flown before. Twenty hours?"

Si Hamimi paused, then nonchalantly, looking towards the sky, said, "You know, in 20 hours, the aircraft will have ample time to crash."

I laughed heartily and we parted on these good words.

Chapter 21
First Taste of America

Why do they call it rush hour when nothing moves?
Robin Williams

The more I study it [the Constitution], the more I have come to admire it, realizing that no other document devised by the hand of man ever brought so much progress and happiness to humanity.
Calvin Coolidge, 1929

◆

The Tunis Air Caravelle that we boarded on February 1, 1962, took us to Rome, and while we waited for our connecting flight in the departure lounge, we had a fortuitous encounter that surely saved me from a terrible misadventure. I saw, standing no more than 20 meters away, M'hammed Yazid and Saad Dahleb, respectively Minister of Information and Minister of Foreign Affairs in the Algerian Provisional Government. When I told them that we were heading to Washington, Yazid asked to see my ticket. As soon as he consulted it, he exclaimed, "Your flight makes a stop in *Paris*!"

My heart skipped a beat and I thanked God for continuing to watch over me. The ticket did not indicate a stop in Paris, but Yazid knew that long-haul flights stopped there to refuel before crossing the Atlantic. The U.S. Consulate, which had booked our tickets, did not know that I was wanted by the French security services for my guerrilla activities. With a stop in Paris, I could have been arrested and interrogated. My U.S. adventure would have been over before it began.

Yazid collected our passports and tickets and made the necessary changes in our itinerary. The rerouting proved painful: we crossed the Atlantic in a propeller plane that made stops in Madrid, Lisbon, and the Azores before finally landing in New York. In New York customs officers thoroughly inspected our luggage, tore open packets of couscous, confiscated the dried meat one of my companions had brought with him, checked the X-rays of our lungs and our immunization cards, and at last let us embark on a continuing flight to Washington, D.C.

Of course, when we landed around six o'clock on a Sunday morning, no one was waiting for us because of the last-minute changes made in Rome. The only contact we had was the Institute of International Education (IIE), our sponsor. My few weeks of English classes at the Bourguiba School now proved useful as I managed to explain our situation to an airport staff member. He dialed several numbers but the response was the same every time: "No answer." We were exhausted after a 30-hour journey, hungry but not anxious, thanks in part to our companion Majid Aïnouz's delightful sense of humor.

Outside, the ground was blanketed with snow and porters were drinking coffee out of paper cups. We enviously eyed the mist rising from the hot beverage. After an hour, the whole airport staff knew our history and a compassionate porter brought us each a cup of coffee which we savored with gusto, not minding that our first cup of American coffee tasted like hot water to us.

It was not until noon that an airport agent was finally able to contact the IIE. Twenty minutes later a fair-haired gentleman with glasses, cold as the weather, showed up and took charge. He briefly introduced himself as "Steve" and we shook hands. Steve made no effort to conceal his annoyance at being disturbed on a Sunday. His stern, expressionless face and the long silences that prevailed at the restaurant where he was kind enough to take us, conveyed his bad mood. Naturally, we all ordered the same dish as his, roast chicken with mashed potatoes, except for Ben Youcef, who ordered a halal meal of spaghetti with tomato sauce. There and then began our long and painful acculturation. No bread was served—two slices the color and taste of cotton hardly counted. We wrestled with our bland chicken thigh with a frustratingly blunt knife, all the while copying Steve's moves and actions.

We were surprised that, with snow covering the ground, we were served water with ice; for dessert, most patrons ordered ice cream. Even the cheesecake which we ordered was freezing cold. After the meal, Steve handed us each a few dollars as an advance on our monthly stipends and drove us in his immense and silent car to the Cairo Hotel in downtown Washington. There he left us, ordering us to be ready at eight a.m. the next day.

On Monday, a different gentleman came to pick us up and take us to the IIE offices where our designated supervisor, Mrs. Culver, gave us a lesson in political morality, the purpose of which I did not understand until much later. She reminded us that our home country of Algeria needed our services after our graduation. We were to return there, not marry an American and stay in the United States. She insisted so tactlessly on the necessity to abstain from outings to night clubs and other places of ill repute that I finally replied, in an irritated tone, that "We did not come to the U.S. to party."

"Good, good," she said, changing the subject. She informed us that she had made reservations for us at the Hartnett Hall boarding house, breakfast included, at Dupont Circle for the month of February.

"It's a short walk from Georgetown University, where you will take intensive English courses at the American Language Institute until you are able to take classes at the university regardless of your chosen field."

After two days at the Cairo Hotel where we sequestered ourselves because of the wet and freezing weather, we moved

241

to the boarding house. We quickly discovered that it reflected a microcosm of Washington society: Latin Americans, Europeans, U.S. citizens from all over the country, and even FBI agents, or at least individuals who introduced themselves to us as such. A group of Texans was very friendly, but we carefully avoided them because of their accent which, initially, made them impossible to understand.

The copious American breakfast gave rise to some comical situations. When we were served, for the first time, cornflakes in a bowl with a glass of milk next to it, we didn't understand that they should be combined before consumption. We munched on dry cornflakes and drank the milk afterwards, deriding the strange American eating habits. After trying three breakfast items, fried eggs, boiled eggs, and scrambled eggs, we decided to order a fourth item listed on the menu as "eggs any style." But the waiter, who engaged in a lengthy explanation too complicated for us to understand, forced us to revert to the familiar items.

English classes began immediately and were intensive—five hours per day, five days a week, with plenty of homework. Most of our fellow scholars were Latin American students or professionals. I retain a vivid memory of Mrs. Maguire, an excellent English teacher who was so fussy about grammar that she interrupted us each time we attempted to construct a full sentence. "Now, let me correct your grammar," she would say. One day a Brazilian student who was an outstanding actor burst into the classroom, panting and distraught, and haltingly managed to gasp out, "Mrs. Maguire, Mrs. Maguire, me find corpse in room bath, dead with knife in chest..." Unfazed, Mrs. Maguire cut off the Brazilian with, "Now, let me correct your grammar." A burst of laughter from the Brazilian told us that he was testing Mrs. Maguire's dedication.

Chapter 22
View from the United States:
Bittersweet Independence

Are you a politician asking what your country can do for you or a
zealous one asking what you can do for your country?
Khalil Gibran, *The New Frontier*

Dry your tears, Africa!
Your children are back,
Hands full of toys
And hearts full of love,
They return to adorn you
With their dreams and their hopes.
Bernard Dadié,
translated from French by the author

Our group had been attending the Language Institute for barely a month when news of the ceasefire in Algeria made the front page of every newspaper. On March 19, 1962, articles reported on the ceasefire as well as the terrorist attacks waged by the Secret Army Organization (OAS). Formed around the diehards of "French Algeria" who had opposed independence, the OAS vowed to sabotage, by any means, the agreement signed on the Algerian side by Krim Belkacem, Vice-President and Minister of the Interior of the Government in Exile.

With independence no longer in doubt, everyone in Washington wanted to know our opinion on the future of Algeria. I quickly understood that a major American concern was Algeria falling into the Communist orbit. We were interviewed by the *Washington Post* and our picture appeared with the headline: "Problems in Algeria Seen Just Beginning." During the interview we focused on three primary needs. First and foremost, the government had to restore the security threatened by the OAS, and then had to stabilize the country by a fair redistribution of land almost totally in the possession of the European minority. Just as important was eradicating the illiteracy of more than 80 percent of the population.

On March 29, a Provisional Executive composed of French and Algerian representatives and presided over by a "moderate," non-National Liberation Front Algerian, was formed. Its charge was to organize a referendum to approve or reject the Evian Accords ending the eight-year-long war of independence. The accords received a resounding vote of approval of more than 90 percent.

An immense joy, mixed nonetheless with sadness and anxiety, overwhelmed us. We had reason to be alarmed. The massacres and bombings, the tortures and humiliations that Algerians had suffered for 132 years had not stopped our countrymen from achieving their objective in one of the fiercest struggles in the history of colonialism, but we knew that the OAS had not yet had its last word. The stated aim of the organization was to bring Algeria back to the state in which the French had found it when they conquered the country between 1830 and 1847—according to colonial propaganda, merely a huge encampment of nomads still living in the Middle Ages. On June 17 representatives of the National Liberation Front and OAS struck a deal: OAS commandos

244

would stop random killings in exchange for their safe passage out of the county. It was far too late, however. Some 800,000 French Algerians, the elites who could have made a difference in the modernization and secularization of the new nation, had already left the country in a massive exodus. The improvement of our English had a sadly ironic twist to it: we could read the news, but it was not cheerful.

In addition to our English classes, we took a course in "American Culture and Civilization." The professor began his class by asking each one of us what feelings and ideas the United States evoked in us.

"Excessive individualism," I said. I had realized immediately that extreme individualism was considered a virtue in America.

"Non-intellectual," ventured Majid Ainouz. His observation did not seem to please the professor, who launched into a long lecture on Europe, as if we were Europeans, culturally divided between the self-styled intellectual, dogmatic Left and the equally dogmatic Right. He showered praise upon the pragmatic and practical Americans who did not waste their time splitting ideological hairs.

"Fascism and communism," the professor claimed, "are generated by collectivist ideologies of European nation states, not an individualistic culture that fosters the autonomy of the individual." What characterizes the American psyche, he stated, was the will to act on and transform things, regardless of the end product of human action.

In the weeks and months that followed, we discovered that a quite a few Americans, intellectuals and ordinary citizens alike, considered communism and fascism to be equally totalitarian, even when we pointed out that communist ideology, like Christianity or Islam, was universalist, while fascism was based on the so-called superiority of the Aryan race or a military caste. But Americans seemed convinced that proclaiming the superiority of the Aryan race or the virtues of the dictatorship of the proletariat were similar in that adherents of both ideologies excluded, through violence, those who did not swear allegiance to their views.

As our English improved and we were introduced to American customs and political institutions, we gradually began to understand the unique cohesion of American society. Unlike in Europe, characteristic American individualism is reflected in the Constitution. That document does not encompass nor guarantee any social right, such as the right to employment, education, or medical care, all of which are enshrined in European constitutions.

What struck us, at first, was the unanimous veneration

for the Founding Fathers. Every American we met attributed the power and greatness of the country to the political genius of the framers of the Constitution, rarely considering the country's wealth of natural resources or its geographical extent in relation to the size and density of the population. Many citizens knew by heart famous passages of the Declaration of Independence. "We hold these truths to be self-evident, that all men are created equal" was a statement apparently memorized by primary-school children just as Algerian children learned by heart verses from the Koran.

The Cold War was in full swing. Fallout shelter signs were ubiquitous on street corners and read, reproduced in large letters, Soviet Premier Nikita Khrushchev's famous statement at the Polish embassy in Moscow on November 18, 1956: "We will bury you." Khrushchev was referring to the superiority of socialism that would inevitably triumph over capitalism when he said "Whether you like it or not, history is on our side, we will bury you." But this statement was widely interpreted as a nuclear threat. Even on Washington buses, we read: "We will bury you! says Khrushchev. Will they 'bury' us? Never, you answer. But are you sure? What are you doing to oppose Communism? One sure way is to help Radio Free Europe."

Unconditional patriotism was the rule. President John F. Kennedy, in his 1961 inaugural address, had just launched his celebrated slogan taken almost literally from the works of Khalil Gibran: "Ask not what your country can do for you, ask what you can do for your country." Like most patriotic presidential oratory, the statement went unchallenged. It seemed never to have occurred to anyone we met that the United States of America had been colonized and populated by men and women who did essentially the opposite: they asked their mother country what it could do for them in terms of jobs, security, freedom of religion, and dignity among other things, and the answer being "not much," they emigrated to the United States. This was a sentiment I understood well: after all, my father and his family, in order to survive, were forced to defy an ancient tribal tradition and leave their ancestral village.

It was only when I began to understand English well enough that I became interested in the history of the United States and understood the factors that shaped this pragmatic political culture that contrasted so sharply with Europe's. I discovered that space and resources in relation to population size were important–but perhaps more crucial was the quality of American leadership. Great leaders were decisively instrumental in the survival and adaptation of American institutions to new situations and to addressing major

246

crises, such as the Civil War, which threatened to irreparably fracture the nation.

My teacher in Tunis, Monsieur Brunswic, knew what he was talking about when he urged me to decline the Bulgarian scholarship and earn my degree in a great country. Coming to America provoked many questions about the mechanisms that drive revolutions and the crucial importance of leadership. In the *New York Times* on April 10, 1962, under the dateline "Cairo," there were two ominous headlines: "Algeria's Ben Bella Threatens Israel" and "Ben Bella Also Predicts: Continuing Algerian and All-African Revolution." The two stories raised the alarm that "Castro, in his plan to export Communism to other Latin American nations, has now imported seventy-six [Algerian] FLN rebels to train Cuban terrorists and saboteurs." Then on April 14, 1962, while returning from Cairo and the pernicious influence of that other demagogue Gamal Abdel Nasser, Ben Bella proclaimed, "We are Arabs, we are Arabs, we are Arabs." He instantly generated a defiant reaction among Berbers like me: "Speak for yourself, Mister, we are Algerians. A few thousand Arab invaders in the seventh century could not possibly turn the Berber people into Arabs."

Thanks to the intensive pace at which we learned English, we were able to attend college-level courses after only three months. We were soon to be dispatched to various universities in accordance with our selected major. For my part, before attending Wesleyan University, I stayed in Georgetown and took summer courses in economics. At my first class, I was stunned when the professor invited us to join him in prayer. That's how I discovered that Georgetown was a Catholic university where almost each class began with a prayer, just as in Algeria devout Muslims would begin any action with the ritual "in the name of God, the Compassionate, the Merciful."

The Georgetown University cafeteria offered meals a bit bland for our Mediterranean tastes, but had an impressive fountain of fresh milk where we could fill and refill our glasses without restriction. Whenever I remembered the hunger and deprivation we had experienced during the war in the no man's lands drained of life and laughter, I would get up from the table to refill my glass. It made me feel like I was living in the paradise of rivers of milk and honey promised to the faithful, according to the family midwife of my childhood. The latter, however, had the unfortunate mania to annihilate the dizzying benefits of paradise with the fear aroused in us by the prospect of first facing God's mythical inquisitor, Azrayen. If only he spoke Berber and not Arabic...

The summer of 1962 was a studious one, almost painfully

247

slow. My English fluency was improving from day to day, but I had still to grasp the intricacies of idiom. I remember spending quite some time reading and rereading a chapter in my economics text and failing to grasp its logic until a fellow student explained to me that "slow down" was not the opposite of "slow up." I still managed to pass my exams at the close of the summer semester and, at the end of August, I was informed that Wesleyan University in Middletown, Connecticut, would grant me a full scholarship while the Institute of International Education would continue to pay me a monthly stipend to cover the cost of books and personal expenses.

Meanwhile, with the historic installation of an Algerian Embassy in Washington, I obtained my first Algerian passport. For a brief moment, I thought of my first symbolic act when I joined the freedom fighters—burning my French-Muslim I.D.card.

In Algeria, following another referendum on July 1, 1962, citizens voted 5,975,581 to 16,581 for independence. France officially recognized Algeria's sovereignty on July 3. On that same day, the Government in Exile, the Provisional Government of the Algerian Republic or GPRA, entered the capital city of Algiers. Two days after that, on July 5, Algerians celebrated their hard-won independence. I was saddened beyond words not to be present for that historic celebration.

But the euphoria that gripped us all soon vanished—instead of peace and reconciliation, a national tragedy was in the offing—and this time the crisis was triggered by a race for power. Backed by four out of six Wilaya Military Commands and, more importantly, by the Border Army led by Boumediene, Army Chief of Staff, Ben Bella declared his opposition to the GPRA and participated in the formation of a Political Bureau openly hostile to the Provisional Government. By the end of August, bloody confrontations resulted in hundreds of casualties. In September the army, led by Boumedienne, entered Algiers like conquerors. The rancor between the Border Army and the freedom fighters, which had faded with the passage of time, was revived even more intensely as border troops fired on valiant guerrillas attempting to stop them from entering Algiers. I couldn't help but remember the prophetic words of Commander Yazourène, who predicted the implosion of the fragile unity maintained in Tunisia. Henceforth, I decided to focus on my studies and ignore the news from home that shamed all us Algerian students living in the United States.

I arrived by bus at Wesleyan University, where I was greeted by the Foreign Student Advisor. I engaged in a lengthy negotiation with the admissions office and, by counting the credits earned for my French baccalaureat and for the summer courses at Georgetown, I was admitted to college as a junior.

Almost immediately I received an invitation to join the Algerian Student Association, which numbered a little over 100 students. The President of the Association, Abderrahman Megateli, the only other ex-guerrilla fighter in the U.S., sent me a copy of the student journal entitled *Connaissance de l'Algerie* (Knowing Algeria) with a request for articles. My piece on my war experience with Colonel Amirouche was very well received by the Algerian student community. At a meeting in Ann Arbor, Michigan, during Christmas vacation, I was elected Secretary General of the U.S. Chapter of the Association, in charge of editing the bilingual student journal.

At Wesleyan, I was assigned a room in the only non-fraternity residence hall, the John Wesley Club. With my Jewish roommate from Chicago, Lawrence Alschuler, I engaged in endless discussions on the Arab-Israeli conflict and Algerian Jews. At the time in 1962, that is to say, five years before the June 1967 war and the occupation of East Jerusalem, the West Bank, Gaza, the Golan Heights, and Sinai, the overwhelming majority of American Jews that I met dreamed of recognition of the State of Israel within its 1948 borders, and Larry Alschuler was no exception.

Like many Wesleyan students, Larry's knowledge of history was colored by ideological bias regarding Arabs and Islam. He was, however, open to other cultures and points of view, a rare model of pragmatism and tolerance. I had to point out to him that I was Berber, not Arab, and that I disputed the Algerian President's claim that Algeria was "Arab." More knowledgeable about the Middle East than Larry thanks to my two Jewish professors in Tunis, Lucette Valensi and Jean-Pierre Darmon, I had no difficulty showing him that what was presented in the media as Arab anti-Semitism was actually anti-Israel to the extent that the Arabs themselves were of Semitic origin. I reminded him that the animosity between Arabs and Jews, even if it went back at least to the end of the 19th century when European Jews began to settle in Palestine, was exacerbated by the creation of the State of Israel on what Arabs viewed as Arab land—and where Jews were a minority.

"Are there any Jews in Algeria?" asked my roommate.

"Very few, Larry. What I do know is that the Crémieux Decree of 1870 granted French citizenship to all Algerian Jews. When the Algerian Revolution broke out, the overwhelming majority of Jews chose the wrong side, the side of French Algeria. On the eve of independence, they left the country along with the other French citizens."

I remembered what Jean-Pierre Darmon had taught me in Tunis and added, "In Algeria, and North Africa in general, virtually all Jews were probably ethnic Berbers, like me. Some of them may have been converted to Judaism with the arrival of Jews among the Phoenicians who established trading posts in North Africa as early as 1200 B.C. The Jews lived in peace among the Muslims until the colonial regime enacted the divide-and-conquer Crémieux law granting to Jews—and to no other Algerians—French citizenship.

"But why do Arabs refuse to recognize the State of Israel?" asked Larry.

"I think they should. But it takes a bit of history, long history, to explain it. The Arabs unrealistically dream of liberating Palestine, which they consider to be occupied by European settlers. Suffice it to state that it's all a matter of leadership on both sides."

Larry listened intently and sharply said, "They do not and will never have the means to free Palestine as you say. They'd better recognize the State of Israel and live in peace with it."

"I agree with you," I replied. "But it is clear that Israel does not seek peace, either. Why else would they have participated in the invasion of Egypt alongside the French and the British in 1956?"

To this, Larry had no answer. Despite our sometimes heated discussions, our relations remained warm and friendly and I even participated in an experiment conducted by his brother, a student at Harvard. Secluded in a forest near Middletown, he gave me two spoonfuls of a transparent liquid, which I suspected much later to be LSD, and asked me to describe its effect: essentially scary hallucinations and a splitting headache. He paled when I told him about recklessly walking towards a cliff and showing utter contempt to the danger of falling a few hundred feet. He never asked me to undergo another experiment.

As we were studying hard for our degrees, Larry announced that he was soon to get married with a French girl. "With or against?" I asked jokingly, suggesting a clash of cultures that Larry had to be aware of. He introduced his fiancée to me and invited me to his wedding after graduation. To help Larry impress his in-laws to be, I taught him a few crucial phrases such as "j'aime ma femme, j'aime ma belle-mère, et j'aime mon beau-père." (I love my wife, I love my mother-in law, and I love my father-in law.)

Wesleyan was a small, private, men-only university organized into fraternities and was exceedingly conservative except, perhaps, for the John Wesley Club, where I resided. I was undergoing enormous difficulties of acculturation and

250

adjustment. Wretchedly lonely, I went through moments of great discouragement and unbearable isolation. Middletown itself, populated mostly by Sicilian immigrants, had no relationship to the university, except commercially. To meet a girl, students had to drive to an all-female school such as Bennington in Vermont or Wellesley in Massachusetts.

I was often invited to parties but was too shy to flirt and, even after costly dancing lessons in Hartford, my confidence remained low. I couldn't crack a joke because of my insufficient mastery of English. When I did manage to secure a date, the woman would firmly state "I don't want to get involved emotionally," to which I mentally—and bitterly—added, "and least of all with an Algerian Muslim." At parties I would silently watch couples dancing and, hearing the women laughing in the arms of their partners, I thought of an Arabic saying claiming that "a woman is never weaker than when she is laughing." Unable for months to overcome my repulsion for alcohol, which would have lessened my timidity, I would sit in a corner for a while and then, stealthily, leave the party and hitchhike back to Middletown. I grew a beard and took to composing verses extolling my melancholy:

Searching day and night for an identity,
Ever evanescent, in the midst of shadows
I only behold a keen consciousness
Paining to surmount my sadness in exile.

It was not until the fall of 1963 that I built an intimate relationship with the daughter of a French visiting professor. But at the end of the semester she left the country with her family. In this time of great loneliness following the departure of my French girlfriend, I continued to take courses in political economy and political science, but the two years I spent at Wesleyan were marked by a great longing for friendship. A perpetual fear of failure haunted me, but whenever I felt my will falter, the mission that Amirouche entrusted to me, to get an education, kept me going.

The library, where I often found refuge among the 400,000 books for about 1,000 students, offered untold treasures for anyone who wanted to learn. I found Ibn Khaldun's *Prolegomena* translated into English as well as works by Albert Camus, such as *Actuelles III*. And in the music library, I was thrilled to find and check out discs by the Algerian singer-musician, Mohammed Al Anka.

While immigration was restricted for most nations, Sicilians continued to arrive and settle in Middletown on an almost daily basis. Curiously enough, as soon as they arrived, they began to invoke, with a pronounced Italian accent, "our Founding Fathers," adopting these bewigged gentlemen as if they were their own ancestors. This instant acculturation and assimilation, I quickly discovered, was a salient feature of many immigrants, bordering on the grotesque when they refused to teach their native language to their children.

In Algeria, meanwhile, where a civil war was narrowly averted in 1962, the power of President Ben Bella, or rather Colonel Boumediene, was firmly founded on the weaponry of the former Border Army. The army-controlled government quickly replaced the emblematic National Liberation Army with the National Popular Army. Ben Bella and Boumedienne rejected the plea made by Aït Ahmed, one of the nine leaders of the revolution, for a constitutional convention, drafting in a movie theater, with a group of their followers, a constitution tailor made for them. In September 1962, Ben Bella, the sole candidate, was "elected" the first president of independent Algeria. Aït Ahmed formed an opposition party, the Socialist Forces Front (FFS) in September 1963 and led a guerrilla movement based in Kabylia against the government. But a Moroccan invasion of contested border areas in October 1963 restored national unity. Aït Ahmed could no longer count on Kabyle support and was arrested in 1964.

Calm had returned to Algeria and I stopped having to avoid the biting remarks of a French student from Alsace who missed no opportunity to proclaim sarcastically, "We should have stayed in Algeria to prevent you from slaughtering each other."

I was soon given the opportunity to get even with him. When the university organized a debate between the two of us on the war in Algeria, I had no difficulty getting the better of him. I had the huge advantage of a better mastery of the English language, political maturity, and, above all, an edge in historical knowledge. I convincingly swept aside his allegations and his sophistry regarding France's accomplishments in Algeria and the dubious, self-serving myth of President de Gaulle "granting independence" to Algeria.

"France's achievements in Algeria?" I sneered. "Ninety percent rate of illiteracy at the time of independence."

"France, a land of Human Rights?" I asked. "Forty-five thousand Algerians killed in 1945 just because they were protesting their conditions of servitude and demanding rights: justice and freedom. Ten percent of the population liquidated in almost eight years of colonial war. Twenty percent thrown in so-called regrouping camps."

Then I added: "De Gaulle granted us independence? Don't make me laugh. It was under his reign that the most genocidal, most lethal military operations were organized against the Algerian freedom fighters. To no avail. He traveled to Algeria in December 1960, convinced that his army had brought an end to the insurgency, and hundreds of thousands of Algerians confronted him in the streets of Algiers, demanding independence. A year later, he sat at the negotiating table with the "terrorists" and the "rebels.""

Some time later, at the beginning of 1963, I engaged in a heated debate with a colonel in the Marines. That sharp exchange occurred in a seminar on U.S. foreign policy in Southeast Asia. Because I was an ex-freedom fighter, common knowledge since the debate with the French student, I was often asked to give my views on the conduct of that other anachronistic and inherently senseless conflict, the Vietnam War. The colonel, who was preparing to rejoin his unit in Saigon, developed the outline of a war plan based on strategic hamlets and the organization of counter-guerrilla forces living and fighting in exactly the same conditions as the Vietcong guerrillas in the jungles of South Vietnam. The colonel was convinced that this strategy would be certain to defeat the Viet Cong. I pointed out that the strategic hamlets were nothing more than a new label for regrouping camps, an unsuccessful strategy practiced by the French Army in Algeria.

Of course, I added, one can easily surmise from a cursory reading of *Revolutionary War* by Mao Zedong that when guerrillas live among the people like fish in water, the enemy need only remove the water—the people themselves—to asphyxiate the fighters. But to kill those fish, one has to take away gigantic amounts of water, to displace millions of people and thereby turn them into deadly enemies. As for counter-guerrilla forces, the French Army suffered a stinging defeat in Algeria during Operation Blue Bird. In 1956, I explained, French Special Forces equipped hundreds of Algerian guerrillas with modern weapons, who promptly joined their revolutionary brothers and staged two deadly ambushes against units of the colonial army.

I had great difficulty convincing the colonel that the Vietnamese, contrary to myth, did not fight for the triumph of communism in the world, but to liberate and unify their country. I recalled that French propaganda during our war of independence constantly raised the specter of communism engulfing North Africa if France abandoned Algeria. I tried in vain to persuade my audience that the Vietnamese were first and foremost patriots and nationalists; the Vietcong primarily a liberation movement. But I was preaching in the arid desert of political bias and propaganda

253

fed by the press and the White House, all of which allowed the noxious mixture of lies, deceptions, and rationalizations to go unchallenged for almost ten years.

Of course, my ideological positions were perceived as leftist, hardly endearing me to Wesleyan's overwhelmingly conservative students. The Algerian leader who captured the headlines, Ben Bella, only exacerbated the increasingly tense U.S.-Algerian relations. When he arrived in New York on October 5, 1962, for the admission of Algeria as the 109th member of the United Nations, my feelings were mixed. On the one hand, I bitterly resented the fact that Ben Bella rode to the presidency on the shoulders of the do-nothing Border Army, safely sitting in Tunisia and staffed by Algerian deserters from the French Army. I felt that Ben Bella, Boumedienne, and their troops should be held accountable for the spilled blood of those guerrillas who, after thwarting for years deadly French Army operations mounted against them, were felled after the ceasefire by those who chose an ignominious path to seizing power.

But on the other hand, I found that this demagogue's high-risk stands echoed my own ideological inclinations. When the *New York Times* of October 9, 1962, featured Ben Bella on the front page embracing Cuban President Dorticos at the United Nations, I was not upset. I was invited to the reception hosted by the Algerian Permanent Mission to the U.N., and was not displeased that President Ben Bella projected the image of a man of the people. On this occasion, I met a remarkable diplomat and a true gentleman, Raouf Boudjakdji, future ambassador of Algeria to India, Switzerland, and the Vatican. In addition to his diplomatic duties, Boudjakdji served as an advisor to Algerian newcomers like me. He constantly argued against mixed marriages, and I had to laugh as he abruptly changed his tune, when he himself tied the knot with an American journalist.

Almost immediately after the ceremony admitting Algeria as a U.N. member, Ben Bella breached what the White House called diplomatic rules by flying directly from New York to Havana. I remember telling myself that the Algerian President was pushing too far the international nonalignment stand that he had just affirmed in his speech to the U.N. When he landed in Cuba, Ben Bella accused the United States of feeding tensions in the Caribbean with the 1961 Bay of Pigs invasion of Cuba. I thought at the time that moving from guerrilla tactics into the diplomatic arena and placing Algeria on a collision course with the strategic interests of a great power could be very dangerous for the Algerian president. His legitimacy was based almost exclusively on the political indifference of the people, focused on recovering from so many years of war, suffering, and grief.

The leftist orientation of Ben Bella's regime was particularly criticized by *The New York Times* and by Franco's Spain, especially immediately after the October 1962 Cuban Missile Crisis. At Wesleyan students of all nationalities lived through these dramatic moments in unbearable anguish, breathing a sigh of relief when the crisis was peacefully resolved. But the threat of global cataclysm made me more aware of my expatriate condition. I had no desire to be annihilated in a senseless war before having a chance to see my now independent country.

I was also intensely eager to reunite with my fellow combatants who had survived the war and, most of all, to see my parents. My father had just been released from the concentration camp of Berrouaghia. My mother stubbornly refused to believe that I was still alive, since nothing could justify my absence now that we had driven the French out of Algeria. Unable to understand the difference between primary school and university, she wouldn't buy the story that her son was still attending a school at the age of 26. I thought with a pang in my heart of the feeling she invariably expressed whenever one of her many sons upset her: "Some of my sons will be loving and affectionate, some might be like the French." There was no phone line in 1962 over which she could speak to me and recognize my voice. Illiterate, she could not read a letter from me and recognize my handwriting. She was one of the 6 or 7 million illiterates that 132 years of the French "civilizing mission" had bequeathed to those who took over the country.

I resolved to write to President Ben Bella himself to state my case for returning to my homeland. I argued that my position as a mujahed, personal secretary, and companion to Colonel Amirouche entitled me to a round-trip ticket to free and sovereign Algeria. A few weeks later, in early summer 1963, I was astounded to learn from my country's embassy in Washington that the Algerian presidency would bear the travel expenses of all Algerian students in the United States, on the condition that we participate in a literacy campaign launched by the president. I prepared feverishly for the journey but told none of my family members, not even my brother Lahcène, with whom I corresponded frequently.

255

Chapter 23
Return to Algeria:
Euphoria and Melancholy in a
Liberated Land

◆

A powerful depravity perpetually drives certain individuals.
Ahitous the Blacksmith

I landed in Paris in July 1963, without being subjected to the humiliating procedures that the French require of Algerians applying for a visa today: proof of accommodation, bank statement, round-trip ticket. At Orly Airport, it seemed to me that the face of the customs officer tightened a fraction of a second when he read the name "Amirouche" on my passport. But perhaps it was only my imagination. I felt uneasy strolling through the streets of Paris, a city I was visiting for the first time in my life. Years later, during a Damascus-Paris flight, a French Jew sat beside me and wanted to know why I had never spent a holiday in his country. I answered that I felt in France what a Jew who survived the Holocaust must feel when he visits Germany. He changed the subject.

Forty-four hours after that first stop in Paris, I arrived in Algiers, tense with emotion. I have often tried to recollect my initial impression on that day when I first set foot in my free country. But the Algiers of the summer 1963, I have never been able to reconstruct. I do remember, though, that I was quite surprised to be surrounded by younger and older men alike offering to carry my suitcase. In my naïve vision of post-independence Algeria, I had always associated the miserable task of porter with the French occupation and colonial exploitation, but of course these men still needed to make a living, independence or no. I booked a hotel room not far from the railway station and took a walk along the waterfront to the former Horse's Square where a statue of the Duke of Aumale had once stood. As Governor-General, the Duke had received the surrender of Emir Abdelkader in 1847. The statue had been toppled with independence and the plaza renamed Martyrs Square. Along the way, turning left and right, I almost expected to encounter a patrol of green locusts, those notorious French paratroopers in camouflage uniforms. The last time I had visited Algiers was in 1955 during the Easter break. I remember filling the large pockets of my fur-collared parka with books acquired for a few francs. W.E. John's tales of Biggles, a British fighter pilot in the First World War, had fascinated the village blacksmith I had been, even after spending a year at the vocational school in Bejaia. It was then that a patrol of soldiers surrounded me and asked, "What have you got in your pockets?"

"A few *Bigglaès*," I replied. But the patrol leader had already started pulling out and examining the books.

258

"It's pronounced 'Biggles,'" he corrected. He must have decided that any Biggles reader with blue eyes could not harbor evil intentions, for he let me go.

I continued my stroll to Chartres Plaza. It was in that neighborhood that, during the height of the revolution, the young militant undergoing his initiation into guerrilla ranks met his fate against a barbed-wire fence. The obstacles that had turned thoroughfares into dead ends were no longer there. Also gone were the *chevaux de frise*, the defensive structures blocking traffic. I returned to my hotel somewhat gloomy but keenly aware that I was living my first moments of freedom in my homeland. The next day I took the Bejaia train towards my hometown of Tazmalt.

On the way, in the region of Palestro, the site of fierce fighting during the war, I saw where trees had been chopped down and caught a glance of the watch towers left behind by the colonial army. I never imagined that they would serve again when the *Algerian* Army sought to suppress an Algerian insurgency 30 years later. The train stopped at Beni Mansur to allow travelers from Constantine to board. It was at this station in 1955 that I had seen my father chained and escorted to the toilet by two gendarmes. I relived the extraordinarily bold exchanges between prisoners and peasants. They were no longer afraid—rather, it was the policemen who were nervous. I smiled at the memory of the coded phrases exchanged. "How is the country?" asked the prisoners.

"The sauce is quite hot and will burn the locusts," replied the peasants standing on the platform. Even under colonial oppression, their sense of humor had not lost its bite. The patriotic flame had melted the chains of servitude. We were free, we had cut loose our nation's ship—but soon incompetent leaders, for whom the lust for power and authoritarianism is pathological, would run the ship of state aground.

To think I was going to see my dear father again, after seven years of separation. What a journey his had been! Activist at the North African Star, member of the radical nationalist party PPA/MTLD, and finally of the National Liberation Front. The hideous walls of the Civil Prison in Bejaia had closed in on him for the first time in 1945, then again from 1954 to 1955. Abuse and torture had marked his time in Algerian and French prisons until independence was proclaimed in 1962.

The same monotonous voice as in 1955 interrupted my thoughts. "Travelers bound to Bejaia, please board, the train is about to depart." After a quarter of an hour we were in Tazmalt. At four o'clock in the afternoon, it was still very hot. I spotted the only taxi parked at the station, put my suitcase in the trunk, and told the driver, in the local accent, which direction to take. He stared at me for a moment and tried to guess what family I could possibly belong to. Finally, unable to control his curiosity, he asked, "You come from France, right?"

"Yes," I replied. Our home was less than a mile from the station, so he had no time to figure out what kind of immigrant worker dressed in white pants and a plaid jacket. I paid for the ride, took my bag out of the trunk, and, for a few moments, stood frozen in front of our house. I glanced toward the majestic Djurdjura Mountains.

The door to the forge was not locked. I left my bag in the shop and walked into the courtyard. My mother was sitting on a wooden bench with a glass of tea, surrounded by my brothers and sisters. She was wearing the typical Kabyle scarf of yesteryear, it seemed to me, black and yellow, and a yellow dress held by a long braided belt shimmering with colors. Tattoos covering her neck were her only adornment. A sudden silence fell over the family circle. My mother stared at the bearded stranger in dark glasses. I still don't know who recognized me first and cried out, "It's Hamou, it's Hamou!"

Everyone rushed towards me. My mother's smile sparkled with tears and she offered a spontaneous gesture deeply engraved in my heart: her hand on my head, she invoked divine protection.

"It's the jackal's feast," she murmured to explain her tears of happiness. In Kabyle folklore, the jackal's moment of joy comes when a rain shower falls in bright sunshine, accompanied by a beautiful rainbow. During this blissful moment of reunion I hardly recognized my siblings, for they had changed so much. They were now teenagers in high school and my two sisters, Djamila and Aziza, seemed symbols of a new era. Unlike my mother and my sister-in law, they could read and write.

After a quarter of an hour, my father appeared in the courtyard, completely out of breath. Ignoring the dignity of age, he had run across the village when he learned of my arrival. A broad smile as I had never seen before was on his face, and his blue-gray eyes, bright as stars, reflected boundless happiness. Wrapping me in his powerful arms, he nearly choked me. He was not wearing the elegant suit and tie of the pictures taken in Paris. That had been a disguise, he explained to me later, which, combined with the color of his eyes and fair complexion, allowed him to avoid for three years the nuisance of being profiled in the street and subjected to questioning. Back in his home, he was dressed in a white shirt and pristine white robe, sleeveless as if air-conditioned.

What a joyous day in the home of Ahitous! From the terrace

of the house next door, no Senegalese mercenary would ever again threaten my youngest brother, Smail, now an adolescent and as clever and mischievous as ever. Kabyles, he asserted, don't know what self-criticism is. When they feel they deserve a reprimand, they briefly claim an Arab identity, to criticize themselves: "*We Arabs,* never we Kabyles, are worthless" and then they would resume their lofty poise of *Imazighen,* men of heights.

The next day I savored, bit by bit, many small and simple pleasures. The whole family was gathered at full strength for the first time in seven years and I had much catching up to do. I learned, for instance, of the miraculous survival of my older brother, Sharif, a fundraiser for the National Liberation Front. Taken to the notorious prison camp of Tizi Neslev to "fetch wood," a phrase coined by the French soldiers for summary executions, he was rescued by my mother's nephew Moussaoui. Also a blacksmith, Moussaoui was delivering tools ordered by the French Army; he arrived at the camp just in the nick of time.

"But that's my cousin!" Moussaoui cried when he saw my brother tied up on the truck. An extra-judicial execution could not be carried out with a member of the family witnessing.

"Are you sure?" asked the officer in charge of the camp.

"See our identity cards, sir." The officer reluctantly obliged: Moussaoui was indeed the name of our mother. My brother was helped down from the truck and released a few months later, but not before he had been routinely abused by the French soldiers.

The second day of my return, I set out to gather information on my fellow combatants, those still alive and native to the region. I visited Brahim Berkani, director of a hospital in Akbou, to whom I had left my automatic pistol when I departed for the United States. I also found Hamiti, a machine-gun ace, and many others. I knew that the Revolution had arrived just in time to spare Hamiti a sinister career in the local mafia, and to erase the stain of being the first, in the history of the village, to be jailed for robbery.

However, it was with my quiet childhood friend Messaoud Ouchouche, another hero of the Revolution, that I lived a moment of bliss. I had not seen him since the Battle of Ouzellaguene where the famous warrior Chaïb had been killed. Messaoud seemed to be in buoyant health; he appeared intact but not quite, since a burst of submachine-gun fire had destroyed a good part of his left forearm shortly before the end of the war. He suffered a great deal and barely escaped amputation before being treated with the utmost dedication by the same doctor that Colonel Amirouche had almost sentenced to death for refusing to join the guerrillas.

I spent days receiving and greeting family members as well

as friends and war comrades who came to salute the companion of the great Amirouche. In conversation with my mother, I regained my fluency in the pure Kabyle language, untainted by Arabic or French. I never imagined that I could forget my mother tongue but, away from home for so many years, there had been few opportunities to use it. Only illiterate people like my mother, those who do not master a foreign language, or our modern-day troubadours, seem to have preserved or restored the purity of the language of our ancestors.

It's this unpolluted language that I rediscovered again in 1980 in, of all places, Damascus, during a reception at the Algerian Embassy. The Ambassador, the late Abdel Kader Ben Kaci, introduced me to a Kabyle whose grandfather had accompanied, in his exile, the Emir Abdelkader in 1855. He spoke to us in the Tamazight of the late 19th century, which Ben Kaci and I had great difficulty comprehending. This was the Kabyle language that many poets and singers strove to restore many years later—but which my mother had no difficulty understanding.

For now, radiating happiness, she would not leave my side. She had difficulty acknowledging me as an adult, repeating that I was too young or too old. "You're too young, my son, to sport a beard, shave it off," she said, or "You're too old to go to school, you have studied enough, you must marry now."

"Yes, Yemma," I replied in a conciliatory tone. "I will marry an American girl as in the song: 'Wake up, my son Mohand, your wife is not pretty,'" I hummed. "Never mind, Yemma, for me she's an American…"

She began to laugh, then frowned at the possibility, and finally concluded, "What is decreed by God is decreed, my son." And it was decreed, as we shall see, that I would return home, four years later, with my American wife, Mary Elizabeth Doyle.

During that summer of 1963, my exchanges with my father were of an entirely different nature. Of all members of the family, he was the one who had suffered the most from occupation and oppression. I wanted so much to hear him tell his story and describe the appalling prison system into which he was plunged in 1945, 1954, and 1960. His confidences were subdued and his face contorted whenever I mentioned abuse and torture. He would begin his narrative in a whisper, looking down, but would never finish it. He was not the kind of militant to parade his woes.

Clenching his teeth, he told me that the ignoble constable M.M., the object of my childhood hatred for confiscating my slingshots, arresting me in a classroom, and handing me over to the police, was now secretary to the mayor of Tazmalt.

"As Algeria's independence became imminent," he told me, "a few days before the announcement of the Evian Peace Accords, French authorities planted a gun in his desk drawer, detained him, and claimed for all to hear that he was a National Liberation Front militant. Shortly after independence, the sinister ex-constable, an administrative agent barely able to read and write, became the town clerk and was awarded a veteran's card and a pension.

"When the police arrested me in November 1954," my father reminded me angrily, "they came to search the house but found nothing incriminating. But this scoundrel led them to the secret room a block away where Si Larbi Oulebsir and I held our meetings. And there they found incriminating documents. You know the rest."

Yes, I did know what happened next: torture, a 16-month prison sentence, five years of banishment from Tazmalt, and subsequent confinement in St.-Maurice-l'Ardoise in France and the Berrouaghia prison camp at the confines of the Sahara desert.

"And you didn't denounce him?" I exclaimed.

"What for? Let the abject character answer to God's judgment. Besides, do you know who one of his family's daughters married? A National Liberation Army officer."

"So what? A traitor is a traitor and must account for his cowardly deeds," I answered.

"Forget it," my father ordered me in a gentle but assertive voice. "It's enough that he looks down and switches sides on the street when he passes me."

The contempt and loathing the ex-constable aroused through his double betrayal could not be clearer in my father's voice. Kabyle like my father, the man had breached kinship solidarity and shamed his tribe; and as a collaborator and informer for the colonial police, he betrayed a national cause. My father's touchy pride was certainly a factor that came into play: he would not condescend to challenge this obsequious licker of colonial boots, whose family hastened to consent to the marriage of two of their daughters with senior officers of the National Liberation Army, thus warding off his prosecution for treason.

For a moment I thought of one aspect of the relations between social classes that the Revolution had dramatically altered. It would have been unimaginable before independence that Constable M.M.'s family, belonging to the wealthy land-owning *bourgeoisie*, would consent to the marriage of their daughter with the son of a peasant National Liberation Army officer. The Francophile bourgeoisie declined in the social scale as the patriotic peasantry ascended. The revolution had brought them together in

263

its own way.

I thought about the other betrayal of May 1945. Again, my father was convinced that he had been fingered to the French police. How else could one explain that the pack of French soldiers and Moroccan Tabors invading our home had headed, without the least hesitation, to the vine where the war rifle was buried? It was obvious that my father knew the culprit who had turned him in. However, there again, he opted for God's judgment. He used exactly the same phrase as 16 years ago: "Let God sentence him."

So I let it go. Out of respect for my late father's injunction, I refrain today from revealing the name or even the initials of this disgusting character whose children were granted French citizenship by the grateful nation of France.

Perplexed by my father's tolerance, I wondered if the influence of Imam Abdel Malek Foudala's sermons had inspired his forgiveness. In the noblest and most generous spirit of Islam—or Christianity for that matter—Abdel Malek preached brotherhood and harmony, constantly reminding us of a saying of the Prophet Mohammed: "None of you is a true believer if he doesn't wish to his fellow man what he wishes for himself; and that if a man avenged the evil that was inflicted on him by his fellow man, he stooped to his level of baseness and became his equal. By contrast, if he forgave him, he hovered over him and was morally incomparable."

That Abdel Malek Foudala was himself betrayed was firmly established. An informer had reported Abdel Malek's journey to Algiers, where he was assassinated, execution style, by French paratroopers. I raised with my father the hypothesis that the informer might have been the constable. He remained silent for a moment before giving me his terse response. "When someone opens the door of betrayal, he can't close it. A powerful depravity perpetually drives certain individuals. Forget all that and keep focused on your studies."

Then he added, in a lighter tone, "How about showing us some war pictures?"

With that, the treacherous constable who intruded into our conversation vanished, a ghost without humanity and therefore without substance. I went to my room and brought back the treasured photo album. Still today, whenever I lose track of it among my countless books, newspapers, and war memorabilia, I almost faint with panic and despair. I held the album on my lap while my mother, four brothers, two sisters, and a swarm of unruly nieces formed a circle around me.

With a mixture of pride and melancholy, I showed the

264

photographs taken between 1956 and 1958. "You see these two handsome guys with me," I said. "They were Colonel Amirouche's aides-de-camp. This one was killed in the same battle as Amirouche on March 28, 1959. That one, a year later, not far from Tazmalt. Not one of these warriors, officers, or soldiers that you see here has survived the war. This is Colonel Si Mohand Oulhajj of Wisgane who took over after Amirouche was killed, with other officers of the Third Military Command."

"Mohand Oulhajj is from the Akli family," clarified my father who had known him before the war.

"This soldier is Sliman Laïchour, Amirouche's trusted courier. Sliman and I were sent together on a mission to Tunisia."

I told of our epic march of more than 40 days and our perilous crossing of the Algerian-Tunisian border. I showed my favorite picture that I can never contemplate without being overwhelmed by a deep emotion: Colonel Amirouche, his arm nonchalantly resting on my shoulder. When I came upon the photo of Lieutenant Chaïb Mohand Ourabah, battalion commander who was killed the day we became acquainted with the horror of napalm, the words stuck in my throat. In the midst of my exuberant family, I was nonetheless surrounded by the ghosts of my fellow mujahedeen. They will haunt me to the last days of my life. I stood up and let the family continue looking through the album amidst the bustling toddlers.

Chapter 24
Pilgrimage and
Childhood Memories of Life
Under Colonialism

First they ignore you, then they laugh at you,
then they fight you, then you win.
Mahatma Gandhi

The days were long in July and I had well over two hours before sunset. I went out into the former Alexander Celio Street, now Mosque Street, and walked to the river, that idyllic place where I had enjoyed the simplest and purest pleasures of my childhood. In 20 minutes I was greeted by the cooing of doves and the ruckus of myriad sparrows preparing to spend the night in the giant eucalyptus foliage along the river.

This bucolic spot carried me back 15 years. It was nearby that friends and I, fishing with a blanket, would catch small mullet and the rare eel. One day a peasant walking by with his wife and daughter, furious to see us splashing half naked in the river, was about to chastise us. My friend Mohand Cherradou took off his jacket, and we understood why he had kept it on despite the heat. He had a pistol tucked into his belt. We were greatly impressed, and the farmer even more so.

"What exactly do you want?" yelled Mohand, who at 15 was the oldest among us. "Is this river your father's?"

Mohand was from Taqarvuzth, a village which was derided quietly—very quietly—for the primitive ways of its insolent and bellicose inhabitants. It was extremely rare to meet a Qarvuzi who was not proudly wearing at his belt a sharp knife of respectable length that would come swiftly out of its sheath as soon as someone angered him. That day by the river, the passing peasant was not aware that he was dealing with a Qarvuzi, but he had no need to know: after one glance at Mohand's gun, he kept silent. He continued on his way with his family while his daughter cast a sidelong glance at us each time her father's vigilance slackened. Remembering this incident, I could not help laughing heartily and promised myself to ask about my childhood friend.

Monsieur Merlot's vineyard was still there, thanks probably to the powerful eucalyptus roots that had protected it from erosion by the stream, meager now but wide and swiftly flowing in fall and winter. This beautiful vineyard, the delight of hungry children recruited for the grape harvest, was to become part of the self-managed nationalized farms. "The country is ours, but the land is theirs," our farmers had often said before independence. This was no longer the case: the land would now belong to those who tilled it. That, at least, was the slogan of the Ben Bella regime. After the expulsion of the settlers the peasants now tilled the land that was, for the time being, state owned.

I saw an elderly woman weighed down by a bundle of wood, the only fuel used for cooking, one measure of the huge gap between our society and the one to which I was becoming accustomed in America. A farmer dressed in rags and leading his donkey loaded with hay was a faithful reflection of a time that, in my imagination, I thought was now gone. The donkey made me think of all those animals who had participated in the revolution with us. We gathered more or less reliable statistics on the countless number of Algerians killed or missing during the war, but nobody will ever know how many donkeys, mules, sheep, and goats had been targeted by the French Air Force, nor the number of dogs that we deliberately slaughtered ourselves to prevent their warning bark.

Goats, as we have seen, were the first to learn to lie down under a bush as soon as they heard the deafening roar of a war plane. That instinct for self-preservation, combined with a learning process, is characteristic of every living being. Years later, snorkeling near Algiers, I encountered a grouper, famous for its impressive size, that a swimmer could approach and admire as long as he or she was not carrying a spear gun. But when a hunter appeared with a crossbow, the grouper disappeared in a flash.

Except for a narrow stream, the wide riverbed was now dry. In autumn or winter, flash floods swept away everything in their path, including careless humans. We said that these unfortunates had been eaten by the river and spat out as if by Tseriel, that ogress of our childhood tales. Memories besieged me, but my perception of the surroundings had drastically altered. This favorite place of my childhood would forever be associated with the war. One evening in 1957, a French Army operation forced us to wade across an icy waist-deep river in the middle of the night. When we arrived at a safe house shivering from cold, it was out of the question to take off our uniforms to dry them. We approached the fireplace and dried ourselves as best we could before lying down on a mat to get a little rest.

This day I crossed the river, jumping from rock to rock between islands of tamarisk bushes and a few puddles of still and greenish water. I looked at the trickle of the stream gradually thinning under the blazing summer sun. What a difference between this and the Potomac River in Washington where, for a few dollars, I rented a canoe and learned to row, or the 407-mile-long Connecticut River that flowed through Middletown half a mile from my university. The strange names of these rivers intrigued me. I discovered that these were Algonquian Indian names: Potomac meant "place where one is trading" and Connecticut "Long River."

269

I thought of Indians, equally victims of land expropriation and massacre, tribes whose languages had completely disappeared. They survived by selling tourist trinkets to the condescending white race, smug like the French settlers in their superiority over the unsophisticated heathen. I thanked God that our people had thwarted the tragic fate of the natives of America.

Colonialism had not only taken everything from us, it had also deprived us of the dignity of life. Today's Algerian youth have no idea of the cruel nature of colonial occupation. Many of them reproach us for having fought in a revolution that dispossessed them of the inestimable privilege of being born "French"—as if it were entirely our fault that many of them drown trying to cross the Mediterranean to France.

In our family, thanks to my father's trade, we never went hungry. But I vividly recall some of my classmates in primary school overcoming their shame to beg me to bring them a slice of bread, even was an old crust dry and hard as a rock. Under French rule, we rarely had a congenial gathering for a cookout, a birthday celebration, or toys for the children. When one of our comrades, of less wretched parents, brought a rubber ball, we were thrilled to improvise a soccer match in the dust of a waste ground. Those who had no shoes required—baring their teeth and clenching their fists—that every kid play barefooted. Wading in the river, clustering around a rubber ball, and hunting birds were our only entertainments.

On this day by the river, the sky was blue and cloudless. In the bush, especially in the flat and barren areas of the Wilaya I Military Command stripped of vegetation by the French to facilitate the incursions of their troops, we had been frustrated by cloudless skies, perfect conditions for sweeps and aerial bombardments. We favored a low sky, even streaked with lightning and threatening a downpour. We preferred the night darkness to the sun; a gray and gloomy sky, a thick and chilly fog, to a clear blue sky.

A light breeze along the riverbed brought a hint of freshness from the Mediterranean, 80 kilometers away. In the distance, a few storks perching on their long legs took advantage of the last rays of daylight to snap up a frog. I thought of these small amphibians, so graceful with their mottled green, a gold ring around the muzzle. They were fun for target practice with a slingshot, and as we killed them we rationalized that we were easing the task of the storks who would spot our targets, floating white belly up in the blue stream.

Thinking of the cold winters of Connecticut, the unbearably humid and mosquito-infested summer heat of Washington, I breathed the fresh air in my liberated land reluctant to exchange it for any other place in the world. As twilight slowly descended over the valley, I also had a fervent thought for the hundreds of thousands of martyrs who had made possible the magic of these moments of freedom and harmony. I could never have imagined then that Algerians themselves, in the name of republican values, and so-called Islamists in the name of God, would turn our country, 30 years later, into a slaughterhouse of terror.

With dusk, the chorus of sparrows and cooing of doves subsided and gradually faded away; it was time to go back home. Standing on the doorstep before entering the house, I looked at the dark imposing mass of the Djurdjura Mountains a few kilometers away. A few scattered lights began to flicker like stars up in the village of Aït Hamdoun. It was in that blessed town, which had endured so much hardship during the war, that I had met Amirouche, the legendary hero who changed my destiny. I still felt so vividly his arm resting affectionately on my shoulder. I could still hear his powerful voice, unaltered by time and space as if echoed by the mountain: "God, alone, is great."

Eighteen of us gathered for the evening meal. In my honor and contrary to custom, it was not my sister-in-law but my mother who meticulously prepared dinner. To her, I was still the capricious kid who demanded fine-grain couscous and threw a tantrum each time he caught sight of the skin of a fresh tomato floating in the sauce. I realized with some chagrin that the portions of meat, except for mine, were as meager as ever. And for good reason: a year after independence, nothing much had changed economically, either in the country or in my family. But now, at least, the girls went to school, unafraid of life as in the past. They were no longer born to find their seat at the table taken; they were no longer trembling and hiding behind the skirts of their mother when, last to be fed, they ventured to ask for food.

After dinner, while we were drinking our mint tea, I was peppered with questions about almost everything regarding my life during the past seven years: as a guerrilla, in Tunisia, and in the United States. My older brother Sharif, a passionate lover of Westerns, had introduced us not only to the Arabian Nights, but also to the Texas Rangers who hunted down bandits dead or alive; he asked me about the "Redskins" and the "Wild West."

"You know, Sharif," I replied, "there are nearly 3,000 kilometers separating the state of Connecticut from the state of Texas. Indians no longer wear feathered costumes, except to impress tourists. They wear neckties and three-piece suits and speak American English without any accent. Their native languages have almost completely disappeared."

In my turn, I too asked a lot of questions. I learned that my Uncle Ravah, after 20 years of marriage, had taken a second wife in the hope of having offspring at last. In the tradition of the time, it was common for a family without sons to adopt a nephew, always on the brother's side, as an heir. But my uncle had chosen to turn his back on this tribal tradition. When I went to greet him in his shop the day after my arrival, I saw that he was not much changed by age. His small and sunken eyes, as piercing as an eagle's, accentuated his sinister features—until a friendly smile lighted up his face. As soon as he saw me, he broke into a grin and hugged me affectionately. Then he opened his box of chewing tobacco, took a generous pinch and, before placing it under his tongue, said, "I hope you're finally home for good."

"No, Uncle Ravah, I have not finished school." And because he was famously miserly with his money and sensitive to the purely material aspect of my absence, I added, "I will earn more money if I study a few more years."

"You apparently don't know the story of the jackal," he chided me.

"Which one, Uncle Ravah?"

My uncle lifted his cap with one hand, scratched his shaved head with the other, and spat tobacco juice onto the dirt floor of his forge. Then he answered, "One morning, the jackal decided to treat himself to a lamb. So he lay in wait to ambush the flock when it came into view, led by a huge ram.

'This one is too big,' thought the jackal. He sized up the next sheep as too thin, the next as too big, and so on until the last of the flock disappeared. Once the shepherd and his mighty dog were out of sight, the jackal cried, 'Quick, the droppings while they are still warm!'

I burst out laughing and promised my uncle to retain the moral of this fable: to get a job before all the best positions were filled.

That night, jet lag and the excitement of the day made it difficult to sleep. Before finally drowsing off in the early morning hours, I made plans for the following day: I was going on a sacred pilgrimage. I set up an appointment with ghosts.

My battlefield pilgrimage began with the sun blazing into my room to wake me up. I heard with incredible pleasure the familiar sound of the hammer on the anvil as cooking aromas penetrated my room. Quickly washing at the outside faucet, I joined the family in a room with a fireplace that served as our kitchen.

My sister-in-law was frying donuts, surely in my honor again, since we were normally entitled to this delicacy only to celebrate Eid Sghir at the end of Ramadhan. I savored with pleasure this flavor of the past. The last time I had eaten one of these shoe-shaped donuts, size 16, was in the mountain village of Semaoun in the fall of 1957.

"What do you take my son, black coffee or with milk? asked my mother.

"Just coffee, Yemma. I'm fed up with milk."

I explained that in America we could fill and refill, endlessly, our glasses with milk in the Georgetown University cafeteria—"a milk fountain, Yemma." I'm not sure she believed me.

Immediately after breakfast, I put on sneakers and announced to my mother that I had some business to attend to; that she should not worry if I came back very late. Unlike her, my father had ceased long ago to wonder about my strange disappearances. I found him at his forge, busy with my older brother repairing farm machinery. As a former blacksmith myself, I surveyed the tools waiting to be repaired, assessed the work load, and left reassured.

I took Mosque Street towards the railroad station. Along the way, I made a brief stop at the imposing mosque, and had a thought for Imam Foudala who had filled the vast prayer hall with his exceptional—and seditious—oratory. Across the street, the former Catholic Church, where now was displayed the Algerian flag, had changed vocations and been transformed into an office of the National Liberation Front. The Christian invaders of 1830 had experienced no qualms turning mosques into churches, and even into bars or stables. With independence restored, a number of churches regained their original status as mosques, while convents were closed, illustrating the degree to which the messages woven into the Abrahamic religions had been twisted. Regrettably, the spirit of the Crusades was stubbornly alive.

I remembered the day when, in front of this place of worship, I sat on the low wall that enclosed the church. While I was bird watching, a passing gendarme ordered me to leave the premises. Often when Algerians resigned themselves to their state of servitude, the contemptuous arrogance of the occupier woke them up like a slap in the face. I still remembered the incident after so many years because my self-esteem was deeply wounded even then, at the age of eight or nine. Architects of their own downfall, the French had never missed an opportunity to stir up Algerian hatred.

Before reaching the train station, I made my last stop in front of the primary school. I spared a loving thought for Monsieur

Fernand Avril, the most dedicated teacher I have ever known, the man who stubbornly guided eight of his pupils to receive the first primary school diplomas in Tazmalt's history. Yet because the teacher had dared to slap one of Mayor Robert Barbaud's sons, Monsieur Avril was banished from Tazmalt.

At the railway station I felt the oblique stares of other travelers, certainly because of my American jacket and dark glasses, and especially my beard which was rare in 1963. I purchased a round trip ticket to Ighzer Amokrane, wondering what effect my pilgrimage would have on my psyche.

The train pulled into the Ighzer Amokrane station shortly before noon. The blistering July sun kept people inside and animals under the shade of olive trees. Standing in front of the station, I surveyed the mountain before me. Then I took the narrow path between two rows of cacti which, like the town's inhabitants, were slowly coming back to life. Because they provided excellent cover for guerrillas, the colonists had bulldozed cactus stands.

The upward climb began about a mile from the station. With no submachine gun, ammunition belt, or briefcase to slow my progress, I felt light as a feather. Besides, I was walking in broad daylight in my liberated country, having driven out the occupiers. I quickened my pace; I had an appointment with spirits and souls who must not be kept waiting.

After two hours I entered the village of Ifri, site of the historic Soummam Convention that organized the Wilaya military commands in 1956. I could see, here and there, the rubble of huts partly or completely destroyed, most probably belonging to guerrillas who had been betrayed. I could not remember where, exactly, the safe house we had stayed in was located and where, at about eight o'clock in the morning one day in February 1958, we were alerted by a blast of gunfire. Nor could I tell under which grove of trees Colonel Amirouche had deployed our small group. But I knew it was halfway between the village and the wild and barren peaks of Aït Zikki.

I climbed another 500 meters and decided that the exact spot where we had outlasted the hellfire of the French artillery and aircraft did not matter. Sitting against an oak tree, I surveyed the fields and low stone walls behind which Chaïb Mohand Ou Rabah's battalion had wiped out the first row of the French force. I saw him again, tall and lanky, recklessly exhibiting his scarlet cap despite stringent rules requiring each one of us to conceal our military headgear in daylight. I thought I still could hear the 105-millimeter cannon shells exploding around us, scattering chunks of earth and fragments of rock, muffling the crackle of submachine gunfire. So close to meeting our Creator, I remembered that I had looked up to Heaven for help.

But Heaven remained silent and indifferent. Only B-26 bombers circled above our heads, dropping their deadly cargo. Closing my eyes, I could still hear Amirouche's voice so soft and brotherly, anxious to instill courage under bombardment, speaking directly to me. "You're scared, eh?"

Of course I was afraid, Colonel, sir. I was only 20 years old and did not want to forsake my blank page of a life, hardly sketched, barely started; I did not want to face Azrayen, God's feared inquisitor.

Now, five years later, in subdued and silent meditation, I looked around as if expecting to see, emerging from behind the bushes, the ghosts of my dead companions. Dead? No, they are in every home and the unborn child, in their country liberated from the paratroopers. They are in these bare and majestic peaks of the Aurès and Djurdjura Mountains. They are reincarnated in this sacred land soaked with their blood. They are the wind that gently sways the olive trees. They are in each one of us, where they will live forever.

After my pilgrimage, I pledged to myself that I would perform dozens of others, travel hundreds of miles in daylight for a change, through the territories of the Wilayas I, II, and III Military Commands. I would visit all the villages where we found hospitality, where men and women spread over us, like an invisible mantle, their protective blessing. More than anything else, I was determined to go to Azrou, or what remained of it, to ensure that it was rebuilt—and do everything possible to find the old lady who, watching her village burn to the ground, uttered that heartbreaking blessing that so deeply moved me. Unfortunately, and this is one of the biggest regrets of my life, I was unable to honor my oath because almost immediately after I retired in 1987, the combination of disastrous leaders and Islamists determined to displace them, led to major upheavals in the country.

It was with a heavy heart that I walked back to the railroad station and returned home. Despite my mother's insistence that I was too old to go to school, four weeks later I was back at Wesleyan University, for the mission entrusted to me by Colonel Amirouche to get an education had yet to be accomplished.

Chapter 25

Falling in love with Colorado and Betsy

Those who love deeply never grow old;
they may die of old age,but they die young
Arthur Wing Pinero

At Wesleyan University, the years 1963 and 1964 were marked by hard work not only to satisfy the requirements for a Bachelor's Degree but also to keep the Algerian student journal going. I edited material sent by my fellow students and wrote articles analyzing the impact of the French-Algerian exodus to France, advocating land reform, and defending the Non-Aligned Movement of which Algeria was a prominent member.

The kitchen facilities of the Wesley Club, where I lived, allowed me to prepare my breakfast and lunch. For dinner, fraternities took turns feeding me. The protocol was so strict and so irritating, requiring a jacket and tie, that one evening all the students of the EQV Fraternity came down to dinner completely naked except for the ties hanging from their necks. Embarrassed by this incident in front of a foreigner, the head of the fraternity apologized to me.

On weekends, I would no longer hitch a ride to Bennington or Wellesley but travel two hours southwest to New York City, which had become my weekend headquarters. Naturally, one of my first visits took me to *le machin*—the thing, as French President de Gaulle had contemptuously referred to the United Nations.

In June of 1964, at the age of 27, I was awarded a Bachelor's Degree, along with my roommate Larry who immediately left for Chicago to be married. Although I was invited, I couldn't afford the trip. Instead, I sent him a humorous gift with my heartfelt congratulations. Besides, before leaving the U.S. for good, I had to attend a meeting of the Algerian Student Association in Boulder, Colorado. Instead of a week, I ended up staying there three years!

I fell in love with the Rocky Mountains, which reminded me of my native Kabylia and the Djurdjura Range. My friend and "eggs-any-style" Washington companion, Majid Aïnouz, who was completing his engineering degree in Boulder, hosted me for a while. I found a job as a French teacher and could afford to register for graduate courses in political science. The University of Colorado, numbering 30,000 students, was a microcosm of the world, boldly contrasting with the tribal-like social homogeneity of Wesleyan. "Welcome where the West remains" was the sign that greeted every newcomer, and to me the West symbolized open minds and a cultural diversity in which Saudis and Hippies, supporters and opponents of the Vietnam War, found a peaceful coexistence. Soon I made more friends, both male and female,

278

than I could handle. In the three extraordinarily gratifying years that I spent at the University of Colorado, I never heard from a young woman that loathed phrase, "I don't want to get emotionally involved." Ironically, although I never actually said it, I was now the one who was occasionally inclined to pronounce the words that had pained me so much at Wesleyan.

When a close friend, Margie Davis, introduced me as Algerian to her roommate Mary Elizabeth Doyle, called Betsy, she pulled back, eyes wide open. Betsy had just spent a year studying in France, associating with French-Algerian diehards who convinced her that Algerians, among other evil inclinations, specialized in pinching women's bottoms in the Metro. It was a sad reminder of how easily prejudices can be manufactured. Luckily in this case, they were just as easily dispelled.

Despite my newfound ability to befriend young women, I took on a more exciting challenge: to earn the friendship of the only girl who exhibited outright suspicion towards Algerians. Betsy was of Irish ancestry from Boston. Seven years older and a graduate student, I soon became like a brother and mentor to her. There was no telephone in the studio I rented, so Betsy served, for all intents and purposes, as my operator. She scheduled my meetings with students and dates with young women, meeting me every day for coffee and a briefing in the University cafeteria. I also joined the University soccer team, got my driver's license, and purchased an old Studebaker, which made life even easier for me and my friend Betsy.

I remained intellectually active, speaking in churches on Islam and Muslims and the Algerian war of liberation, and participating in debates on the Vietnam War. The mainstream media's interest in Algeria and its vexing pro-Cuba stand had not relented three years after independence. At the end of the 1965 academic year, I was invited to give a talk at the University to assess the situation in North Africa and provide insight on the Algerian political system. In a packed room on June 18, 1965, I pointed out that for a government to endure, regardless of its configuration, the consent of the governed is not required. All that's needed is the indifference of the governed. Since that was the case in Algeria, I maintained that the Algerian regime, under President Ben Bella, was the most stable in Africa. The day after, that very regime was overthrown!

Luckily I had just been accepted for a summer teaching position at Manchester College in New Hampshire and could escape without having to endure sarcastic comments about my political prescience. My sharp-tongued friend Majid, however, never misses, to this day, an opportunity to remind me of my poor reading of Algerian power politics.

At Manchester, I taught a course on French Culture and Civilization and founded and edited a newsletter called *La Plume Enragée* (The Rabid Pen). Before the end of the summer term, I was offered a permanent position but declined. I wanted to complete my graduate studies at the University of Colorado. Perhaps my friendship with Betsy came into play as well. So, when she invited me to spend the weekend in Boston to meet her parents, I quickly accepted. At that time, "getting emotionally involved" to the degree of proposing marriage to an American woman never crossed my mind, so I was not particularly worried about the impression I was going to make on Betsy's family. Her mother, Mary, although a devout Catholic, was also spiritually close to Christian Scientists and a fan of Theihard de Chardin, the French philosopher and Jesuit priest.

Betsy's father, J. Paul Doyle, a lawyer, architect, and retired Massachusetts Commissioner of Corrections, was known for quelling a 700-inmate prison riot with a speech and a promise to dramatically improve conditions, a promise that he kept. I was impressed by a clipping from the *Boston Evening Globe* of March 1, 1946, with the headline, "Doyle Meets Committee of Convicts." In that article, the journalist pointed out that "Massachusetts penal precedents were broken today when State Commissioner of Corrections J. Paul Doyle conferred this morning on grievances with a 12-man committee chosen by inmates of the State Prison at Charlestown." To think that a man of his standing exhibited the political courage to oppose the Vietnam War made me admire him all the more. Back in 1965, such opposition was depicted by some vocal and influential media as akin to condoning communism and capitulating to evil.

Although J. Paul Doyle attended and sang regularly at the Boston College parish church, he transcended, like me, the stringent injunctions of scripture. He demonstrated a remarkable degree of tolerance, even if, as Betsy later told me, he pointed out the precedent of her older sister who dated a Frenchman while studying in Paris, ultimately breaking off the relationship because of major cultural differences. He reminded his younger daughter, then just 21, that the cultural chasm would be even wider with a Muslim Algerian. Happily, our future proved him wrong.

Back in Boulder, Betsy and I continued to see each other almost every day and, without being fully conscious of it, our relationship grew deeper during the years 1965 and 1966—as well as worrisome for me.

"A bourgeois girl, born to upper-middle-class parents, who own multiple homes, and vacation in Europe, or Florida in winter and Cape Cod in summer, will never adapt to life in Muslim Algeria," I kept reminding myself. So I began cautiously to broach the subject. One day, over a pizza and a beer, I raised the sensitive issue of religion and quietly said, "You know, Betsy, I am convinced that the stronger you believe in a particular religion, the more you exclude all others, and that breeds intolerance."

"You mean to say that you don't adhere to any religious beliefs?" she asked.

"That's what I mean. I don't, except for their ethical underpinnings."

Betsy didn't even finish her pizza. She got up to leave and said, "I don't think we have much in common if you don't believe in *any* religion. Good bye."

I couldn't believe it. (No play on words!)

How vividly I remember that late autumn conversation in 1965. Students were spilling out of a Colorado vs. Oklahoma football game and soon the pizza joint was crammed with young people, shouting over the music playing "Go Away Little Girl."

I ordered another beer and assessed the situation. At first I seriously considered forgetting about Betsy, completing my graduate work, going home, and letting my parents arrange a marriage with a good Berber Muslim. But I liked Betsy very much. My relationship with religion and the Almighty being what they were, I thought that our different perceptions of religion were not sufficient cause for ending a promising relationship.

Back at my studio, I drew a picture of myself looking gloomy, recognizable only by the beard. Under the drawing I wrote, "I am sad." I put it in an envelope, wrote Betsy's name on it, walked to her dorm, and left it with the resident advisor. Returning to my studio, I tried to focus on my courses and the preparations for the French classes I was teaching. In the late afternoon, when I answered the doorbell, Betsy stood there. She fell into my arms and, figuratively at least, has never left them since.

Nevertheless, although our relationship had reached a point of no return and the moments spent together incredibly gratifying, I never said the word marriage. I was not convinced that our love would overcome the daunting challenges of cultural adjustments, nor that my family would welcome her as their own daughter.

The summer of 1966 provided an opportunity to find out. I was elected by the Algerian Student Association to represent the U.S. Chapter at a national convention in Algiers and, after the convention, I spent more than a month in Tazmalt with my parents. Naturally, my mother reminded me how old I was and how urgent it was for me to get married before she passed away. I had anticipated this.

"You know, Yemma," I said, "I think I found the girl that I will marry." And I showed her Betsy's picture.

My mother looked at the photograph, nodded, and said, "She is pretty. What's willed by God is willed. Does she speak Kabyle?"

"No, Yemma, but you will teach her." I entrusted her to announce the news to my father, knowing that if he had objections, he would convey them to me before I left Algeria.

During the long stay in my hometown, I missed Betsy to a degree that I had not anticipated. At night, before falling asleep, I looked at her picture and agreed with my mother: she *was* beautiful and still is. Slightly built, she stood five feet six and was always impeccably dressed. Aside from her long auburn hair, her most striking feature was her blue eyes in her peaches-and-cream complexion. I imagined her living in Tazmalt, learning enough of my native tongue to communicate with my mother, gradually adapting to Kabyle ways. Could love overcome such cultural barriers? I didn't know the answer, but it was in Tazmalt that my decision to propose to Betsy was made. Almost as soon as I returned to Boulder, I proposed. Her eyes, welling with tears, said yes, but she managed to say, "I'll have to think about it." And while she was thinking, we began to make plans.

I had to complete my Masters' thesis that year, 1966, and decide if I wanted to pursue a Ph.D. Betsy had to graduate from college the following year and then, perhaps, we would marry. Still harboring great misgivings about her ability to meet the daunting challenges of cultural adjustment, I began telling her what life in Algeria would be like. If she wanted to roast a chicken, for example, she had to buy it live, cut its throat facing east to Mecca, clean it, and cook it. Canned and frozen vegetables and refrigerators were unheard of. Then one summer day at Boulder Creek, I rolled up my pants, waded into the shallow stream and said to her, "To eat chicken in Algeria, I told you what you will have to do. For fish, it will be much easier. Watch me!" I reached to the bottom of the brook, and using a trick I learned in the Soummam River as a kid, I came up with a fish in my hand.

"Wow!" she exclaimed. "With you, I'll never go hungry." Still, I knew that she would be taking a chance if she married me. "She is only 22, for God's sake," I kept reminding myself. I did not want to ruin the life of a young girl who clearly was ready to jump into the unknown and follow me to Algeria. An opportunity

282

to dissuade her was soon provided.

One morning as I entered my office, I found two pigeons sitting on the desk. Trapped in the room, they had soiled exam papers. I remembered what I had told Betsy about catching live chickens and cutting their throats and saw a way to shock, once and for all, the wits out of my fiancée. I caught the birds, sliced their throats, wrapped them in an old newspaper and, after cleaning my desk, called Betsy to invite her to dinner at my studio. When she arrived, I said: "Here is dinner" and opened the newspaper. When she saw the birds and the bloodstains soaking the newspaper, she nearly fainted.

"That's what you will have to expect from life in Algeria. Pigeons are fowl in Algeria. Only fish don't get their throats sliced before being consumed."

Betsy did not break up with me and found the pigeons cooked with peas quite tasty. That was an encouraging sign.

At the end of 1966, I completed my thesis, took my comprehensive oral exams, and was awarded a Master's Degree. While waiting for Betsy to finish her senior year and graduate, I took advanced courses towards a Ph.D. We were now informally engaged and as soon as she graduated, we left for Boston in an old Ford Galaxy which we had just purchased together. Although I had completed almost all requirements for a Ph.D., I suddenly felt tired of it all and, using the pretext of a sharp argument with one of my professors, abruptly decided to leave the U.S. after the wedding—for good, or so I thought.

During the long journey to Boston, we discussed wedding preparations. Having considerably changed her position on religion, Betsy proposed a civil marriage.

"You are a Muslim, I am a Catholic," she said. "A judge or a commissioner for civil marriages will marry us."

"No," I replied. We'll get married in a Catholic church. Personally, I really don't care one way or the other. But for your mom, it's important." Surprised, her beautiful blue eyes sparkling, she didn't say anything but reached for my hand and squeezed it.

A few days after we arrived in Boston, I began religious instruction with a charming priest who showed an unusual eagerness to learn about Islam. When I told him that Saint Augustine was a Berber from Algeria like me, he instantly became my friend and ally.

A Sicilian and an American, a gay couple from the University of Colorado, served as my best men. We exchanged vows in a Brookline Catholic church on June 24, 1967. Champagne flowed unrestricted the rest of the day as a number of guests eyed me with curiosity, but were apparently reassured that I was at least a white African Muslim.

Betsy and I headed to Maine for our honeymoon. In a log cabin built on a lake by Betsy's Uncle Frank Egan, our lyrical promises of unconditional love alternated with preparations for traveling to Algeria. We knew our plans could be hampered by the situation in the Middle East and North Africa. In the aftermath of the Arab-Israeli war, hardly three weeks old, Algeria had severed diplomatic relations with the United States.

After two weeks of bliss, marked by romantic outings on a rowboat, water skiing, and lobster dinners, we returned to Boston. Betsy took her passport to change her name, but the passport office stamped on it "No travel to Algeria" and most of the Middle Eastern countries. Stranded in Boston, unable to find work, I decided to write to the State Department myself. My letter began "I am an Algerian who wants to go home…" It did the trick. The ban was lifted, for us anyway.

My brother Lahcène, now a prominent agricultural engineer, the first ever of our tribe to earn an engineering degree, met us at the Algiers airport. His wife Hacina, a schoolteacher and the first Algerian woman Betsy met, was lively and exuberant, immediately putting her new sister-in-law at ease. After spending the night in Algiers, Lahcène drove us to Tazmalt where a huge celebration was waiting for us. A lamb was slaughtered and the local Muslim cleric blessed our union. Betsy could not communicate with my mother or other elderly women, but she got along quite well with my two teenaged sisters. While I was chatting with friends and family on the first floor, Betsy was surrounded by a platoon of kids and women on the second. One of my nieces rushed down to tell me that Betsy was crying. I dashed upstairs and sure enough, she was in tears.

I couldn't take her into my arms; the customs of Algerian culture did not permit it. So I just said soothingly, "Come on now. Everybody loves you. I am staying here with you." I had, in fact, anticipated such a rude awakening. Was it finally dawning upon her that her patience and understanding of the Berber culture were going to be sorely tested, and that love alone might be powerless to help her adapt?

After spending three days in Tazmalt, Lahcène drove us in his old jalopy to a beach near Bejaia, the city where so much of my destiny and my father's had been determined. We stopped near the sinister civil prison which still hosted undesirables just as under French rule, but now they were political prisoners opposed to an Algerian government. We rented rooms in a hotel right on the beach, and I will never forget Betsy's thrill when she entered the waters of the Algerian Mediterranean for the first time in her life.

"It's so warm," she cried. I was recording every factor that would ease her adjustment to her new life in Africa, and the temperature of the sea was one of them. "Yes," I said, "it's not the melted ice of Boston beaches."

I also knew that the bonds that she would make with my parents would be the decisive factor. After an unforgettable week at the beach, Lahcène drove us back to Algiers where we found a temporary residence in my older brother's villa, while I looked for a job and an apartment to rent.

The first six months we lived in our first home together took a toll on our patience and tested the harmony of our marriage. Betsy could not find a job in Algiers, and for lack of transportation, she could not accept a position she was offered teaching English in a high school in Blida some 50 kilometers away. The house had no heating system, so during the freezing winter months Betsy stayed home, reading novels in bed under heavy blankets. For the first Thanksgiving we celebrated in Algeria, Lahcène supplied us with a live turkey which we kept in the yard for a few days. On Thanksgiving Day, I handed a knife to Betsy and matter-of-factly said to her, "Catch the bird, face east to Mecca, and cut its throat."

She said, "I'd rather make my reservations and face west to Boston if I have to do that."

I relented. "Okay, I'll do it and you help me clean it."

Although the bird was skinny by American standards, it was quite tasty since it was a free-range turkey.

In my quest for a job, I made my first formal visit to Colonel Mohand Oul Hajj, then a member of the Executive Secretariat of the National Liberation Front. He received me affectionately in his sparsely furnished office and immediately sensed that the purpose of my visit was to ask for some favor. While my intention was to put myself under his orders, I changed my mind when I realized that the army alone wielded power in the country: the National Liberation Front "ruling party," by any measure, ruled nothing.

My second visit was to Belaïd Abdessélam, the Industry and Oil Minister who, unwittingly, had determined part of my destiny by sending me to the United States. He greeted me warmly and offered me a position in his cabinet, which I immediately accepted. As soon as I took office at the end of the summer of 1967 as counselor, I was petitioned by my former comrades-in-arms seeking employment. The compelling case of one of them, an immigrant worker settled in West Germany when the Revolution broke out, determined my attitude.

"I was married to a German woman and had two children," he told us. "I earned decent wages as a skilled worker. I could even send remittances to my father in the village. For months, I pretended not to hear about the war, not to see anything in the news. And honestly, I thought that the November 1954 insurrection was going to be just another May 1945, crushed again in blood and iron. Then one day in the cafeteria, a German comrade made a remark that I felt like a slap in the face: 'I can't figure you out, Tahar. Your brothers are fighting and dying every day to free your country and you...' A sudden silence wrapped our table and my fork remained suspended in the air. I didn't say anything. A few days later, I asked for my pay and left."

I saw a cloud of sadness darken his face and I was sure he was thinking of his two daughters who had stayed in Germany. But he quickly pulled himself together and, in a lighter tone, remarked: "You, the educated, you will occupy high positions of responsibility in independent Algeria. And when we ask to see you for a job, you will tell your secretary that you're not in your office."

Of course not, I protested in good faith. During the long years that I spent at the Ministry of Industry and Oil, the leading provider of nonagricultural employment in the nation, or as a chief executive of an Algerian-British engineering company, whenever my secretary announced a former mujahed, I remembered Tahar's remark and made myself immediately available. I felt I was reliving the moments with Amirouche who, in every place he visited, granted an audience to any villager with a grievance. Luckily, the 20 years I worked in the oil and industrial sector coincided with the launching of major job-creating projects. So my positions in Belaïd Abdessélam's cabinet and later in the engineering company enabled me to secure employment for my fellow guerrillas, most of whom were illiterate.

But for now, my position as advisor to the Minister was quite challenging: I was in charge of monitoring industrial development studies entrusted mostly to U.S. firms, and negotiating joint stock ventures designed to benefit Algeria with badly needed transfers of technology. Although I was earning a fairly high salary, because of the lengthy bureaucratic procedures to process my file, I did not receive my first pay until some eight months after I started work.

Luckily, we had hinted before our marriage that, as far as wedding gifts went, dollars traveled much better than crystal or silverware. While eagerly awaiting my first pay, we lived on the $2,000 we brought with us and, when that money was gone, had to borrow from my brother.

"You're not crazy about life here, are you?" I asked Betsy in a tone which couldn't disguise my sadness.

"Do I have to be crazy about it? You're here now. I wait the whole day to hear the outside gate squeak, knowing it's you." Choking with emotion, I didn't say anything; I just took her into my arms and hugged her.

In those interminable months, spring took forever to bloom. Poor Betsy, underfed in a freezing cold house, never complained, and her patience and love never wavered. I remember telling myself that if she did not return to the cozy bourgeois life of Boston, if our marriage did not dissolve then, it never would.

Then one day, I was notified that my eight months' pay was ready to be picked up. The equivalent of some $5,000 was handed to me in cash, checks being unknown in Algeria in the 1960s. When I arrived home I found Betsy under the covers, although it was spring. I opened the bag containing the cash and poured the banknotes on the bed.

"Wow!" she cried. "How much is that?"

"The purchasing power for 10,000 pounds of fresh Mediterranean jumbo shrimp or 5,000 bottles of the choicest Algerian wine."

"Let's go buy a bottle. Who said that money can't buy happiness?"

"Usually, I am the one who has the good ideas," I joked. "But today, you beat me. Let's go."

It was a short walk to the small grocery store that sold the best red wines I have ever tasted. We chose a 1949 Frederick Lung which the French settlers had had the good sense to leave behind. It sold for the equivalent of 60 cents a bottle. Everything we wanted to buy was suddenly underpriced.

That day marked the beginning of a major transformation of our life together. Soon, less than a year after we arrived, Betsy was hired to teach at the American School of Algiers. She remained there throughout the 70s and early 80s, until she was appointed Director of the United States Information Services Language Institute. She became Principal of the American School in the late 80s. Meanwhile I was promoted to Chief Executive of an Algerian-British engineering company, a position which provided Betsy with a chauffeur and a full-time maid and cook, both paid for by the government as part of compensations granted in kind in "socialist" Algeria.

We moved from the damp and unheated villa to a government-owned three-bedroom apartment just before Betsy's parents came to visit in 1968. They were anxious to find out how their youngest daughter was living among the nomads. They had noticed that we bought a small tent and a sleeping bag before we left for Algeria. When her father asked Betsy what the tent was for, she answered with a straight face that "in Algeria, they don't have houses."

The same day they arrived we took them to dinner at one of the fanciest restaurants in Algiers, The Tent. During the few weeks they spent with us, they obstinately refused to try another restaurant. Eventually Betsy's two sisters and her brother came visiting. By then, we had rented from the government a beautiful 12-room villa overlooking the Mediterranean, which we later purchased when real estate was privatized in 1986.

My parents visited regularly as well. Betsy found in my mother the love and affection she never expected to receive in a Muslim land. Eager to see Betsy pregnant, as soon as she arrived in our home, my mother would put her hand on Betsy's abdomen and ask: "Boy or girl?"

"No, Yemma, chocolate cake."

It was not until 1971 that we had our daughter, Malina, and then, in 1973, our son, Djorf.

The way Betsy conquered the hearts of my mother and father is worth telling. Betsy's Irish ancestors had fled the terrible Irish famine of the 19th century, and she demonstrated some characteristic features of a people who suffered from hunger in their brains and not in their stomach, as my Uncle Ravah would say. This cultural similarity immediately attracted my mother's attention. While her other three daughters-in-law threw away stale bread, my mother noticed that Betsy used it as raw material to bake a delicious bread pudding. The American instantly became her favorite daughter-in-law.

"This girl is my girl, my son; she really shows respect for bread," observed my mother.

My father, inclined to sweeping generalizations like most autodidacts, concurred with a nod, "No wonder the Americans are so rich."

If I ever raised my voice towards the American, my father would instantly take me aside and reprimand me. "Don't you ever forget our noble traditions, my son; this girl is an exilee and, as such, sacred; she has no father, mother, or brother nearby to look after her, from whom she can seek protection."

I must say that Betsy was instrumental, among other feats, in bringing about a *ghazw al-thaqafi* or a cultural invasion, to borrow from Islamist ideology: the joyous celebration of my parents' birthdays for the first time in their lives. My American also

288

submitted with sardonic humor to the 1984 Family Code passed by Parliament, making her a minor who could not leave the country without my written authorization duly stamped and notarized. Inspired by Islamist conservatives in the National Assembly, the Code also legalized the practice of polygamy.

Throughout the late 60s and 70s Betsy had been welcome among Muslim families everywhere, from the Sahara Desert to the Djurdjura Mountains, to the cities of Algiers, Oran, and Bejaia. Feeling love and affection wherever she traveled in Algeria, she celebrated with the same uninhibited enthusiasm Christian as well as Muslim holidays. All this played a decisive factor in her acculturation. But by the mid-80s, as was evidenced by the Family Code, the semblance of secularism that had pervaded Algerian society became a thing of the past. More and more veiled women and more and more robed and bearded men in the streets were the first warning signs that fundamentalists were beginning to assert their authority in our country.

"She is pretty," said Yemma, "does she speak Kabyle?"

Chapter 26
The End of Socialist Utopia

The security of a republic or of a kingdom does not depend upon its ruler governing it prudently during his lifetime but in so ordering it that, after his death, it may maintain itself in being.
Niccolo Machiavelli, The Discourses

If the building of a bridge does not enrich the awareness of those who work on it, then that bridge ought not to be built and the citizens can go on swimming across the river or going by boat.
Frantz Fanon, *The Wretched of the Earth*, 1963

For a decade after independence, gigantic domestic industrial projects sustained the firm belief among Algerians that their nation had the means to develop a modern economy and build an army capable of dissuading any aggression against the country. But we soon lost the pretense that we could "catch up with Spain," ultimately discovering that self-sustaining economic and social development was a delusion without the effective participation of the people. It dawned upon us that no real stability was possible without legitimate political institutions resting on universally accepted conventions, on the conditions for the acquisition, use, and transmission of political power. We became helpless witnesses to the bloody riots generated by a general strike in May-June 1991. Ordered by the Islamists to protest an electoral law outrageously favoring the ruling party, the strike sparked off violent confrontations. Calm was restored only after several hundred peaceful protestors were killed.

On December 26, 1991, when I cast my ballot in the first democratic legislative elections ever held in Algeria, I told myself that the ultimate case for democracy was that it worked in one crucial way: it eradicates arbitrary rule and violence from politics. The first fair and unfettered elections in the Arab World, which the Islamic Salvation Front was poised to win in a crushing landslide, occurred in Algeria 19 years before a young Tunisian torching himself triggered the so-called "Arab Spring."

However, the reckless decision by the Algerian Military to cancel the democratic process on January 12, 1992, set the stage for the protracted civil war that tore the country apart for the next ten years. The military coup instantly raised an issue of decisive importance: if free elections bring to power antidemocratic and fundamentalist groups bent on putting an end to the alternation of power inherent to the political process, is their suspension justified?

Because the drama was the first of its kind in the Arab world, it generated what came to be known as the "Algerian Complex"—dreading elections which produce an Islamic state. Until the Arab Spring resulted in the popular overthrow of autocrats in Tunisia, Egypt, Libya, and Yemen, the stunning triumph of the Algerian Islamists seemed to sound the death knell for democracy in the Arab world. The ideological rationale hastily put forward by the Algerian Army, and endorsed by influential Western media, was that democracy cannot benefit a party vowing to end it once in power.

To be sure, the dubious argument was put forward that an Islamist party that comes to power through universal suffrage will not act the same way as one that gains power through revolution, as in Iran, or in a coup as in Sudan. But the Islamists could not overcome the suspicion harbored towards "fundamentalists."[76]

The Algerian Army could not reconcile itself to the notion that democracy, by definition, signals the end of military rule. Just as in Egypt 21 years later in 2013, the army, fearing that an elected civilian president might get "Western" ideas and proclaim himself commander-in-chief, put an end to the democratic process. The Algerian nation's rulers reflected the paradoxes that ultimately undermined their power: they underestimated the creative force of intelligent thinking and could not anticipate the tragic events that were to tear apart the nation.

I held a enduring grudge against Boumediène for the more than 2,000 mujahedeen his troops killed in 1962 to seize power and impose the demagogue Ben Bella as the first president of the Algerian Democratic and Popular Republic. I hated him even more when he chose to overthrow Ben Bella's regime and become president himself at the very moment that I was stressing its stability in my talk at the University of Colorado.

I met President Boumediene only twice during my professional career. The first time was in 1975 when Abdessélam, a colleague, and I submitted to the president a study projecting Algeria's needs for the next 20 years in terms of cereals, milk, meat, fruit, and vegetables. We pointed out that, in order for the country to cope with the vital necessities of a population growing by 3.2 percent per year—one of the highest growth rates in the world—Algeria needed either to develop the equivalent of 75,000 additional irrigated farmland acres per year, or to enforce nationwide birth control measures.

Drawing in on his seven-inch Cohiba cigar, Boumediene exhaled and dictated his decision: "Altering the rate of population growth is out of the question."

Algeria was to pay a heavy price for that rash pronouncement. A unique phenomenon in modern times, Boumediene governed for 11 years without a constitution, without the usual makeshift parliament, without a political party, and with near total impunity. Populist policies, thanks to oil and gas revenues, offered free mass education, free medical care, full employment, and free electricity and gas to the most remote mountain areas, keeping alive the illusion that the government was for the people if not by the

293

people. Externally, Boumediene's authority and leadership in the Non-Aligned Movement made Algeria, at one point, "the single most influential country in the United Nations,"[77] in the words of a U.S. diplomat.

Boumediene, in the wake of his takeover in the June 1965 coup, pledged to create "the conditions for the establishment of a democratic State capable of surviving governments and men," but he ruled for 12 years with a tailor-made constitution and a parody of Presidential elections in which he was the only candidate and died without delivering on his promise. Aggravating this legacy, his successor Chadli Bendjedid charted a disastrous economic course fraught with corruption and nepotism after assuming power in 1979. The Iranian revolution had just boosted oil prices to levels unseen since the 1850s, when oil was first discovered. However, instead of pursuing and, above all, adapting the policies of his late predecessor—austerity, productive investment, and creation of jobs—Bendjedid took actions that led directly to the popular riots of 1988. His regime recklessly introduced a new consumption model, including massive imports of consumer goods ranging from exotic fruits to VCRs and Hondas, for the nomenclatura.

In the process, the government cancelled several crucial industrial projects—automobile manufacturing, steel, cement and petrochemical plants, oil refineries—along with huge contracts for the sale of natural gas to the United States and Europe. The regime thereby cut the country off from needed financial resources for self-sustaining economic development. When Algeria's oil revenues plummeted by more than 42 percent in 1986, the regime resorted to costly short-term credit and borrowing to maintain the level of vital imports. The subsequent servicing of the accumulated $26 billion foreign debt drained 75 percent of Algeria's foreign exchange. To add to our woes, technological innovations and the discovery of North Sea oil undermined the power of the OPEC oil cartel and choked small producers such as Algeria. The safety net holding up the mass of the population was shredded. The rescheduling of the debt and the structural adjustment program dictated by the International Monetary Fund and ending most government subsidies could only make things worse.

Meanwhile, a spiraling birth rate increased population by 800,000 annually, and the education system threw more than 200,000 young people into the streets as the lack of space in universities forestalled high-school graduation for more than 80 percent of the students. With an administration and an economy still functioning in the French language, the "arabized" graduates and dropouts formed an army of "hitists" (leaners against walls),

294

who expressed bitter resentment towards the "French Party." Agriculture was moribund due to cheap subsidized imports such as grain, vegetable oil, and milk. The major cities swelled as thousands of youngsters drifted away from the countryside and began sleeping in packed apartments, spawning shantytowns and increasing the burglary and petty crime rate to unprecedented levels. A major popular revolt was in the offing.

Living in a huge villa, we could hear, loud and clear, frequent comments from the street, that it was unfair that a family of four lived in a palace, while a family of ten had to share a single room.

Acute shortages, ranging from spare parts to flour, sugar, and potatoes, began in October 1988. Labor strikes crippled the large industrial complexes near the capital and fed rising social tensions. Police vanished overnight from streets and public squares. Mysterious provocateurs roamed the city in unmarked cars, firing randomly at demonstrators setting fire to symbols of the state: police stations, empty state-owned supermarkets, and the National Liberation Front headquarters. The riots were crushed by troops commanded by a former officer of the French Army, resulting in several hundred casualties.

The inability of the regime to respond to urgent social demands and buy social peace marked the end of an era and brought into the open an irrepressible demand for political change mustered by secular, essentially Berber, groups as well as Islamists. A generation after independence, blatantly incompetent leaders and the collapse of oil prices turned the same fringe Islamist movement of the 60s and 70s into a popular and powerful revolutionary force. The stage was set for one of the most vicious civil wars in modern history, a tragic repeat of the War of Independence.

The 1991 strike unfolded with the same fateful sequences as the bloody riots of 1945. History was not repeating itself, but it began to stutter. The massacres of 1945 led to the establishment of the first nationalist secret armed group, the Special Organization, in 1947. Similarly, the bloody 1991 crackdown on peaceful demonstrators resulted in the organization of the first armed Islamist groups. Structured and led by veterans of the war against the Soviets in Afghanistan, [78] which had ended in 1989, the Islamists engaged the Algerian government in a conflict from which the country is still reeling to this day.

Events picked up speed and caught everyone by surprise. A massive anti-Islamist demonstration by democrats on January 3, 1992, was led by one of the nine leaders of the Revolution, Hocine Aït Ahmed. His faction chanted "No police state, no

Islamic state," but proved powerless to stem the tide of violence that would tear the nation apart. Just as the colonial administration in 1945, and again in 1954, ordered the people to surrender their arms, the Algerian government issued a similar proclamation in 1992 requiring the people to hand over their hunting weapons.

I found myself brought 30 years back. We were experiencing not only "us at their age," but also the mobilization of army reservists by the Minister of the Interior, himself a former deserter from the French Army, just as French Army reservists had been recalled in 1955. I was reading again in the Algerian press, "twenty-one terrorists were killed... by the police... the Casbah lived yesterday a special day. Early in the morning, members of the security forces surrounded the area and conducted a sweep... a large quantity of weapons was recovered... by the police."

In my free country, I intensely relived the nightmare of occupation and war. I had the feeling that I was reading the infuriating columns of the 50s and 60s in *L'Echo d'Alger*, the settlers' daily, and not in the Algerian newspaper *El Watan* of November 26, 1996.

The terrorists began targeting foreigners. Twelve Croatians working on a dam were slaughtered in one attack in December 1993. Spaniards, Italians, South Koreans, Russians, citizens of various nationalities working in Algeria, were assassinated. Foreign schools were closed; the families of U.S. diplomatic personnel were evacuated, but Betsy adamantly refused to heed the advice of friends and family that she close the American School.

"The American kids are gone, but Nigerians, Indians, Pakistanis, and Bangladeshis are still attending my school," she said. "They're entitled to finish the school year too." The school was relocated to a dangerous cul-de-sac outside the security area of the Embassy premises. Although U.S. citizens had never been attacked, I was not about to take any chances.

So, leading a German shepherd in one hand and a great Dane/boxer in the other, I inspected the neighborhood every morning. If everything was clear, Betsy put on a head scarf and got in the car in the garage, with the German shepherd and a loaded automatic rifle in the back seat. We left at a different hour every day, varying our itinerary to and from school. Often, to foil possible traps, we spent the night with friends or at one of my brothers' homes. At the end of the day, when we were safely home, I would go down to the cellar, select the best wine in our reserve, and, with our two dogs at our side and my rifle leaning against the fireplace, polish off one more bottle to spare the fundamentalists the trouble of smashing it.

Our daughter would call me collect from the University of

Virginia and warn me, in tears, that if something happened to her mother, I would be the one held accountable.

"All foreigners have left Algeria," she repeatedly reminded me. "All foreign schools are closed. What is she still doing there?"

"Talk to her, not to me," I would wearily answer.

At the end of the school year in May 1994, we began to prepare for our departure. A Boston friend, Jane Howell, offered to host us until we found work and a place of our own. Betsy immediately sensed my reluctance to leave. "I spent 27 years in your country, more than I lived in my own," she said. "Now it's your turn."

I announced the news to my parents. Almost instantly, the indestructible blacksmith fell into a semi-coma and refused to take any food or liquid. It was almost as if he chose to pass away, a week before we left, at the age of 90. We buried him as a free man in the cemetery where, as a young militant, he had conspired to end his condition of servitude.

I entrusted our villa to my sister and her family. Two weeks later we landed in Boston where we were treated like war refugees, with benevolence and sympathy, by Betsy's two sisters, Bunny and Frances, Jane Howell, and her husband George Harrison. Betsy was home but I wasn't. As an ex-freedom fighter, I suddenly felt uncomfortable. Now everyone who knew me would pass judgment on my bravery: I had chickened out and fled my country, cowering before the Islamist terrorists who occasionally shot former mujahedeen who supported the January 1992 coup, thwarting their access to power.

A month or so later, I was back in Algeria. This time, it was Betsy who couldn't hold back her tears when she called me. And I missed her so much: 27 years of marriage had not altered our extraordinary love and devotion.

I strolled in my neighborhood, clean-shaven and dressed like a European, without my dogs, went shopping in Islamist strongholds in the Algiers suburbs, and for almost two months exhibited ridiculous, brazen postures sending the message that I hadn't cowered before the terrorists. But I began to feel more and more like an alien in my native country. I gave up deluding myself and entertaining the hope that some miracle would occur, that a secular Muslim like me, let alone a Catholic, could again live in the peace and harmony in which we had bathed for more than 20 years.

It was not to be. In pursuit of their objective, the establishment of an undefined and amorphous Islamic state, the armed groups were ruthless. They waged indiscriminate war on whole categories of people, rather than on the armed security forces defending an illegitimate government. Finally I gave up on Algeria and flew back to Boston.

The author with the late Indian Prime Minister in 1982 at a United Nations Industrial Development Organization conference in New Delhi.

EPILOGUE
No, Amirouche Is Not Dead

I wondered how anyone who survived war could ever be cruel to anything, ever again.
Anonymous

I was a mujahed and high-school student when I wrote the first lines of this story in the din of a smoky cafe in Tunis in the wake of Colonel Amirouche's death. Now, more than half a century later, the university lecturer that I have become is about to conclude the story in San Diego. During the years between, I have been a sad witness to a score of convulsions and tragedies in the world and in my native country.

The sight of my father's abuse in 1945, when I was seven years old, combined with the virtues of armed resistance, love of country, and pride of being Algerian that he instilled in me, forged my political consciousness and drove me to take up arms against the occupier when I was 19. Then Colonel Amirouche was instrumental in turning a blacksmith into an academic, graciously helped by the unforgettable friendship and private tutoring of a Jew, Alexis Stern, who refused to take up arms against the Algerian insurgents.

As I wearily observe the turmoil besetting the planet, one of my firmest beliefs is reinforced: the greatness of a nation lies not in the profusion of its natural resources, nor the size of its territory and the power of its armed forces, but in the wisdom of its leaders. Thucydides' (460-395 BCE) "Melian Dialogue" continues, regrettably, to define international relations: "In the discussion of human affairs the question of justice only enters where the pressure of necessity is equal, and that the powerful exact what they can, and the weak grant what they must."[79] When the weak, be they Algerians, Vietnamese, Iraqis, or Melians, rise in righteous anger and dare confront the powerful, the price exacted is dreadful, inflicting irreparable havoc on their societies for generations. But in a democratic system, when wars, massacres, and massive population displacements, whether in Algeria or Iraq, are committed following a "democratic" decision, it's out of the question to indict a whole people or a majority for war crimes at the International Criminal Tribunal. Nevertheless, a cursory study of history tends to substantiate the claim that it is hardly more than events underlying the rise and fall of empires. "Empires drive history."[80] Empires are the principal actors in the history of the world.

The Algerian President Abdelaziz Bouteflika and other political leaders, who insist that the French Government apologize for invading and colonizing Algeria, deserve the middle finger shown to them by French Minister Gérard Longuet.[81] They should be reminded that the French are equally entitled to demand apologies for a Muslim invasion from North Africa in the eighth century, when the Umayyad Empire occupied Spain and then invaded France, and was finally turned back at Poitiers in 732. After the Ottoman Empire became the "sick man of Europe," one of its protectorates, Algeria, was invaded and occupied for 132 years.

Ever since I inhaled tear gas during the bloody riots of June 1991, a sense of *déjà vu* has haunted me. During those demonstrations, my childhood friend and war companion Messaoud Ouchouche and I watched the young anti-government protesters who demanded an Islamic state, shouting, "For it we shall live and for it we shall die."

"Don't you think they are us at their age?" Messaoud said.

I felt that the comparison was superficial, so we let the mass of demonstrators go by, sat in a café, and continued talking.

"No, not quite," I said. "In any insurgency, ideology plays an essential role. For us, the struggle was waged in the name of the fatherland; for them it's for the cause of the Islamic state and, occasionally, the Arab Nation."

"How so?"

"Remember Sheikh Ali Benhadj's march last January and his declared desire to go fight for a secular, unrepentant Saddam Hussein, after saddling him with the name 'El Haddam' [the demolisher]? But ultimately, you're probably right. It amounts to the same thing. It's the same social revolt against a government's contempt for the citizens. Although articulated differently, it's the same quest for justice."

"Wait a minute," replied Messaoud. "What kind of injustices have they suffered? Have they ever experienced hunger and wretchedness? They have barely entered life and have taken to whining and complaining about lacking everything."

"Still," I said, "the current government is seen by some as alien and as tyrannical as that of the colonial rulers, even if the rebelling youngsters were almost all born after independence."

"I see nowhere any signs of their woes," said my friend. "If they want to take power, they must provide proof of their values and their virtues. What good have they ever done for the nation or for their fellow Algerians?"

"Messaoud, their ideology is a caricature of that homegrown saying, I'll play with you or ruin your game. Our politicians are not projecting uplifting qualities. In a democracy, when the citizens are unhappy with their leaders, they vote them out of power. In our

301

country, it's just the opposite. When the government is displeased with citizens, it gets rid of them. The nation no longer generates inspiring leaders such as Amirouche. Even among Islamists. Although the Islamic Salvation Front inherits a healthy revolt that they could have steered towards major and peaceful change, its leaders are novices in political strategy."

"I don't agree," said Messaoud. "They did win last year's local elections and control the majority of municipal and provincial assemblies."

"Yes, but look at how they are running them. They are self-serving instead of attending to the people's problems. Religious fervor conspicuously and vocally displayed belies the flagrant lack of morals in their actions."

My friend replied, "God bless the martyrs, the founders of the nation who have left us too soon. But I am optimistic that this is just a slump. We went through a period of despair when Ferhat Abbas had virtually dismissed the notion of an Algerian nation rising from the ashes, after consulting with the dead [82] as well as with the living. Algeria will eventually empty its bowels of these leaders that impose their rule. If Colonel Amirouche had survived, the nation would not be in this state today."

"It is impossible to gauge the 'if's' of history." I said. "One thing is certain: if Colonel Amirouche were still alive, he would have devoted his whole being to the causes he espoused, defense of justice and equality."

Messaoud said, "And what makes you think he would not have ended up managing a restaurant like Colonel Saddek, a gas station like Colonel Ouamrane, or a brick factory like Boudiaf?"

"Never! He would never have tolerated the anti-popular drifts, economically and socially disenfranchising so many citizens. I believe he was a born statesman who would have played a decisive role in modernizing Algeria and empowering the dispossessed. Having said that, I often think of a book about the Russian Revolution that I read in high school, *How the Steel Was Tempered* by Nicolai Ostrovsky. There is a passage where the author observes that the same men, legendary superhuman heroes during the revolution, turn into pathetic and commonplace citizens in civilian life. War acts as a great revealer of human nature. Don't forget that Colonel Amirouche, was a modest tailor and jeweler before the Revolution. Perhaps the thought of imminent death unleashes in humans sublime actions and makes them transcend their insignificant pettiness. War brings out in men the noblest qualities and the willingness to accept the ultimate sacrifice for a just cause."

"Or the other way around," Messaoud wryly observed.

"Yes, you're right. War brings out the worst, too."

"Is it not us, at their age?" Messaoud mused again at the sight of the rising tide of protesters surging through the streets of Algiers, shouting their quest for an Islamic state just as we, at their age, had demanded a free and independent Algeria. It *was* us all right, except for the beards and the robes ostensibly proclaiming a religious rather than a national identity. A spontaneous outpouring of sympathy had drawn us towards these young demonstrators. We realized that dialectics were at work, that a nebulous process, bordering on the absurd, was unwinding and would soon unleash violence and senseless killings, a tragic continuation of politics by other means.

In taking stock of our lives, as my war companion Messaoud suggested, I thought of the men who most influenced the course of my destiny. Chance and fate placed in my path the great leader Amirouche, without whom I might never have gone beyond a humble vocational school diploma. Living abroad, I see myself accused by members of my "tribe," just as my father was, of breaching ancestral tribal rules and abandoning the land where I was born.

Reliving the times that have so deeply affected Messaoud and me, I think of his unshakable conviction that the nation will eventually uproot from its ranks the self-appointed leaders that have led us to disaster. Naturally, I have a fervent thought for all those humble and anonymous heroes of the war of liberation, such as our revered Imam and my father the blacksmith. Driven by an indestructible faith in our struggle, they mingled their diverse voices in the patriotic chorus.

In concluding my story, I tell myself that there is no perfect hero in the history of the Algerian Revolution, unless one, perhaps, who died in battle. Other colonels, fierce warriors, ended their careers managing restaurants or gas stations, serving as ushers, or were lured to chair a High State Council and then assassinated. They had risked their lives to accomplish a sacred duty, without bombast or clamor. They had their moments of glory and their combat cannot be erased from the history of the nation, yet few people sing their legend. How many of them still among us, watching their nation rebuilt with blood and tears, have resigned themselves to the unjust and arbitrary rule that explains Algeria's endemic violence? Do those unsung heroes mean anything at all to today's young boat people attempting to cross the Mediterranean to Europe? Or to potential suicide bombers still fighting the Islamist battle? Born after independence, some of them douse their clothes with gasoline and set themselves on fire. Few of them ever asked me about the heroic actions of the War of Independence. They would stare at a future that rejects them, at a government that represses them, and, after repeated tourist visa denials by the French Consulate, say to me, "Monsieur Amirouche, why did you fight in the war? You know, if you hadn't, I'd be French now."

The tragic end of my chief, Colonel Amirouche Aït Hamouda, inspired me to write the first melancholy verses of a poem in March 1959. Decades later, I completed it in San Diego. My verses are powered by the infinite sadness I felt as violence again tore apart my beloved country, and they offer a benediction to all those fighters, makers of history now gone, and to a fabulous people who spread over them—over us, guerrillas—their protective wings.

No, Amirouche Is Not Dead

Do not cry, my sister; dry your tears, my brother,
Behold in silence these lofty mountains,
Soiled by mercenaries in cowardice at ease,
Profaning the rocks proclaimed "French owned,"
Trampling the bushes, or setting them on fire,
Hunting fierce patriots defending their land.

He is in every home and unborn child,
In his liberated homeland, driving out the beasts.
He is this clear stream flowing down the valley
Through rubble and boulders, digging new alleys,
Pressed to fertilize this tormented terrain,
Scorched by the sun and so bloodthirsty.
He is this raging torrent that impetuously thunders,
Challenging obstacles in its wandering race.

Listen and hear the whisper of the spring
Which chants his legend at this time that stings.
Listen to the night wind that shakes the mighty oaks
Of the tough fighters softening the shock.

Amirouche is not dead and buried deep,
It's his breath, Sister, in the tree that shuddered.
Amirouche was killed, but he never departed.

ENDNOTES

[1.] Historically, revolutions are often triggered or instigated by small groups. The "Group of 22," as the Algerian founders are referred to, are hardly any smaller than the 56 American patriots who signed the Declaration of Independence in 1776 or the 39 delegates who signed the United States Constitution in 1787.

[2.] Maurice Challe, Notre Révolte, Presses de la Cité, Paris : 1968 p. 42.

[3.] Ramdane Abane was arrested in 1950 for his activities within the paramilitary Special Organisation (SO) set-up in 1947 to prepare for the armed struggle. Sentenced to five years in jail, he joined the FLN immediately after his release in 1955. He was considered one of the most prominent leaders of the Revolution until he was assassinated by his peers in 1957. Larbi Ben M'hidi, co-organizer of the Soummam Convention that institutionalized the armed struggle was assassinated by the French paratroopers during the "Battle of Algiers" the same year! French General Paul Aussaresses stunned France--or France pretended to be stunned-- when he confessed to the media that he routinely tortured and summarily executed dozens of prisoners including Larbi Ben M'hidi. See the New York Times 05/12/ 2013

[4.] Harbi, Mohammed, and Meynier, Gilbert, Le FLN, Documents et Histoire 1954-1962, (Fayard : Paris 2004), p. 820.

[5.] Charles de Gaulle, Mémoires d'Espoir, le Renouveau, 1958-1962 Plon 1970 p. 18

[6.] On May 1, 2011, the Algerian Press Agency reported that a child was killed by a land mine. Since 1963, special units of the Algerian Army have destroyed 8,267,971 landmines, or an estimated 69-75 percent of the total planted by the French Army along the Tunisian and Moroccan borders.

[7.] Islamist is to be contrasted with Islamic; Islamism, or political Islam, is an ideology and refers to the use of the religion of Islam for political gain.

[8.] The Association of Islamic Scholars, an Islamic reform movement founded in 1931 by Sheikh Abdelhamid Ben Badis, shunned politics and focused on education. This organization rallied the

FLN *two years* after the outbreak of the war, in 1956.

9. Alistair Horne, *A Savage War of Peace*, New York: *New York Review of Books*, 2006 p.131.

10. Michael R. Beschloss, *The Crisis Years, Kennedy and Khrushchev 1960-1963* (New York: Harper Collins: 1991) p.19.

11. Benjamin Claude Brower, *A Desert Named Peace*, (New York: Columbia University Press, 2009) p. x

12. The Mokrani revolt was triggered by the French confiscation of tribal land combined with serious drought and crop failure. An estimated 20 percent of the Muslim Algerian population died over a three-year period in the Constantine region. In 1871 the civil authorities repudiated guarantees made to tribal chieftains for loans to replenish their seed supply. It was against this backdrop of misery and hopelessness that the Algerians rose in revolt when Sheikh Ahaddadh proclaimed jihad. The revolt was crushed after a year.

13. Vincent Confer, *France and Algeria*, (Syracuse: 1966), p. 117.

14. Although Tunisia was dubbed a "Protectorate," it was administered by France as a colony under the provisions of the Treaty of Bardo [Empire by Treaty!) signed on May 12, 1881. France was the occupying power in Morocco, except for areas in the North and the South, since the March 30, 1912, Treaty of Fez, which made Morocco France's Protectorate.

15. An offshoot of the Union inter-coloniale, a satellite of the French Communist party, NAS united workers from countries living under colonialism, and was immediately invigorated by its call for the intensification of anti-imperialist struggle launched by the Third Communist International. See Ben Youcef Benkhedda, *Les Origines du 1er Novembre 1954*, Editions Dahleb, Alger 1989, p.48.

16. *Ibid.* p. 49. This was during the anti-imperialist convention held in Brussels in 1927 where Messali represented the NAS with his mentor, Hadj Ali.

17. There are four Berber groups in Algeria: the Kabyles in the North, the Shawiya in the Aurès Mountains, the Mozabits in the South, and the Tuaregs of the Sahara Desert.

[18.] Henri Alleg, *La Guerre d'Algérie*, T.I, Temps Actuels, Paris 1981, p. 258.

[19.] Ali Habib, *"Mai 1945: répression à Sétif"* in *La Guerre d'Algérie*, "Le Monde et Librio" (Paris: 2003) p.18.

[20.] *Ibid*. p.19.

[21.] *Ibid*. p.19.

[22.] *Ibid*. p.19

[23.] The Emir Abdelkader led the resistance to the invasion and occupation of Algeria by France from 1832 to 1847.

[24.] Ben Youcef Benkhedda, *Les Origines du 1er Novembre 1954*, *Op.Cit*. p. 262.

[25.] *Ibid*. p.263. Sheikh Mohammed Abdu (1849-1905), one of the founding fathers of Islamic reformism, was writing to his friend Abd-al Halim Ben Smaya, a professor at the Arabic school of Algiers.

[26.] Charles de Gaulle, *Mémoires d'Espoir*, le Renouveau, 1958-1962 Plon 1970 p. 18.

[27.] There is a consensus among historians that Abane masterminded the Soummam Conference. It established the 5-member executive committee, the CCE (Comité de Coordination et d'Execution) and the 34-member revolutionary Parliament, the CNRA (Conseil National de la Révolution Algérienne), elected from the various parts of the "Interior."Abane succeeded in getting two important principles enshrined in the 40-page-long Soummam Convention: the primacy of the political leadership over the military, and the primacy of the "interior" (i.e., the fighters) over the "exterior" (i.e. Aït Ahmed Hocine, Mohamed Khider, and Ahmed Ben Bella.) These three leaders had represented the PPA/MTLD since 1950 at the Arab League and the FLN until they were captured when their flight was hijacked by the French Air Force on October 22, 1956. However, at the CNRA meeting in Cairo (August 20-27, 1957), the founding members of the FLN, Krim Belkacem, Lakhdar Ben Tobbal, and Abdelhafid Boussouf, staged a "soft coup" endorsed by almost all members except Abane and Colonel Saddek, who abstained from voting. The CNRA membership was increased from 17 holders and 17 deputies to 54. A major amendment to the decisions of the Soummam Convention was approved: "...the CNRA reaffirms: All those involved in the struggle for national liberation, with or without uniform have equal status and therefore, there is no primacy of the 'political' over the 'military,' and no difference between the 'interior' and the 'exterior.'" The same year, mafia-type executioners under the orders of Colonel Abdelhafid Boussouf strangled Abane in a Moroccan farm belonging to the FLN. See Mohammed Harbi and Gilbert Meynier, *Op. cit.* p. 18; Mabrouk Belhocine, *Le Courrier Alger-Le Caire 1954-1956*, (Casbah Editions: Alger: 2000) p. 65; Mohammed Harbi, *Une Vie Debout, Mémoires Politiques*, T. I, (Casbah Editions: Alger 2001), p. 242.

[28.] "When you go to the market, explain who we are. You hear vocal French claims that we are outlaws, bandits. We are patriots who fight to liberate their country." Yves Courrière, *Les Fils de la Toussaint*, (Paris: Fayard, 1969) p. 428.

[29.] André Mandouze in *Le Monde Diplomatique*, July-August 2001.

[30.] What a prominent First of November 1954 revolutionary, Ali Zamoum, claimed is the truth: joining the insurgents was voluntary. "I want to testify at this time," he writes, "... that commitment to the ALN was totally a free choice... This is why our two comrades [nationalist militants who declined to engage in armed struggle] were able to withdraw without fear... and go home a few hours before launching the revolution. A few days after the insurrection was triggered, we were harassed by requests from people who wanted to 'take to the bush.' " Quoted in Mohammed Harbi, Gilbert Meynier, *Le FLN, Documents et Histoire 1954-1962, Op. Cit.* p.35.

[31.] François Maspero, *L'Honneur de Saint Arnaud*, (Algiers: 2004 Casbah éd.) p. 80. Quoted by *El Watan*, 18-20 July 2005. It is fully documented that the French Army continued this abominable tradition during the war of liberation.

[32.] The Moussebline were not recruited due to an acute shortage of arms. Some of them may have been armed with ancient Foucher shotguns. They continued to live in their villages, serving as watch guards for guerrillas and responsible for their supplies. Entrusted with sabotage missions, the Moussebline could be called upon to join in battle using the weapons of fallen guerrillas.

33. Prime Minister Sid Ahmed Ghozali initially declared that the December 26, 1991, Parliamentary elections were clean and honest. But he later changed his mind to claim that there was fraud, signaling his implicit support for a coup that canceled the democratic process, triggering a bloody civil war which, although subsiding, continues to this day.

34. I was to learn what exactly happened only on September 3, 2011, from Cherif Mahdi, ex-Defense Ministry Secretary. A French captain, in exchange for an authorization allowing his Algerian wife to leave with him to France, disclosed the place where Colonels Amirouche and El Haoues were buried. Under orders by Boumediene to keep total silence or risk death, Mahdi and a fellow officer recovered Amirouche's remains on December 13, 1962, and buried them in El Alia, Algiers. It was only in 1982, three years after Boumediene's death, that the national heroes received a decent burial. Cherif Mahdi published the story in *Le Soir d'Algérie* on December 7, 2011.

35. Alistair Horne, *A Savage War of Peace. Op. cit.* p. 131.

36. *El Watan* July 20, 2009; *El Khabar* July 20, 2009; *Le Quotidien d'Oran* October 31, 2009; *Liberté* August 13, 2009, April 14, 2011 and February 23, 2012; *Le Soir d'Algerie*, July 28 2009, March 24, 2010, and April 12, 2011.

37. Quoted in *El Watan*, May 14, 2006.

38. This case of summary execution occurred before the 1956 Soummam Conference established a strict procedure of "due process," not always respected, before sentencing a soldier or an officer to death.

39. Yves Courrière, *Les Fils de la Toussaint* (Paris: Fayard, 1969) p. 425.

40. *Le Monde*, 8-20-1958.

41. *Libération*, 8-20-1958.

42. *L'Humanité*, 5-21-1959.

43. Djoudi Attoumi, *Le Colonel Amirouche, Entre Légende et Histoire* (Imprimerie Hasnaoui, n.d.: Alger) pp. 244-247.

44. Saddam Hussein could have avoided the destruction of his army and part of his country in 1991 if he had only listened to the Algerian Minister of Foreign Affairs, Sid Ahmed Ghozali. Dispatched by the President of Algeria to convince Saddam to evacuate Kuwait before the ultimatum expired, the Minister insisted that the U.S. was going to use cruise missiles and fighter-bombers, not foot soldiers. It seems that Saddam completely ignored or foolishly underestimated the decisive role of the control of airspace in the outcome of a modern war. According to the Minister, Saddam kept muttering "al harb al bariya, al harb al bariya" [ground warfare, ground warfare]. According to Lawrence Friedman and Efraim Karsh, Iraqi troops retreating under American firepower were massacred like "rabbits in a bag or fish in a barrel." Attacked from the air or by cruise missiles launched from warships, the Iraqi soldiers had neither the opportunity to raise a white flag and surrender, nor the ability to die fighting. And the American High Command rationalized that "We have no choice but to treat retreating combat units as a threat." (Lawrence Friedman and Efraim Karsh, *The Gulf Conflict 1990-1991 and Diplomacy War in the New World Order*, p.401.)

45. Yves Courrière, *Le Temps des Léopards*. (Paris: Fayard, 1969) p. 160.

46. *Ibid.*, p.162.

47. Ben Khedda, the Nationalist Party's General Secretary, initiated a process of actions and reactions that led to conflict between members of the Party's Central Committee (referred to as "Centralists") and Messali Hajj, the President of the Party, who sharply criticized Ben Khedda for "the removal of Messali's faithful assistants from the Directorate." Thus Moulay Merbah, Messali's spokesman and confidant, who had actually proposed Ben Khedda as Secretary-General on behalf of Messali; Mézerna, one of his oldest companions; and Bouda were rejected outright by Ben Khedda, without consulting either the Central Committee (CC), let alone Messali, who reacted by "withdrawing his confidence in the Directorate and demanded full powers to revitalize the Party." The CC argued that Messali's demand was inadmissible as it contravened the Party's statutes and was antidemocratic in nature. The fracture between Messalists and Centralists was officially endorsed when the two factions held parallel Conventions in

311

the summer of 1954. When the insurrection was triggered, two rival armed groups, the National Liberation Front (FLN) and the Algerian National Movement (MNA) waged a protracted civil war.

48. The daily *Le Soir d'Algérie* of June 12, 2014, reported the death of a 117-year-old woman of Azrou and pointed out that the villagers of "Azrou, considered a stronghold of the revolution, do not exclude the hypothesis that it is that woman's courage that Hamou Amirouche, secretary of Colonel Amirouche, honored by dedicating his book *A Year with Colonel Amirouche*," to her.

49. *L'Echo d'Alger*, May 21, 1959.
50. Yves Courrière, *Le Temps des Léopards*, (Librairie Arthème Fayard: 1969) p. 249.

51. *Ibid.* p. 261.

52. Henry Alleg, *La Guerre d'Algérie*, v. 2, *Op.cit.* pp. 135-136; Yves Courrière, *Le Temps Des Léopards*, *Op.cit.*, Paris 1969, p.216.

53. Paul-Alain Léger, *Aux Carrefours de la Guerre*, Albin Michel, (Paris: 1989) pp. 217-219.

54. Alistair Horne, *A Savage War of Peace*, *Op. cit.* p. 260.
55. Yves Courrière, *Le Temps des Léopards*, *Op. cit.* p. 570.
56. Alistair Horne, *A Savage War of Peace*, *Op. cit.* p.258.

57. Paul-Alain Léger, *Aux Carrefours de la Guerre*, (Albin Michel: 1983 Paris) pp. 217-219.

58. *Ibid.* p. 250.
59. This information was revealed by Jean-Louis Rioual, journalist at France Culture. During an interview that I granted to him in December 2007 in Algiers, the journalist raised the Bleuite episode. When I pointed out that it's peculiar that only Colonel Amirouche is incriminated for the several hundred soldiers executed, never the instigator and main culprit Captain Léger, the journalist replied: "Mr. Amirouche, Légers widow confessed to me that the Captain was tortured by his conscience before he passed away."

60. Patrick Eveno, "Premier Bilan," *La Guerre d'Algérie*, 1954-1962, Librio 1985, p. 109.

61. Alistair Horne, *A Savage War of Peace, Op. cit.* p. 220

62. Quoted by Alistair Horne, *Op. cit.* p. 221

63. Based on Agathe Logeart's article in *Le Nouvel Observateur*, October 21, 2004, pp.15-16.

64. *El Watan*, April 20, 2008.

65. At the time I wrote these lines, the number of Iraqi refugees in neighboring countries such as Syria and Jordan reached two million people; refugees within their own country also reached two million. Who in the United States, or France for that matter, is accountable for this crime against humanity? The Melian Dialogue provides the answer. See http://answers.yahoo.com/question/index?qid=20080424184701AAbapQf

66. Agathe Logeart, *Op. cit.*

67. Following the death of the head of Wilaya I, Mustapha Ben Boulaïd, killed on March 22, 1956, anarchy threatened to reign in that Military Command. The Soummam Convention appointed Amirouche to head to the area and help restore unity. Amirouche nominated Youcef Yaalaoui, "a leader with a strong national consciousness," Political Commissar and dismissed Messaoud Aïssi in the process. The latter refused to accept the measure and, with a group of followers, engaged in dissidence. His fierce hatred of Kabyles led him to slaughter an entire company of young recruits, among them students, heading to Tunisia to fetch arms. See Mohammed Harbi, Gilbert Meynier, *Le FLN, Documents et Histoire, Op.cit.* p. 453.

68. The village was Messalist General Bellounis' headquarters. Following attacks against National Liberation Army soldiers, lieutenant Abdelkader El Bariki was dispatched to that Messalist stronghold. He gathered the villagers the night of May 28, 1957, and attempted to rally them to the National Liberation Front. Their contemptuous rejection of El Bariki's offer provoked their massacre. Nearby Melouza, on the other hand, was an FLN/ALN stronghold. The massacre that occurred there was perpetrated by Messalists with the help of French troops on June 2, 1957. See Footnote 47, Chapter 10, for the origin of the conflict.

69. Abane's assassination on December 27, 1957 is still shrouded in mystery. Krim Belkacem, along with Abdelhafid Boussouf and Ben Tobal, were probably the assassins. An authoritarian leader, highly educated and often displaying contempt towards his military

peers, Abane paid the price for imposing the principle of the "primacy of the civilian over the military," in effect threatening to marginalize the uneducated colonels. His tragic death at the hands of his peers inaugurated the practice of political assassinations and coups d'état continuing in Algeria to this day.

[70.] Yves Courrière, *Les Feux du Désespoir*, Fayard (Paris: 1969) p.32.

[71.] When 35 years later, in December 1994, I read that the Algerian terrorists who had hijacked an Air France airliner had intended to crash it into the Eiffel Tower, I thought of my own fanatic hatred that inspired the same desire for revenge. While condemning any action targeting innocent people, I concluded that no human being is born a fanatic. It's no use expressing indignant incomprehension and condemnation if we do not address the causes of terrorist violence, which are political and not religious. The terrorist group, which currently holds the world record for suicide actions, the "Tamil Tigers" of Sri Lanka, is a Marxist-Maoist group.

[72.] Mohammed Harbi and Gilbert Meynier, *Op. cit.* p.428.

[73.] At a picnic organized by the Algerian community in San Diego, one Algerian selected an isolated corner in which to enjoy his halal sandwich, authorized by religion, with a beer that clearly was not. Another Algerian chose that same corner to provocatively spread his prayer rug. "Why did you come to pray before my beer?" yelled the beer lover. Two opposing camps instantly formed.

[74.] Redha Malek, *L'Algérie à Evian, Histoire des Négociations secrètes 1956-1962*, Editions le Seuil, Paris 1995, p.49.

[75.] Boumediene initially refused to obey the Government's orders to hand over to the Red Crescent a captured French Air Force pilot. It took long negotiations by President Ferhat Abbas and pressure from the Tunisian authorities to obtain the prisoner's release. This episode confirmed that the Government in Exile had lost all authority which could be bestowed only by the Interior of Algeria itself, and the Interior was beginning to rebel.

[76.] Fundamentalism: Webster's Dictionary: "A movement in 20th century Protestantism emphasizing the literally interpreted Bible as fundamental to Christian life and teaching".
The American Heritage Dictionary: "An organized, militant Evangelical movement originating in the US in 1920 in opposition

to liberalism and secularism." It is regarded as referring to those who wish to return to and replicate the past, the golden age. Example: the puritanical revivalist movement (Wahabism) founded in Arabia by Mohammad ibn Abdul-Wahab in the 18th century and still very much alive in Saudi Arabia. Its guiding principle: the need for Islam to return to the purity of the first community of Muslims founded by the Prophet Mohammed in the 7th century A.D. However, the term "fundamentalism" presents problems, because its application to believers of any faith-- Jewish, Christian, or Muslim--implies a return to the fundamentals or basics of that faith, but does not necessarily connote political activism or the intrusion of the religious into what is considered a temporal sphere. Hence, the use of "Islamism" to which the meaning of "political Islam" has been assigned by most scholars in the field.

77. Stanley Meisler, United Nations, The First Fifty Years (New York: Atlantic Monthly Press, 1995), pp.209-210.

78. The first terrorist attack, against a border post at Guemar (El Oued), inaugurating more than ten years of appalling bloodshed, occurred on the anniversary of the death of a famous Afghan veteran, Abdallah Azzam, assassinated by a car bomb in Peshawar, Pakistan, in 1989. (See *El-Moudjahid,* November 29-30, 1991.) Much of the violence that followed, possibly culminating in President Boudiaf's assassination in June 1992, was staged by "Afghans," as they are known in Algeria. Thousands of Arab/Muslim volunteers, including about 2,800 Algerians, were stationed around Peshawar, Pakistan, to fight the Soviet Army in Afghanistan. Money for the operation came from huge Saudi slush funds and from the CIA. See John K. Cooley, "Algeria: Has Cold War Blindness Struck Again?" *The International Herald Tribune*, July 2, 1992.

79. http://www.shsu.edu/~his_ncp/Melian.html

80. Niall Ferguson, Foreign Policy, September-October 2006.

81. Le Monde, November 2, 2012.

82. Ferhat Abbas, leader of small Algerian group of French-educated intellectuals, organized into a political party, the Union du Manifeste Algerien (UDMA), struggling for civil rights and integration, published in 1936 a widely quoted article in which he said: "I have questioned the living and the dead. No one spoke to me of such a thing as the Algerian Nation."

BIBLIOGRAPHY

1. Belaïd Abdesselam, <u>Le Gaz Algérien Stratégies et Enjeux</u>. Algiers: Bouchène, 1989.

2. Lounis Aggoun, Jean-Baptiste Rivoire, Françalgérie, <u>Crimes et Mensonges d'Etat</u>. Paris: Editions La Découverte 2004.

3. Alleg, Henri, <u>La Guerre d'Algérie</u> v. I and II. Paris: Temps Actuels,1981.

4. Attoumi , Djoudi, <u>Le colonel Amirouche, Entre Légende et Histoire</u>

      "   "   <u>Le colonel Amirouche A La Croisée des Chemins</u>

      "   "   <u>Avoir 20 Ans Dans les Maquis</u>. Algiers: Imprimerie Hasnaoui, n.d.

5. Ben Khedda, Benyoucef, <u>Les Origines du 1er Novembre 1954</u>. Algiers: Editions Dahlab, 1989.

6. Bennoune, Mahfoud and El Kenz, Ali, <u>Le Hasard et l'Histoire</u>, Entretiens avec Belaid Abdessélam, Tome I et II. Algiers: Enag Editions, 1990.

7. Chabane, Nordine, <u>L'Aigle du Djurdjura</u>. Algiers: Enag Editions, 2006.

8. Challe, Maurice, <u>Notre Révolte</u>. Paris: Presses de la Cité, 1968.

9. Courrière, Yves, <u>Les Fils de la Toussaint,</u>

      "   "   <u>Le Temps des Léopards,</u>

      "   "   <u>L'Heure des colonels,</u>

      "   "   <u>Les Feux du Désespoir</u>. Paris: Fayard, 1969.

10. Daniel, Jean, <u>De Gaulle et l'Algérie</u>. Paris: Editions du Seuil, 1986.

11. De Gaulle, Charles, <u>Mémoires d'Espoir, le Renouveau</u>, 1958-

1962. Paris: Plon, 1970.

12. Eveno, Patrick «Premier Bilan», La Guerre d'Algérie, 1954-1962. Paris: Librio, Le Monde et E.J.L. , 2003.

13. Grandmaison, Olivier Le Cour «Quand Tocqueville légitimait les Boucheries.» Le Monde Diplomatique, Polémiques sur l'Histoire coloniale, juillet-août 2001.

14. Fanon, Franz-Omar, Les Damnés de la Terre. Algiers: Editions Anep, 2006.

15. Habib, Ali «Mai 1945: répression à Sétif,» La Guerre d'Algérie. Paris: Le Monde, Librio et E.J.L., 2003.

16. Harbi, Mohammed, Les Archives de la Révolution Algérienne. Algiers: Editions Jeune Afrique, 1981.

17. Harbi, Mohammed, Une Vie Debout, Mémoires Politiques v. I: 1945-1962 Algiers: Casbah Editions, 2001.

18. Harbi, Mohammed, L'Algérie et Son Destin-Croyants ou Citoyens. Paris: Arcantère, 1992.

19. Harbi, Mohammed and Gilbert Meynier, Le FLN Documents et Histoire 1954-1962. Paris: Fayard, 2004.

20. Horne, Alistair A Savage War of Peace. London: Mac Millan, 1977.

21. Hourani, Albert, L'Histoire des Peuples Arabes. Translated from English by Paul Chemla. Paris: Editions du Seuil , 1993.

22. Khalfa, Mammeri, Abane Ramdane, Héros de la Guerre d'Algérie. Algiers: Rahma, 1992.

23. Léger, Paul-Alain Aux Carrefours de la Guerre. Paris: Albin Michel, 1983.

24. Nicholas Machiavel, Œuvres Complètes, «Le Prince.» Paris: Gallimard, 1952.

" "   " "   The Discourses. London: Penguin Books, 1970.

25. Robert S. Mc Namara, <u>In Retrospect, the Tragedy and Lessons of Vietnam</u>. New York: Vintage, 1996.

26. Malek, Rédha, <u>Tradition et Révolution</u>, (Bouchène: Alger, 1991)

27. Malek, Rédha, <u>L'Algérie à Evian, Histoire des Négociations Secrètes</u> 1956-1962. Paris: Le Seuil, 1995.

28. Mécacher, Salah, <u>Aux PC de la Wilaya III 1957-1962.</u> Algiers: Editions El Amel, 2006.

29. Ministère de l'Information, <u>*Documents: Les Discours du Président Boumediène.*</u> Algiers: Imprimerie Nationale, 1966.

30. Rousseau, J-J., <u>Du Contrat social</u>. Paris: Classiques Larousse, 1953.

31. Madame Saâdi Djamina Mokrane, <u>La Charte Nationale</u>. Algiers: OPU, n.d.

32. Stora, Benjamin, <u>Dictionnaire Biographique de Militants Nationalistes Algériens 1926-1954</u>. Paris: l'Harmatan, 1985.

33. Taleb Ibrahimi, Ahmed, <u>De la Décolonisation à la Révolution culturelle</u>, (1962-1972). Algiers: Société nationale d'édition et de diffusion: 1981.

34. Warner, Keith A., <u>Voix Françaises du Monde Noir</u>. New York: Holt, Rinehart and Winston, inc.,1971.

JOURNALS-NEWSPAPERS:

<u>El Watan </u>December 1-5, 1992; July 18-20, 2005; April 20, 2008; June 5, 2008.

<u>L'Express,</u> June 21, 1962.

<u>The Journal of Strategic Studies</u>, June 25, 2002.

<u>Le Matin,</u> December 3, 2001.

<u>Le Monde Diplomatique</u>, July-August, 2001.

The New York Times, October 9 and 31, 1962.

Le Nouvel Observateur, October 21, 2004.

GLOSSARY

Abbas, Ferhat: Pharmacist, moderate politician. Early in his political career, he advocated equal rights and the abolition of colonialism to bring about the emancipation of the Algerian Muslims as French citizens. In 1956 he escaped to Cairo to join the Front de Libération Nationale (FLN), the organization which launched the revolutionary struggle for independence from France on November 1, 1954.

Ferhat Abbas was appointed President of the Provisional Government of the Algerian Republic proclaimed in Cairo on Sept. 19, 1958. Elected president of the Algerian Constituent Assembly in 1962, when Algeria gained independence, he resigned to protest the drafting of the Algerian constitution by the FLN outside the Constituent Assembly. A declared opponent of the then-president, Ahmed Ben Bella, he was placed under house arrest in 1964 but was released the following year.

Abane, Ramdane: Nationalist activist born in Kabylia. Incarcerated 1950-1955 for his membership in the paramilitary Special Organization (OS) created in 1947. Played a key role in the organization of the Soummam Conference. Assassinated by his peers in December 1957.

Amazigh: plural Imazighen, misnamed "Berbers:" The original inhabitants of North Africa.

ALN: National Liberation Army, the armed wing of the FLN

Belkacem Krim: One of the nine leaders of the Algerian Revolution and the first head of Wilaya III (Military Command). Led the delegation which signed the cease-fire Evian Agreements on March 18, 1962.

Berbers: Berber-speaking original inhabitants of North Africa.

CCE: Comité de Coordination et d'Éxécution, A five-member executive established by the Soummam Conference along with the CNRA.

CNRA: Conseil National de la Révolution Algérienne. National Council of the Algerian Revolution established by the Soummam Convention; a 34 member revolutionary Parliament.

Djebel: Mountain

Djema'â: Berber Assembly of elders

Fellaghas, hors-la loi (HLL): Outlaws in Arabic. Terms used by the French security forces to refer to the Algerian insurgents.

Fellah: Algerian peasant

FLN: National Liberation Front: Militant political organization which launched the war of liberation.

GPRA: Gouvernement Provisoire de la Révolution Algérienne. Provisional Government proclaimed in Cairo on September 19, 1958.

Harki: Algerian Muslim mercenary of the French Army.

Imam: Sunni (orthodox) preacher and prayer leader; politico-religious Shi'a leader.

Islamic: relating to the Islamic Scriptures.

Islamism, or political Islam: an ideology which uses the religion of Islam for political gain.

Kabyle: An inhabitant of Kabylia or Soummam Valley. Also a dialect spoken by the Kabyle Berbers.

Kabylia: North East mountainous region of Algeria where most Berbers live.

Messali Hajj (1898-1974): The father and the leader of the Algerian nationalist movement(1937-1954)and of the MNA, (Mouvement National Algérien 1954-1962)the FLN rival during the war.

Messalist: A nationalist loyal to Messali Hajj; a militant of the MNA.

Morice (and Challe) Lines: Heavily electrified fences (5,000 volts)surrounded by minefields erected along the Tunisian border to block the flow of arms and ammunition to the Algerian insurgents.

MTLD: Movement for the Triumph of Democratic Liberties. Name adopted by the nationalist Algerian People's Party (PPA) after it was banned by the French Government.

PPA: Algerian People's Party banned in 1939 and reappearing under a new name in 1947.

Pieds Noirs: French settlers born in Algeria.

Qur'an or Koran: Sacred book of Islam.

Salafiyya: An extremist Islamic Sunni movement advocating a return to the religious practices of the earliest Muslims of the time of the Prophet.

Shari'a: Islamic Law, based on the Qur'an and the sayings and conduct of the Prophet during his lifetime.

Sheikh: In Algerian Arabic, a teacher or a prayer leader.

Soummam Conference: Held in Ifri, Kabylia on August 20, 1956, it constituted a turning point in the war of liberation in so far as it established the Institutions of the Revolution: A Parliament and an Executive Branch.

Sunni vs. Shi'a Islam: Following the Prophet Mohammed's death in 632, a crisis of succession occurred. A faction (shi'a means party) claimed the right of Muhammed's family members and his descendants to lead the Islamic community while the tribal tradition which represents Sunni, orthodox Islam, was to co-opt a leader respected for his wisdom and virtuous life. Today Sunny Islam represents roughly 85 % of the World's Muslims. Members of the two sects have peacefully co-existed, intermarried and shared for centuries most fundamental beliefs and practices. Today's bloody confrontations are rooted in political and social disenfranchisement and are the direct product of the invasion and occupation of Iraq.

Ulama: Islamic scholars

Vava: Papa in Berber

Wilaya: One of the six military commands of the Algerian insurgents.

Yemma: Mom in Berber

FROM THE AKFADOU FOREST, THROUGH THE ATLAS MOUNTAINS, TO TUNISIA

A 42 Day journey on foot to deliver secret documents and an important sum of money to the Provisional Government in Tunis

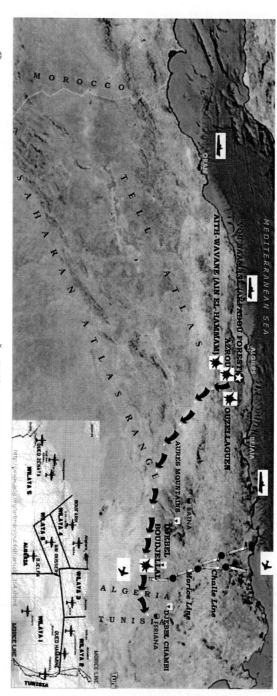

⊘ Point of departure

✳ Clashes with the French Colonial Army

✈ Aerial surveillance

→ French Navy patrols

Itinerary of the commando

Challe and Morice Lines: heavily electrified fences (5000 volts) at the border betwwen Algeria and Tunisia surrounded by minefields and alarm systems

WILAYA: The Soummam Convention (August 1956) divided Algeria at war into six Military Commands called Wilayas. Algiers and its immediate surroundings constituted the Algiers Autonomous Zone (ZAA)

324

FROM THE AKFADOU FOREST, THROUGH THE ATLAS MOUNTAINS, TO TUNISIA

The Wilaya 3 is the departure of a 42 day journey on foot to deliver secret documents and an important sum of money to the Provisional Government in Tunis

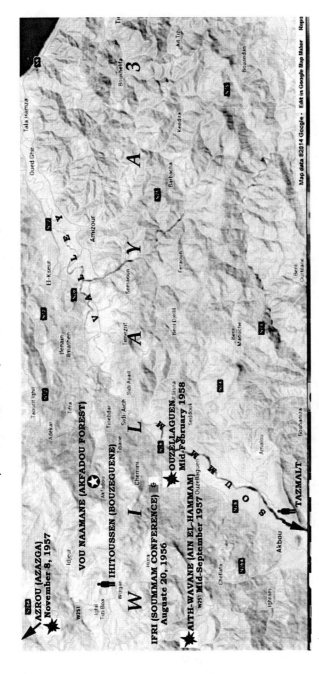

AZROU (AZAZGA)
November 8, 1957

VOU NAAMANE (AKFADOU FOREST)

IHITOUSSEN (BOUZEGUENE)

W I L A Y A 3

IFRI (SOUMMAM CONFERENCE)
Auguste 20, 1956

OUZELLAGUEN
Mid-February 1958

AITH-WAVANE (AIN EL-HAMMAM)
Mid-September 1957

TAZMALT

Map data ©2014 Google · Edit in Google Map Maker

Point of departure

Clashes with the French Colonial Army

Important villages
Ihitoussen: my ancestors' village
Tazmalt: my place of birth

WILAYA 3: The Soummam Convention (August 1956) divided Algeria at war into six Military Commands called Wilayas. Algiers and its immediate surroundings constituted the Algiers Autonomous Zone (ZAA).

IFRI : The Soummam Conference is the founding act of the modern Algerian State

N

325

About the Author

Hamou Amirouche was born in Algeria in 1937. When the Algerian War of Liberation broke out in 1954, he was training to be a mechanic. He joined the freedom fighters and served as the private secretary to a national hero, Colonel Amirouche Aït Hamouda in 1957-1958. In March 1958 the Colonel appointed him to be a member of a commando that routed mail and funds to Tunisia.

While in Tunis, the author was ordered to return to school. After earning a French *Baccalauréat* he was sent to the United States where he earned a BA in Government at Wesleyan University (Connecticut) and an MA in Political Science at the University of Colorado. In 1967, he began his professional career at the Algerian Ministry of Industry and Energy.

He retired in 1987 but was recalled in 1988-1989 to serve as a fellow at the Institute for Global and Strategic Studies. In 1994, he settled in the United States with his family and began a new career as a researcher, and university lecturer first in Cambridge (MA) and, beginning in 1997 in San Diego (CA) where he lives with his wife.

326

Since the publication of his best-selling book, "Akfadou, Un An avec le Colonel Amirouche," in 2009, the author has accepted several invitations to give talks on his work at various institutions in Algeria (2009-2012), Montreal and Ottawa (2011), the University of Texas (Austin: 2010); at the Algerian Cultural Center (Paris: 2011), at the American Institute for Maghrebi Studies (Oran: 2011), Oregon State and Portland State Universities (2012).
Hamou Amirouche is the author of numerous academic articles both in French and English on Islam and politics; democratic rules and principles; prerequisites for democracy to strike roots; asymmetric warfare; how to eradicate political violence and terrorism.

This book is the first published in English by an academic who fought in the Algerian revolution.

CPSIA information can be obtained at www.ICGtesting.com
Printed in the USA
LVOW08s0205301215

468380LV00019B/151/P